Final
Chapters

Final Chapters

How Famous Authors Died

JIM BERNHARD

Skyhorse Publishing

Skyhorse Publishing books may be purchased in bulk at special discounts for sales promotion, corporate gifts, fund-raising, or educational purposes. Special editions can also be created to specifications. For details, contact the Special Sales Department, Skyhorse Publishing, 307 West 36th Street, 11th Floor, New York, NY 10018 or info@skyhorsepublishing.com.

Skyhorse® and Skyhorse Publishing® are registered trademarks of Skyhorse Publishing, Inc.®, a Delaware corporation.

Visit our website at www.skyhorsepublishing.com.

10 9 8 7 6 5 4 3 2 1

Library of Congress Cataloging-in-Publication Data is available on file.

Cover design by Tom Lau
Cover photo credit: Thinkstock

Print ISBN: 978-1-63450-241-2
Ebook ISBN: 978-1-5107-0061-1

Printed in the United States of America

For Ginger

Contents

Contents

Last Words First: An Introduction

WHEN WE HEAR that anyone has died, one of the first things we ask is: "What did he (or she) die of?" And then: "How old was he (or she)?" Such personal details of death are a source of fascination to most people. Dorothy L. Sayers, who killed off a good many folks in her murder mysteries, said, "Death seems to provide the minds of the Anglo-Saxon race with a greater fund of amusement than any other single subject." But she didn't go far enough in her assessment. It's not just Anglo-Saxons who are stuck on death; it's the whole human race.

Death has several characteristics that may explain the attention that we lavish on it. It is both inevitable (so far as we know) and unpredictable (in most circumstances). People who estimate such things tell us that since the beginning of the world, about 107 billion people have been born. Of that total, only a little more than 7 billion are alive today. If you do the math, you'll find that means that out of everyone who has ever lived, 93 percent of them have died. The odds are not in favor of the remaining 7 percent of us.

The Pulitzer Prize–winning writer William Saroyan once said, "Everybody has got to die, but I have always believed an exception would be made in my case." Unfortunately for him, no exception was made, and he died of prostate cancer in 1981. He was seventy-two.

Inevitable as it may be, death is also unpredictable for most of us as to precisely when we might expect it. This quality infuses it with a suspenseful *frisson*, guaranteeing that we will think about it from time to time.

Nobody has expressed the inevitability of death better than William Shakespeare. Hamlet, who pondered the subject more than was good for him, put it this way: "There is a special providence in the fall of a sparrow; if it be now, 'tis not to come; if it be not to come, it will be now; if it be not now, yet it will come. The readiness is all."

One other quality that gives death a healthy dose of *gravitas* is its finality. No matter what one's views are about the possibility of an afterlife, there's no getting around the fact that death permanently ends the life we're in now—the only one we really know anything about. The "lane to the land of the dead," as W. H. Auden called it, is a one-way street. And its destination, as Hamlet puts it, is "the undiscovered country, from whose bourn no traveler returns."

The lives and deaths of the world's poets, dramatists, and novelists are ideal for studying how humans approach dying. The various ways they shuffled off this mortal coil could fill an encyclopedia of disease and mishap. They were snuffed out by infections (especially in the days before antibiotics); by frequent lung disease (particularly in the nineteenth century, when tuberculosis and pneumonia were rampant); by the expected quotient of heart attacks, strokes, and cancer; by stomach and kidney disorders and a few rare and unknown diseases; plus a fair number of suicides, murders, assassinations, and bizarre accidents. Alcohol, tobacco, and narcotics played leading roles in many cases.

Death came to some in startling ways. The Greek playwright Aeschylus had a fatal encounter with a turtle that fell from the sky. Italian theologian Thomas Aquinas was knocked off a donkey by a tree branch and never recovered. French dramatist Molière was mortally stricken while playing the part of a hypochondriac in one of his own plays. The corpse of the *philosophe* Voltaire was transported to his funeral dressed in finery and propped up as if he were still alive.

American poet Emily Dickinson's final illness was difficult to diagnose—because rather than allowing her doctor to examine her, all she would consent to was to walk slowly past the open door of his examining room while he observed her from inside. Writer Sherwood Anderson was felled by an errant toothpick in a martini. Trappist monk Thomas Merton was killed by a fan—an electric one. Did poet Dylan Thomas really die of eighteen straight whiskeys? And was it a stray bottle cap, too many pills and too much liquor, or murder most foul that did in playwright Tennessee Williams?

Ages of authors at the time of death have also varied widely. Curiously, even though average life expectancies have substantially lengthened in modern times, writers do not seem to have benefited from the improvement. The average age at death of the classical Greek and Roman subjects in this book was about seventy. Oddly enough, for the authors of the twentieth and twenty-first centuries, it was earlier—about sixty-five. Ages at death range from Sophocles at ninety-one and George Bernard Shaw at ninety-four, to Percy Bysshe Shelley at twenty-nine and John Keats at only twenty-five.

This book explores not only the individual causes of death and the circumstances surrounding it, but also what each author might have thought about the end of life. Being writers, most have left at least some clues, if not specific exposition, about their attitudes toward death in their poems, plays, novels, diaries, letters, and interviews. They exhibit a wide range of opinions.

Few if any of these famous authors have had the kind of "near-death" experiences that have spawned many recent sensational books that often climb to the top of bestseller lists. The array of such alluring titles is dizzying: *Proof of Heaven, Return from Tomorrow, My Descent into Death, 90 Minutes in Heaven, Life on the Other Side, Waking Up in Heaven,* and *Heaven Is For Real* are a few of them. One classic author who stands out as an anomaly for his unwavering certainty about the existence of an afterlife is Arthur Conan Doyle, Sherlock Holmes's creator, who insisted that he was able to converse with folks who had passed over to the other side.

For the most part, however, the creators of our literature, from the classical era to modern times, have expressed the same kind of uncertainty the rest of us feel about what to expect from a visit by the Grim Reaper. Like anyone else's, the authors' views about death are shaped by their religious and philosophical beliefs, which span the gamut from polytheism and Stoicism in the classical Greco-Roman period; to Christianity, prevalent in the European Middle Ages and Renaissance; to Deist and Transcendental thought, developed in France and America in the eighteenth and nineteenth centuries; to the questioning agnosticism or blatant atheism that pervades the contemporary "Age of Anxiety." Attitudes toward death differ widely, ranging from fear to acceptance to indifference.

The selection of authors may strike some readers as arbitrary, and it is. It is based on purely personal preferences, appearing in a chronological sequence by date of birth. Despite glaring omissions or idiosyncratic inclusions, the list does represent an approximation of what might be found in a history of Western Lit. The historical arrangement of the authors is purely for the convenience of the reader. The periods have been divided into Classical, Medieval, Renaissance, Enlightenment, Romantic, Victorian, and Modern, generally following the usual pattern of literature courses.

As for historical documentation, this is not a textbook or a reference work and should not be held to strict academic standards. Other than quotations from the works of the authors themselves, sources include online and printed encyclopedias (including but not limited to the invaluable Wikipedia.org), literary web sites, biographies, biographical directories, diaries, news accounts (principally NYTimes.com, Telegraph.co.uk, Theguardian.com, Dailymail.co.uk, Bbc.co.uk), the especially useful web sites Nndb.com, Biography.com, Poets.org, Poetryfoundation.org, Poetsgraves.co.uk, Poemhunter.com, Books.google.com, Shmoop.com, and the always fascinating Findadeath.com and Findagrave.com. *They Went That-A-Way* by Malcolm Forbes also provided a number of informative tips.

While reasonable effort has been made to verify facts, details are nonetheless incomplete and should not be relied upon as having encyclopedic authority. Where there have been differing accounts of the circumstances of an author's death, I have favored the most interesting (or lurid) version (but have also indicated that opinions vary).

As always, I am grateful for the encouragement and (almost all of) the criticism of my devoted wife, Virginia, a historian, whose suggestions have attempted, in vain, to disguise the inadequacies of this volume with a patina of scholarly methods. I must also acknowledge with gratitude the counsel and assistance of Julia Lord, my savvy, gracious, and indefatigable agent. My thanks also go to Nicole Frail, my editor at Skyhorse Publishing.

If there are lessons to be learned from the words of the authors in this book, the best one is probably that of Marcus Aurelius: "Death smiles at us all; all we can do is smile back."

The Classical Age

AESCHYLUS

If plays had been rated in ancient Athens as movies are today, the tragedies of Aeschylus would have earned an "R" for violence, incestuous sex, cannibalism, and gory deaths. You be the judge: In the *Oresteia* trilogy, lurid details tell of Agamemnon's bloody murder of his own daughter while she is bound and gagged; the subsequent butchery and dismemberment of Agamemnon, along with his paramour, Cassandra, by his vengeful wife, Clytemnestra; more revenge perpetrated by their son, Orestes, who with the help of his sister, Electra, fatally stabs Clytemnestra and her lover, Aegisthus. Oh, and don't forget Aegisthus's father, Thyestes, who murdered his half-brother and slept with the wife of his brother, Atreus—who then got even by killing Thyestes's sons, roasting them, and feeding them to their unwitting father. Thyestes then raped his own daughter, who gave birth to Aegisthus, who killed Atreus. Whew! And that's only three of the ninety or so plays that Aeschylus wrote. It's too bad for slasher fans that only seven of the ninety have been found.

First of the three great tragic Greek playwrights, Aeschylus himself was apparently a very gentle and scholarly fellow, born about 525 BC into a wealthy family in Eleusis, twenty-five miles northwest of Athens. He grew up devoutly religious, believing in the Greek pantheon of gods, who were often cruel and violent. He was initiated into the secret cult of Demeter, known as the Eleusinian Mysteries. With his brother, Aeschylus fought in the battle of Marathon, in which the Greeks defeated the invading Persians under King Darius. His brother died in the battle, but Aeschylus lived to do military duty once again against the Persians, this time led by King Xerxes, at the battle of Salamis ten years later. This battle is memorialized in his play *The Persians*.

Murder may have been a horror to Aeschylus, but death itself was a natural and sometimes desirable culmination of life. "Death is a gentler fate than tyranny," he wrote in *Agamemnon*. "There is fame for one who nobly meets his death with honor." In that play the unfortunate Cassandra contemplates her brutal demise with equanimity:

> I willingly endure my death,
> And warmly greet the gates
> Of Hades that open for me.
> Grant me, you gods,
> A clean blow and an easy fall,
> Free from agony!
> Let my blood
> Flow smoothly from my veins,
> So that I may close my eyes
> In peaceful death.

Aeschylus's own death was nothing he would have written a play about. He met his end unexpectedly in the year 456 BC, at the age of sixty-eight or sixty-nine, in a bizarre mishap while visiting the island of Sicily. According to Pliny the Elder in his *Natural History*, Aeschylus had been warned by an oracle that he would be killed by a house falling on him; accordingly, he spent as much time as possible in the open, far from any edifices that might collapse. He was taking an ostensibly healthful stroll in the fresh sea air when what was said to be an eagle (more likely a vulture) dropped a turtle on his glistening bald head, which the not-so-eagle-eyed bird mistook for a rock. Bearded vultures, or Lammergeier (*Gypaetus barbatus*), are known to pick up box turtles (*Testudo graeca*) and drop them from great heights onto large rocks with remarkable accuracy in order to get at the juicy meat and bones inside. The turtle "house" that was dropped on Aeschylus reportedly remained intact, but, alas, the old playwright's head did not.

Aeschylus was buried on the island in a grave that bore an epitaph that he had composed for himself:

"In this tomb in the wheat fields of Gela lies Aeschylus of Athens, son of Euphorion. He fought in the hallowed precincts of Marathon, which can speak of his valor, which is remembered as well by the long-haired Persians."

Aeschylus was survived by two sons, who were also dramatists. One of them, Euphorion, won first prize at the City Dionysia play competition in 431 BC, defeating both Sophocles and Euripides. Even though they didn't win on this occasion, those two were the true heirs of Aeschylus's dramatic legacy.

SOPHOCLES

Waiting eagerly in the wings, Sophocles was about forty years old when Aeschylus died. Born into a wealthy family about 497 BC in Colonus, he was incredibly prolific, turning out more than 125 plays. Like those of Aeschylus, however, most have vanished, and only seven survive—notably *Antigone*, *Oedipus Rex*, and *Oedipus at Colonus*.

Sophocles's first big success came when he was barely thirty—he took first prize at the Dionysia, besting the veteran Aeschylus, who left Athens in a huff shortly thereafter and went to Sicily. Active in Athenian politics, Sophocles served in several civic positions, including city treasurer, general of the army, and priest. Constantly busy, he was known as the "Bee" of Athens. He was married twice and had two sons.

Sophocles held a conventional ancient Greek view of death as a liberation from life's hardships. Antigone tells Creon she would welcome death as a blessing:

> I know I must die, even without your edicts.
> But if I am to die before my time,
> I count that as a gain.
> For when one lives as I do,
> Surrounded by evils,
> What could death bring but gain?
> So for me to meet this doom
> Is but a trifling grief.

For Sophocles, as for most Greeks, the greatest possible good was to live out one's life without encountering the kind of tragic events that filled his plays. As the chorus at the end of *Oedipus Rex* observes:

> This was Oedipus the Great! Upon him
> All the world would gaze with envious eyes.
> But now a sea of trouble overwhelms him!
> Thus we must wait until the day of death,
> Which comes upon us all, and count no man
> Among the blest until his journey ends
> Without calamity befalling him.

Sophocles basked among the blest until he died at the age of ninety or ninety-one in the winter of 406/5 BC. There are several stories about the cause of death. Most famous is that he died from excessive strain while trying to recite a long sentence from *Antigone* without pausing to take a breath. Another account says he choked on a mouthful of grapes at an Athenian festival. And some of his admirers maintained that he succumbed to sheer happiness after winning his final victory at the City Dionysia. There is the possibility that he died of plain old senility, since his sons allegedly tried to have him declared incompetent shortly before the end of his life. Sophocles was buried in a family tomb, no longer extant, on the road between Athens and Decelea.

After his death, the comic playwright Phyrnicus, in a play titled *The Muses*, wrote this eulogy: "Blessed is Sophocles, who had a long life, was a man both happy and talented, and the writer of many good tragedies; and he ended his life well without suffering any misfortune."

EURIPIDES

Playwrights were adulated like Olympic athletes in ancient Athens, and the next gold medalist was Euripides. He wrote about ninety-five tragedies, and eighteen of them survive—among them *Medea, Orestes, Electra, The Trojan Women, Helen of Troy, Iphigenia in Taurus, Andromache,* and *The Bacchae*. From a middle-class merchant family, Euripides was born sometime between 485 and 480 BC on the Greek island of Salamis, about sixteen miles from Athens. He grew up as a skeptic, a humanist who believed, like the philosopher Protagoras, that "man is the measure of all things."

Euripides's plays use some of the same mythological material as those of Aeschylus, but the action depends more on human psychology than on what the gods decree. Some people thought the philosopher Socrates helped him write them, and like Socrates, Euripides was accused of being an irreverent fire-brand. He put into the mouth of Medea words that he probably thought applied to himself:

> If you express new ideas among fools, they regard you as a trifling ignoramus. And if you happen to become more famous than the so-called intelligentsia, they will really hate you! That has been my misfortune. Some people think I am clever—and they resent me. Others think I'm stupid—and they scorn me.

Euripides relished his role as an iconoclast, and the prospect of his own death can only have been regarded as an unwelcome interruption of his productive life. True to conventional Greek beliefs, his Medea, learning that she has been abandoned by her husband, Jason, longs for death as an escape:

> How I wish a lightning bolt from Heaven
> Would split my head in two!
> What good is there in life for me?
> None! There's nothing but woe!
> O let me die and be released
> From this horrid existence.

Not so fast, says the Chorus, in what seems to be Euripides's own voice:

> O, you reckless one!
> Why do you long for that eternal rest
> That comes only with death?
> There's no need to pray for it!
> It will arrive soon enough.

Never accorded as much acclaim as his illustrious predecessors enjoyed, Euripides won Athens's top prize for tragedy only four times, compared with thirteen for Aeschylus and twenty for Sophocles. He was also unlucky at love, and both his wives left him for other men. He became a recluse, making a home for himself in a cave on Salamis. In 408, at the invitation of King Archelaus, he moved to Macedon, and lived there in another cave, happy as a clam, until he died.

How he died is a mystery. Owing to his unsympathetic female characters, like Medea, Phaedra, and Helen, Euripides gained a reputation as a woman-hater, and one legend says a group of angry women did him in. Another story says he was torn apart by wild dogs while walking home from an evening festival. Probably he died in his cave around 406 BC, in his late seventies, of natural causes, exacerbated by the frigid winter weather of Macedon.

Euripides was buried in Macedon near an Athenian settlement in the valley of Arethusa. A memorial inscription reads: "All Greece is the monument of Euripides. The Macedonian earth covers only his bones, for it was there that his life reached its end. His homeland is Athens, the Greece of all Greece. He gave much delight through his muse and is greatly esteemed."

SOCRATES

A troublemaker and proud of it, Socrates technically wasn't an author at all, since the only surviving accounts of his ideas were written by his famous pupil Plato. Born in Athens in 469 BC, Socrates came from a middle-class family; his father was either a stone-mason, sculptor, or woodworker, or maybe all three, and his mother was a midwife. Known around Athens as a philosopher and teacher who delighted

in paradoxical questioning that proved embarrassing to the powers-that-be, he married a woman named Xanthippe, who was as argumentative as he was.

When he stood trial at the age of seventy, he was charged with impiety against the religion of the state and of corrupting the minds of young people. Something of a smart aleck, he defended his role as a gadfly by suggesting that his punishment should be a handsome salary and free dinners for the rest of his life. "Not a chance," said his judges, and instead sentenced him to death by drinking hemlock, a highly poisonous, perennial, herbaceous flowering plant native to the Mediterranean region. It disrupts the central nervous system, and even small doses result in muscular paralysis, causing respiratory failure and death.

That fate didn't faze Socrates. His views on death, and the serene manner in which he approached his own end, are well chronicled in several of Plato's dialogues. In the *Apology*, Socrates observes, "To fear death, gentlemen, is to think oneself wise when one is not, to think one knows what one does not know. As far as anyone knows, death may be the greatest of all blessings, yet people fear it as if they knew for certain that it is the greatest of evils."

Socrates was condemned, by a vote of 281 to 220. Plato tells us that as he was taken away to prison, he told his judges: "The hour of departure has arrived, and now we go our separate ways—I to die and you to live. Which is better only God knows."

This account of Socrates's final moments is from Plato's *Phaedo:*

"In what way shall we bury you?" asked his friend Crito.

"Any way you like," replied Socrates. "But first you have to catch me! Be careful that I do not run away from you. You think the dead body you will soon see is the same Socrates standing here talking. But when I have drunk the poison, I shall leave you all and go to the joys of the blessed. So be of good cheer then, Crito, and remember that you're not burying Socrates, you're only burying my body. Now, we'd better get the poison ready."

Crito said, "It's early. We can wait a little while."

Socrates answered, "I do not think that I would gain anything by waiting. I would only seem ridiculous to myself for trying to squeeze out a few more minutes from a life that is already forfeit. So please, get the poison."

The jailer came with the poison, and Socrates said, "You're experienced in these matters. What am I supposed to do?"

The man answered: "Just walk about until your legs are heavy, and then lie down, and the poison will do the rest."

"I understand," Socrates said. "Now I ask the gods to give me a prosperous journey from this to the other world."

Then he cheerfully drank all the poison. His friends began to weep. "What are you doing?" said Socrates. "Please just be quiet—a man should be allowed to die in peace."

He walked about until he said his legs began to fail, and then he lay on his back. The jailer pressed his foot hard, and asked him if he could feel; and he said, "No, nothing. When the poison reaches my heart, that will be the end." In a while he began to grow cold about the groin. Suddenly he turned to Crito and reminded him to offer a rooster to Aesclepius, the god of healing, in thanks for delivering him from a painful life.

"Of course," said Crito. "Anything else?"

But Socrates did not answer, and they noted that his eyes were fixed.

Such was the end of our friend, who was the wisest and best and most just man of his time.

PLATO

Plato's real name was Aristocles, which in Greek means "highest glory." He was a hefty lad whose wrestling coach gave him the nickname Plato, meaning "broad-shouldered." It must have suited him better than his real name, since that's how he has been known ever since.

Born in 428 BC in Athens to a politically connected family, Plato did a stint in the army, and then, as a civilian, he became a devoted follower of Socrates. In 387 he founded a school in Athens that he called the Academy. Among his prize pupils was Aristotle, who studied there for twenty years, beginning in 367. A prolific writer, Plato left a number of dialogues and epistles, including the *Apology*, *Crito*, *The Republic*, *Phaedo*, the *Symposium*, the *Parmenides*, the *Sophist*, and *The Laws*. He is the principal chronicler of the life of Socrates and the main source of his mentor's teachings.

Plato was not bashful in expressing views on a number of political, artistic, and metaphysical subjects—including death. In the *Symposium*, he recounts the legendary Greek warrior Achilles's heroic death, seemingly with approval:

Achilles was quite aware that he might avoid death and return home, and live to a good old age, if he abstained from slaying Hector. Nevertheless he gave his life to revenge his friend, and dared to die. For this the gods honored him and sent him to the Islands of the Blest. These are my reasons for affirming that Love is the noblest and mightiest of the gods, and the chief author of virtue in life, and of happiness after death.

Plato likely believed that the eternal human soul is in a constant cycle, trapped in a human body, and then escaping the body at death to return to the "realm of the forms," then back to a human body, and so on *ad infinitum*. In *Timaeus*, he paints a picture of a pleasant natural death (as opposed to the pain of a violent one). Plato writes:

> In a natural death the soul flies away with joy. For that which takes place according to nature is pleasant, but that which is contrary to nature is painful. And thus *death*, if caused by disease or produced by wounds, is painful and violent; but that sort of *death* which comes with old age and fulfills the debt of nature is the easiest of *death*s, and is accompanied with pleasure rather than with pain.

Plato's death, in 347 BC at the age of eighty-one, was of the pleasant variety. In his treatise on old age, the Roman poet Cicero characterizes Plato's final years as "a tranquil and serene evening of a life spent in peaceful, blameless, enlightened pursuits." According to a popular account, a Thracian girl played the flute for Plato on the evening of his death. Untrained as a musician, the girl didn't get the tempo right, so Plato began to conduct the piece as she played. He then drifted peacefully into death, music ringing in his ears. Another tale says he dropped dead at a wedding feast—presumably while having a jolly time.

Never married, Plato willed the Academy to his sister's son, Speusippus, and it survived as an institution of learning for nearly a thousand years.

ARISTOTLE

Aristotle, third in the philosophical succession from Socrates to Plato, characterized by Dante as "the master of those who know," was born in 384 BC in Stagira, Chalcide, which is about

fifty-five miles east of the present-day Greek city of Thessalonika. His name supposedly means "highest purpose," which gives you an idea of what his parents had in mind for him. His father, the personal physician to King Amyntas II of Macedon, was named Nicomachus.

Aristotle's parents both died when he was young, and he was brought up by an uncle named Proxenus. At the age of eighteen he was sent to study in Athens at Plato's Academy, where he remained for twenty years; then, after Plato's death, he opened his own school, which he called the Lyceum. Aristotle wrote extensively about politics, ethics, metaphysics, and poetics.

Aristotle was married to Pythias, the foster daughter of his friend and patron Hermias, king of the Greek city-state of Atarneus. They had a daughter named Pythias, for her mother. After his wife's death, her servant, Herpyllis, became Aristotle's live-in mistress, and they had a son, Nicomachus, to whom Aristotle dedicated his famous philosophical work, *The Nicomachean Ethics.*

When Aristotle was in his early forties, he was invited by King Philip of Macedon to become the tutor of his son, Prince Alexander—better known as Alexander the Great. Teacher and pupil didn't always see eye to eye, and at one point Alexander accused Aristotle of wanting to assassinate him, and threatened him with execution. Aristotle skedaddled back to Athens.

When Alexander died in 323 (after a prolonged drinking binge), Athenians were eager to rid themselves of any vestige of the hated Macedonians. Because of his association with Alexander, Aristotle was accused of some of the same crimes that Socrates had been charged with, and rather than stick around to see if he would meet the same fate, Aristotle got out of town fast, saying, "I will not allow the Athenians to sin twice against philosophy."

He retired to his mother's family estate in Macedon, where he died shortly thereafter, at the tender age of sixty-two, from a stomach ailment—perhaps ulcers—that he suffered from much of his life. There is no evidence for either of two stories that were circulated after his death: that he killed himself with hemlock in tribute to Socrates, or that he threw himself into the sea because he could not explain the motion of the tides.

Aristotle believed that soul and body were inseparable, the soul being a component of the body, keeping it alive and enriching it, in much the same way as blood does. When the body died, so did the soul. While Aristotle did allow for the possibility of the immortality of the intellect, it is doubtful that he meant an individual, personal intellect. In *The Nicomachean Ethics*, he wrote:

"Death is the most terrible of all things, for it is the end, and nothing is any longer thought to be either good or bad for the dead."

VIRGIL

"Arms and the man I sing!" are the ringing opening lines of Virgil's *Aeneid*, the epic poem that celebrates the voyage of the Trojan prince Aeneas to Italy after the fall of Troy and his founding of what was to become the Roman Empire. Virgil himself, or Publius Virgilius Maro to use his full name, was far from being the kind of military hero he extols in his poem. Today, he might be called a "dweeb"  or a "nerd"—a virtual recluse, shy and sickly, with digestive problems throughout his life. Born in Andes, Cisalpine Gaul, in what is now Lombardy, Italy, on October 15, 70 BC, he came from a family of landowners. After attending school in several

Italian cities, he devoted himself to poetry, turning out the pastoral *Eclogues* and *Georgics* before writing his masterpiece, the *Aeneid*.

Very much a loner and never married, Virgil was probably a Stoic, basically materialist in his worldview, with no clear notion of an afterlife. He seems to approve of the prevailing sentiment of the time that it would be noble to die in battle, as expressed by Aeneas, his Trojan hero, in John Dryden's sonorous translation:

> "Thrice and four times happy those," he cried,
> "That under Ilian walls before their parents died!
> Tydides, bravest of the Grecian train!
> Why could not I by that strong arm be slain,
> And lie by noble Hector on the plain,
> Or great Sarpedon in those bloody fields
> Where Simois rolls the bodies and the shields
> Of heroes, whose dismember'd hands yet bear
> The dart aloft, and clench the pointed spear!"

Virgil journeyed to Greece in 19 BC, hoping to find the inspiration to revise some parts of the *Aeneid*. While there, he met his friend and patron, the Emperor Augustus, who was also visiting Athens. On his way back to Rome, Virgil came down with a fever, possibly a symptom of tuberculosis. He made it back to Italy, but only as far as Brundisium, where he died on September 21 at the age of fifty. Unable to complete his revisions of the *Aeneid*, he had left instructions for it to be burned—but Augustus, with an emperor's prerogative and a shrewd literary hunch, overrode his wishes and ordered it published anyway. Hail, Caesar!

HORACE

The Roman poet Horace, born on December 8, 65 BC, in Venusia, a military colony in southeast Italy, was named Quintus

Horatius Flaccus—which means Limp, or Feeble, or maybe Flap-Eared Horace the Fifth. What his parents had in mind with that label is anybody's guess.

As an adult, he was known to be short, fat, and prematurely gray-haired. No wonder he took his pleasures when and where he could find them. According to the reliably gossipy historian Suetonius, Horace was a notorious hedonist who was addicted to pornographic pictures and had mirrors installed in his bedroom. It was Horace, in one of his odes, who coined the phrase "*Carpe diem*," usually translated as "Seize the day." He was educated at Rome's finest school and joined the army—unfortunately ending up on the wrong side at the battle of Philippi, where Marc Antony and Octavian defeated Brutus, for whom Horace fought.

Amnesty was granted all around by the new Emperor Octavian, soon to be Augustus, so Horace was able to find a government job and start writing poetry. His *Satires*, his *Epistles*, and his *Odes* became quite popular, and Horace obtained the patronage of Maecenas, one of Augustus's chief advisers. Maecenas lavished Horace with gifts, one of which was an estate in the Sabine Hills, where Horace enjoyed a leisurely life, often sleeping until ten o'clock in the morning. Suetonius reports that Horace, who never married, led a vigorous sex life in his mirrored bedroom. There were reports that he enjoyed having partners of both genders.

Horace apparently accepted the traditional Roman religion, but devoted little speculative thought to the meaning of life and death, either in his works or in his private life. He claimed to have been startled out of his atheism when he heard a clap of thunder in a cloudless sky. His poems embody a conventional belief in the gods, to whom he gives due respect, but for whom there is little evident devotion.

In early November of 8 BC, Maecenas died, and Horace rushed to his patron's villa in Rome, where he himself died suddenly three weeks later, on November 27, just twelve days before his fifty-seventh birthday. Some speculated that he died of grief at the loss of Maecenas, or possibly even committed suicide in order to follow him in death. It is more likely that Horace succumbed to a heart attack or stroke. However he died, it must have been unexpected—while he had begun to draft a will, in which he left all his belongings to the Emperor Augustus (as was expected of Augustus's friends), he didn't live long enough to complete the document. Horace is buried near Maecenas on the Esquiline Hill in Rome.

OVID

Ovid, the enormously popular Roman poet whose *Metamorphoses* is one of the most influential works of Western literature, spent the last decade of his life as an exile in a bleak and remote Black Sea community in what is now Romania, where the winters were bitter cold, savage Cossack barbarians made periodic raids, and no one spoke Latin.

Why one of Rome's leading lights wound up in the boondocks is anybody's guess. "A poem and a mistake" is the cryptic reason Ovid gave for his mysterious banishment by Augustus Caesar in 8 AD. The "poem" in question was undoubtedly *Ars Amatoria* (*The Art of Love*), a racy bit of erotica that might well have required punishment from an emperor supposedly dedicated to restoring public morality. But the "mistake," which Ovid would say only was worse than murder and more harmful than poetry, remains unknown. Most likely it was some form of *lèse majesté*, a personal offense against the Emperor—possibly the discovery of Augustus in incestuous *flagrante delicto* with his own daughter. Be that as it may, Ovid was not a happy camper during the last years of his life.

Born on March 20, 43 BC, in Abruzzo, in central Italy, Ovid is best known for the *Metamorphoses*, a compendium of mythological transformations, which provided source material for such later authors as Dante, Chaucer, Boccaccio, Spenser, and Shakespeare. He is also noted for his love poetry, particularly the *Ars Amatoria* and *Amores*. In the *Ars Amatoria*, Ovid shows not only his cynical take on romance, but also an insouciant view of the role the gods play in human life:

> Promise women anything; women love promises. And be sure to swear by all the gods that you'll be true to your word. Jupiter will just look down and laugh at your lies and toss them to Aeolus for the winds to play with. He used to make the same kind of promises to Juno, down by the River Styx, when he swore he'd be faithful. And you know how well he kept those promises! So take courage from his example.
>
> It's a good idea to believe in the gods and to bring offerings of wine and incense to their altars. You would do well to observe the precepts of religion. Don't lie to anybody, except, of course, women—for that doesn't count!

It's little wonder that Ovid was divorced twice before he was thirty. His third wife, however, was a keeper, and she thought the same of him, for she stuck by him during his exile.

Ovid's poetry turned bitter during his years away from Rome. In his writings he complains of a harsh climate, a general weakness in his body, insomnia, loss of weight and appetite, pallor, a parched tongue, a pain in the side attributed to the winter cold, trembling hands, deep wrinkles, senility, delirium, and depression. These ailments finally caught up with him in the harsh winter of 17 AD, when Ovid died at the age of sixty. He was buried a few kilometers away in a town that was renamed Ovidiu in his honor in 1930.

MARCUS AURELIUS

"Death is a release from the impressions of the senses, from the desires that make us their puppets, from the vagaries of the mind, and from the hard service of the flesh," wrote Marcus Aurelius in his *Meditations.* The future Roman Emperor was to the manner born—his parents were both members of the ruling patrician class—in Rome on April 26, 121 AD. As a young man he was a serious student, devoted to the teachings of the Greek Stoic philosopher Epictetus.

Marcus's early life would make a good soap opera. He came to the attention of the Emperor Hadrian, who arranged for him to be adopted by Antoninus, who was next in line to be Emperor. Antoninus, who had another adoptive son, known as Verus, succeeded to the throne in 138. Marcus continued his studies, married Antoninus's daughter Faustina, and served as consul, the leader of the Senate. In 161, Antoninus died, and Marcus shared the throne with his adoptive brother until Verus's death in 169, after which Marcus ruled alone.

Marcus Aurelius is most remembered for his philosophical *Meditations*, rooted in Stoic philosophy, many of which deal with the meaning of death, characterized as a welcome and nat-ural part of life. "Despise not death, but welcome it, for nature wills it like all else," he wrote. "Live a good life. If there are gods and they are just, then they will not care how devout you have been, but will welcome you based on the virtues you have lived by. If there are gods, but unjust, then you should not want to worship them. If there are no gods, then you will be gone, but will have lived a noble life that will live on in the memories of your loved ones."

Perhaps his final word on the subject is this wry observation: "Death smiles at us all. All we can do is smile back."

Marcus Aurelius, smiling or not, met his death in 180, when he was fifty-nine, near what is now Vienna. He had been ill for some time with an unknown ailment, possibly cancer, and is thought to have died of an infection. There were tales that he had died of the plague brought back from Parthia by his army, or from lead poisoning in the water pipes, or that his son, Com-modus, hastened his departure by administering poison—but these suppositions are all without evidence. Marcus is buried in the Mausoleum of Hadrian at Castel Sant'Angelo in Rome.

The Middle Ages

AUGUSTINE OF HIPPO

Augustine of Hippo, known in many Christian churches as Saint Augustine or sometimes Saint Austin, was no saint as a young man. Born in 354 in Tagaste, a now-vanished city on the site of what is now Souk Ahras, Algeria, he was a pleasure-seeking playboy who lived in the fast lane until his mid-thirties. A professor of rhetoric, first in Carthage and later in Rome and Milan, he had a mistress in Carthage—with whom he sired a son named Adeodatus—and there were other paramours in Milan. He was noted for a prayer in which he asked God, "Give me chastity—but not yet."

His mother, a devout Christian convert named Monica, took a dim view of Augustine's debauchery and tried for years to convert her son. He went through a series of philosophical attachments—Manicheism, skepticism, and neo-Platonism—before renouncing his hedonistic life and adopting Christianity. He later became a bishop in the city of Hippo (Algeria), a revered Father of the Church, and the author of several notable works on theology, which include *The City of God* and the *Confessions*.

Augustine held carefully reasoned and theologically detailed ideas about what happens to people after death, stemming from his reading of the Bible and from traditional Catholic teaching.

He was noted for expounding the doctrine of *amillennialism*, the belief that Christ was now reigning in a symbolic thousand-year period that would be followed, at world's end, by final judgment and the establishment of a permanent Kingdom of God. Augustine taught that the eternal fate of the soul is determined at death, and that the fires of Purgatory purify those who die in communion with the Church, but are still tainted by sin.

Augustine's death came at the age of seventy-six, on August 28, 430, of a virulent fever, aggravated by stress and malnutrition, that he suffered three months into a siege of the city of Hippo by the German tribe known as Vandals. The Vandals kept Hippo under attack for fourteen months, and twenty-five years later, ensuring their name would be known for centuries to come, the same bunch sacked Rome, leading to the fall of the Roman Empire.

Augustine's remains were buried first in the Hippo cathedral, but when Catholic bishops were expelled from northern Africa by the Vandal ruler Huneric in 484, they took Augustine's bones with them to Cagliari in Sardinia. About 720 the remains were acquired by the bishop of Pavia, Italy, who deposited them in Pavia's Church of San Pietro in Ciel d'Oro, where they now reside.

THOMAS AQUINAS

Nicknamed "Dumb Sicilian Ox" by his fellow monks, Thomas Aquinas was heavyset, hardworking, and slow to speak. But when he had something to say, he bellowed. Born January 28, 1225, into a well-connected family in Aquino County, Sicily, Thomas was the youngest son of Landulf of Aquino, a *miles*, or knight, and Dame Theodora, whose family were minor aristocrats in

Naples. He was destined for monastic life from age five, when he was sent to study at the Benedictine abbey of Monte Cassino, where his uncle had been abbot. At nineteen, he joined the upstart Dominican order—to the chagrin of his pro-Benedictine family, who went so far as to kidnap him to try to dissuade him, but to no avail.

Ensconced among the Dominicans, Thomas wrote numerous carefully reasoned theological works, the most famous of which, *Summa Theologica* (sometimes *Theologiæ*) and *Summa Contra Gentiles*, still form the basis of much Roman Catholic thought.

On December 6, 1273, when he was forty-eight years old, he was observed in the chapel of the Dominican monastery at Naples levitating and having a conversation with an icon of the crucified Christ. "What would you have as a reward for your labor?" Christ supposedly said. "Nothing but you, Lord," said Thomas. After this episode—which was either a mystical epiphany or a stroke—Thomas never wrote another line, telling his secretary, "I cannot, for all that I have written before seems like straw, compared to what has been revealed to me."

Thomas's view of life after death was the orthodox Catholic view of reward and punishment in Heaven, Hell, and Purgatory—a view that he himself helped to shape. In *Summa Theologica*, he wrote: "The soul becomes separated from its mortal body, and its merits determine whether it receives the consequences of good or of evil. Therefore, after death the soul either receives or is denied a final reward. The state of final retribution is twofold: for the good, it is Paradise; for the evil, because of unforgiven faults, it is Hell. . . . If, however, the soul is in a state that prevents it from receiving its final reward because of minor sins that have been committed, it is detained in Purgatory, where souls may expiate those faults and defects that detract from the glory of human nature until they are ready to obtain their reward."

In 1274, Pope Gregory X summoned Thomas to take part in a council in Lyon on May 1, and in January he set out from Naples, a distance of some 600 miles, on foot and by donkey. Along the Appian Way, Thomas hit his head on a tree branch and was knocked off the donkey. He was taken to the nearby monastery of Monte Cassino to recuperate. He set out once more, but fell ill again, this time stopping at the castle of his niece, Countess Francesca Ceccano. After a few days, he felt no better, and asked to be moved to the Cistercian Abbey of Fossanova six miles away. "If the Lord wishes to take me," he said, "it's better that he find me in a holy monastery than in a layperson's castle."

Thomas was given last rites by the monks, received the Eucharist, and, with remarkable stamina and syntactical precision for a dying man, offered this lengthy prayer:

> If in this world there be any knowledge of this sacrament stronger than that of faith, I wish now to use it in affirming that I firmly believe and know as certain that Jesus Christ, True God and True Man, Son of God and Son of the Virgin Mary, is in this Sacrament . . . I receive Thee, the price of my redemption, for Whose love I have watched, studied, and laboured. Thee have I preached; Thee have I taught. Never have I said anything against Thee: if anything was not well said, that is to be attributed to my ignorance. Neither do I wish to be obstinate in my opinions, but if I have written anything erroneous concerning this sacrament or other matters, I submit all to the judgment and correction of the Holy Roman Church, in whose obedience I now pass from this life.

He died on March 7, 1274, at the age of forty-nine. The poet Dante Alighieri, in his *Inferno*, claimed that Thomas had been poisoned (possibly by a fellow monk, or a knight, or a physician) on the orders of King Charles of Anjou, with whom Thomas was at odds politically. Thomas's body was given to the Dominican order, and today most of it is in a gold and silver sarcophagus in the Church of St. Sernin in Toulouse, France—except his right arm, which is in the Church of Santa Maria Sopra Minerva in Rome, and a bone from his left arm, which is preserved as a relic in the cathedral of Naples. Canonized in 1323, Saint Thomas now rests in pieces.

DANTE ALIGHIERI

Dante Alighieri had a lifelong obsession with a young woman he saw only twice in his life. Best remembered for his epic poem, *The Divine Comedy*, Dante was born in Florence, Italy, around 1265. His family were Guelphs, members of a political party that supported the papacy in a power struggle with the German emperor, and this affiliation would later cause him much grief.

Dante married Gemma de Manetto Donati, and they had four children—but the love of his life, at least in his own mind, was Beatrice Portinari, whom he met for the first time at a May Day party at her house when he was nine years old and she was eight. Their second and last meeting was a chance encounter nine years later on a Florence street. Beatrice remained a fixation with him, and he wrote extensively of her in his autobiography *La Vita Nuova* (*The New Life*) and in the *Paradiso* section of *The Divine Comedy*, where she appears as his celestial guide.

Through a series of political machinations, in which the pro-pope Guelphs were pitted against the pro-emperor Ghibbelines,

Dante found himself on the losing side and was banished in perpetual exile from his beloved Florence. Dante's vision of life after death pops up often in his writing. Death is viewed as a dreaded calamity in *La Vita Nuova*, where Dante writes (in this translation by his namesake, Dante Gabriel Rossetti):

> Death, always cruel,
> Pity's foe in chief,
> Mother who brought forth grief,
> Merciless judgment and without appeal!
> Since thou alone hast made my heart to feel
> This sadness and unweal,
> My tongue upbraideth thee without relief.

In *The Divine Comedy*, Dante divides the afterlife into the three locales of Catholic theology: Hell (*Inferno*) for really nasty evildoers, Purgatory (*Purgatorio*) for basically good people who backslid occasionally and must be cleansed of minor sins, and Heaven (*Paradiso*) for those righteous few whose souls are pure and receive the beatific vision. The torments of Hell are hard to ignore, as Dante describes them in horrific detail, and the utter despair of those who are unfortunate enough to be sent there is reflected in the famous motto over the entrance: "Abandon all hope, ye who enter here." The Roman poet Virgil is Dante's guide through the *Inferno* and most of *Purgatorio*, but because he is a pagan and cannot enter *Paradiso*, he is replaced as a guide in the final book by Beatrice, the love of Dante's life.

Certainly Dante must have aspired to the celestial glory that he tries to convey in the final canto of *Paradiso*:

> My mind, thus wholly in suspense, was gazing
> Steadfast and motionless, and all intent,
> And, gazing, grew enkindled more and more.
> Such in that Light doth one at last become,

That one can never possibly consent
To turn therefrom for any other sight;
Because the Good, which is the will's real object,
Is therein wholly gathered, and, outside,
That is defective which is perfect there.

Dante reached the ultimate goodness and light in 1321 when he was fifty-six. On the way home to Ravenna from a visit to Venice, he came down with what was probably malaria and died a month later, on September 14. His body is buried in Ravenna, and the tomb erected for him in Florence in the Church of Santa Croce remains empty. Although the Florence City Council formally revoked his exile in 2008, there is no indication that Dante plans to relocate.

GEOFFREY CHAUCER

Jack of many trades—valet, government clerk, forester, soldier, international diplomat, and the first poet buried in Westminster Abbey's Poets' Corner—Geoffrey Chaucer was born in London sometime around 1343, the precise date and locale being unknown. His father and grandfather were wine merchants. Through family connections, he was placed at  the age of fourteen as a page in the household of the Countess of Ulster. Thereafter, he rose in the ranks of royal courtiers, serving in various capacities for kings Edward III, Richard II, and, briefly, Henry IV. His various jobs included valet de chambre, special diplomatic envoy, clerk of the King's Works, forester (a sort of

game warden), and controller of customs. So highly regarded
was he by Edward III that he was granted a gallon of wine daily
for life, possibly as a reward for an early poetical work.

When Chaucer was twenty-three, he married Philippa
Roet, a lady-in-waiting to Edward's Queen Philippa, and the
Chaucers had three or four children (the record is not precise),
one of whom, Thomas, later became Speaker of the House of
Commons.

Chaucer's great achievement—accomplished while he held
down his day job at court—was *The Canterbury Tales*, an
account of a pilgrimage that portrays medieval English travel-
ers from many walks of life in vivid, amusing, and sometimes
bawdy detail. (If you read it in high school, those parts were
probably tactfully omitted.) Although he was a sophisticated
man of the world with a ribald sense of humor, Chaucer was
also a faithful Catholic, and he apparently had some concern
that his writings might stain his immortal soul. As a kind of
insurance policy, he wrote this "retraction" at the end of *The
Canterbury Tales*:

> Now I pray to all that hear or read this little treatise, that
> if there be anything in it that pleases them, that for it they
> thank our Lord Jesus Christ, from whom proceeds all wit
> and goodness. And if there be anything that displeases
> them, I pray them also that they ascribe it to the fault
> of my ignorance, and not to my will, for I would gladly
> have written better if I had had the skill. For our book
> says, "All that is written is written for our doctrine,"
> and that is my intent. Wherefore I beseech you meekly,
> for the mercy of God, that you pray for me that Christ
> have mercy on me and forgive me my sins, namely my
> translations and editings of worldly vanities, which I
> revoke in this retraction. . . . that Christ in his great mercy
> forgive me the sin. But for the translation of Boethius'

Consolation, and other books of legends of saints, and homilies, and morality, and devotion, I thank our Lord Jesus Christ and his blissful Mother, and all the saints of heaven, beseeching them that they from henceforth until the end of my life send me grace to bewail my guilt, and to contemplate the salvation of my soul, and grant me grace of true penitence, confession, and satisfaction in this present life, through the benign grace of him that is king of kings and priest over all priests, that bought us with the precious blood of his heart, so that I may be one of them at the day of doom that shall be saved....

Here is ended the book of the Tales of Canterbury,
compiled by Geoffrey Chaucer,
on whose soul may Jesus Christ have mercy.
Amen.

On December 24, 1399, when Chaucer was fifty-six, he optimistically took out a fifty-three-year lease on a dwelling in the garden of St. Mary's Chapel, Westminster, and it was probably here that he died October 25, 1400. There is some speculation that he was murdered by enemies of his patron, Richard II—possibly even on the orders of Richard's successor, Henry IV. Hardly anybody believes this, and more likely he died of some unknown illness, or maybe that daily gallon of wine. He left no will, and there was no public funeral. By virtue of his status as a tenant of Westminster Abbey, he was buried there, and his remains were moved in 1556 to a more ornate tomb—the first in what has become known as Poets' Corner.

The Renaissance

MIGUEL DE CERVANTES

The early life of Miguel de Cervantes would make a fascinating novel—and, as a matter of fact, it did. Known now as the father of the modern novel, Cervantes was born about September 29, 1547, near Madrid. His father, who was deaf, worked as a surgeon, in those days not a very lucrative trade, and as a young man Cervantes found employment in Rome as an aide to Giulio Acquaviva, a Roman Catholic prelate who later became a cardinal.

Cervantes joined the Spanish military and fought in the Battle of Lepanto in 1571, when an alliance of Catholic nations defeated the Ottoman Turks. Although seriously wounded, losing the use of his left hand, Cervantes stayed in the military several more years. In 1575 he embarked on a new voyage with his brother Rodrigo, and the two were captured by Barbary pirates, who held them for ransom in Algeria. The brothers were imprisoned for five years, making numerous thwarted efforts to escape. Their parents sent two priests with three hundred crowns as ransom, but it was only enough to free Rodrigo. At last, with the aid of an order of monks known as the Trinitarians, the parents raised five hundred gold ducats, which proved adequate to spring Miguel, and he returned to Madrid.

When he was thirty-seven, Cervantes married Catalina de Palacios Salazar y Vozmediano, who was nineteen. They never had children, although Cervantes had fathered a daughter in an earlier relationship.

The year after he married he published a novel, *La Galatea*, but it met with only modest success. After that, he found work as a supplier to the "invincible" Spanish Armada, but some irregularities in his accounts landed him in jail. This misfortune was a blessing in disguise, for during his imprisonment Cervantes began work on what was to become his masterpiece: *The Ingenious Gentleman, Don Quixote de La Mancha.* It is a romantic tale of a would-be knight who sets out to revive chivalry. Don Quixote has many adventures, in the course of which he employs his lance to "tilt with windmills," an amusing but hopelessly futile pursuit. *Don Quixote* is regarded as the earliest example of the modern novel, and it is the most influential work in Spanish literature.

Cervantes viewed death with the eyes of a practicing Catholic. This is his account of Don Quixote's final moments:

Since nothing earthly lasts forever, especially man's life, and since Don Quixote's enjoyed no special dispensation from heaven to stay its course, its end came when he least looked for it. A fever settled upon him and kept him in bed for six days, during which he was often visited by his friends—Carrasco, and the curate, and Nicholas the barber—while his squire Sancho Panza never left his bedside. His friends called in the doctor, who felt his pulse and frowned, and said that he had better attend to his soul, as his body was in a bad way.

Don Quixote heard this news calmly; but his housekeeper, his niece, and his squire began to weep copiously, as if he already lay dead before them. The doctor's opinion was that melancholy and depression were bringing him to his end.

"I feel that I am rapidly drawing near death," said Don Quixote. "Let the curate hear my confession and call a notary to make my will."

When Don Quixote had finished confessing and dictating his will, he felt faint and stretched out on the bed. The house was in confusion; but Don Quixote's niece continued to nibble sweets, and the housekeeper kept on nipping sherry, and Sancho Panza smiled contentedly— for the prospect of inheriting property softens the pangs of grief.

At last Don Quixote's end came, after he had received the last rites, and had in forceful terms declared how much he hated books of chivalry. The notary said that in no book of chivalry had he ever read of any knight-errant dying in his bed so calmly and so like a Christian as Don Quixote, who amid the tears and lamentations of all present yielded up his spirit. The curate asked the notary to attest that Alonso Quixano the Good, commonly called Don Quixote of La Mancha, had passed away from this present life, and died naturally.

Cervantes never got rich from his writing—royalties in the seventeenth century were not customary—and he ended his life in near poverty. As his health began to fail, he worked tirelessly on a new novel, *The Travels of Persiles and Sigismunda*, which he thought would be "either the worst or the best book ever written." He finished it four days before he died at age sixty-eight. He had developed edema, then known as "dropsy," which led to heart failure, and after receiving the last rites, he died in his home in Madrid on April 23, 1616—the same day that William Shakespeare died in Stratford-upon-Avon. Cervantes was carried from the house, "face uncovered," according to the rule of the Franciscans, and buried in the convent of the Trinitarian nuns in Madrid.

Always cheerful, even in the face of his imminent death, Cervantes wrote a personal farewell in the prologue of his final work, in which he recounts discussing his ailment with a young medical student. The student advises him,

"Sir, your malady is the dropsy, which not all the water of the Ocean, no matter how sweet, can cure. You should curtail your drinking, and be sure to eat properly, and without any other medicine, you should do all right."

Cervantes replies, "Many people have told me the same thing, but I can no more give up drinking for pleasure than if I had been born to do nothing else. My life is slipping away, and according to the diary my pulse is keeping, it will come to an end by this Sunday. I have to close my life's account. Good-bye, humours; good-bye, merry friends, for I perceive I am dying, in the wish to see you happy in the other life."

WALTER RALEIGH

Danger lurked around every corner that Walter Raleigh turned, and more often than not, Raleigh pursued it. He was born January 22, 1552, in Devonshire, to a staunchly Protestant family, which had a number of narrow escapes from attempts by England's Catholic Queen "Bloody" Mary to ferret out heretics. Life became easier for the Raleighs when the Protestant Queen Elizabeth I took the throne in 1558. After a brief stint at Oxford University, young Walter left there to roam the Continent—possibly fighting as a mercenary in various skirmishes—but eventually returned to England and may have studied law.

At the age of twenty-six, Raleigh launched his remarkable career—explorer, poet, historian, soldier, courtier, diplomat, and probably spy—with an expedition to America with Humphrey Gilbert, his half-brother. He later returned to the New World and founded a short-lived settlement in a place he named Virginia in honor of Elizabeth I, the "Virgin Queen." In 1587, he sent 117 colonists to Roanoke Island in what is now North Carolina. By 1590, this "lost colony" had vanished without a trace.

Raleigh brought tobacco with him back to the court, where he popularized the "healthful" habit of smoking. The dashing explorer became a favorite of Queen Elizabeth. He became a member of Parliament, was awarded extensive land holdings in England and Ireland, and was knighted by the queen in 1585.

A slight indiscretion—the queen discovered Raleigh had secretly married one of her ladies-in-waiting—briefly made him a prisoner in the Tower of London. Released two months later, he led another expedition to America in search of the fabled El Dorado, "City of Gold." He did not find it, but he worked his way back into good standing with the queen. Elizabeth died in 1603, and her successor, James I, intensely disliked Raleigh. Within a matter of months, the king accused him of plotting against the throne, charged him with treason, and sentenced him to death, then relented and reduced the punishment to life in prison. Raleigh, never one to be idle, wrote his *History of the World* during the twelve years he was locked up in the Tower of London.

At length he was freed to lead another fruitless quest for El Dorado. This time Raleigh disobeyed the King's orders and attacked a Spanish settlement. On his return to England, the outraged Spanish ambassador prevailed upon James to execute him. Raleigh was beheaded on October 29, 1618, at the age of sixty-six.

Raleigh's views of death were those of a faithful Anglican, and he had no doubt that he would be suitably rewarded in the next world. He wrote about a blissful afterlife in "The Passionate Man's Pilgrimage," a poem subtitled "Supposed to be written by one at the point of death:"

> Give me my scallop-shell of quiet,
> My staff of faith to walk upon,
> My scrip of joy, immortal diet,
> My bottle of salvation,
> My gown of glory, hope's true gage,
> And thus I'll take my pilgrimage.
>
> Blood must be my body's balmer,
> No other balm will there be given,
> Whilst my soul like a white palmer
> Travels to the land of heaven,
> Over the silver mountains,
> Where spring the nectar fountains;
> And there I'll kiss
> The bowl of bliss,
> And drink my eternal fill.
>
> On every milken hill.
> My soul will be a-dry before,
> But after it will ne'er thirst more.
> And by the happy blissful way
> More peaceful pilgrims I shall see,
> That have shook off their gowns of clay
> And go apparelled fresh like me.

I'll bring them first
To slake their thirst,
And then to taste those nectar suckets,
At the clear wells
Where sweetness dwells,
Drawn up by saints in crystal buckets.

And when our bottles and all we
Are filled with immortality,
Then the holy paths we'll travel,
Strewed with rubies thick as gravel,
Ceilings of diamonds, sapphire floors,
High walls of coral and pearl bowers.

The night before Raleigh's execution, he was allowed to stay overnight at the Westminster Abbey gatehouse. His wife was with him until midnight. Next morning a friend, Charles Thynne, came to say good-bye, and the dean of Westminster, Robert Townson, brought Communion and spiritual comfort. Raleigh ate a hearty breakfast, smoked his pipe, and then dressed in a satin doublet with black embroidered waistcoat, taffeta breeches, colored silk stockings, an embroidered hat, and a black velvet cloak.

London's streets were crowded because it was also the day of the Lord Mayor's Show, a festive parade and celebration. At the place of execution, the Old Palace Yard at Westminster, Dean Townson and two sheriffs led Raleigh to the scaffold. He turned to the spectators and said, "So I take my leave of you all, making my peace with God." He took off his gown and doublet, then asked the executioner to show him the axe. He observed, "This is sharp medicine—but it is a physician for all diseases and miseries." As he placed his head on the block, he said to the executioner, "Let us dispatch. At this hour my ague comes upon me, and I would not have my enemies think I quaked from fear." His final words, as he waited for the axe to fall, were, "Strike, man, strike!"

Raleigh's head was embalmed and given to his wife. The rest of him was laid to rest at St. Margaret's Church in Westminster. Lady Raleigh kept the head in a velvet bag until her death in 1647, at which time it was placed in Raleigh's tomb with the body.

FRANCIS BACON

Curiosity may have killed the cat, and curiosity (plus a chicken) also had a hand in the death of the scientific genius Francis Bacon. Bacon was born to privilege on January 22, 1561. His father, Sir Nicholas Bacon, was Lord Keeper of the Seal, and his mother, Anne Cooke, was the daughter of Sir Anthony Cooke, tutor to King Edward VI. After attending Trinity College in Cambridge, Francis studied law, then took up a career in politics, becoming known as a politician, lawyer, author, orator, member of Parliament, Queen's Counsel, Lord Chancellor of England, first Viscount St. Alban, and, most notably, philosopher and scientist. It was a scientific experiment that caused his death at the age of sixty-five.

Every undergraduate has at least a vague notion that Bacon was responsible for codifying the "scientific method," the basis of all empirical investigation. He wrote many works on science and natural philosophy, notably *The Advancement of Learning*, *Novum Organum Scientiarum* (*New Scientific Method*), *Nova Atlantis* (*The New Atlantis*), and a series of *Essays* on ethical subjects. Bacon's interests were wide-ranging, and some later scholars have even argued that Bacon wrote the plays attributed to Shakespeare.

In his essay "Of Death," Bacon gives his views on the inevitable end of life:

Men fear death, as children fear to go in the dark; and as that natural fear in children, is increased with tales, so is the other. Certainly, the contemplation of death, as the wages of sin, and passage to another world, is holy and religious; but the fear of it, as a tribute due unto nature, is weak. . . . You shall read, in some of the friars' books of mortification, that a man should think with himself, what the pain is, if he have but his finger's end pressed, or tortured, and thereby imagine, what the pains of death are, when the whole body is corrupted, and dissolved; when many times death passeth, with less pain than the torture of a limb; for the most vital parts, are not the quickest of sense. . . . Groans, and convulsions, and a discolored face, and friends weeping, and blacks, and obsequies, and the like, show death terrible. It is worthy the observing, that there is no passion in the mind of man, so weak, but it mates, and masters, the fear of death; and therefore, death is no such terrible enemy, when a man hath so many attendants about him, that can win the combat of him. . . . It is as natural to die, as to be born; and to a little infant, perhaps, the one is as painful, as the other. He that dies in an earnest pursuit, is like one that is wounded in hot blood; who, for the time, scarce feels the hurt; and therefore a mind fixed, and bent upon somewhat that is good, doth avert the dolors of death.

Bacon was in "an earnest pursuit" of a scientific answer when he became fatally ill. Riding in a carriage with a physician friend from London to his home at St. Albans, he noticed snow on the ground and began to wonder if snow would preserve meat in the same way that salt does. He stopped the coach at a farm near Highgate, bought a chicken, gutted it, and proceeded to stuff it with snow. He spent so much time in the damp, freezing air that he developed a chill and decided to stop and rest at the home of his friend, the Earl of Arundel. This turned out not to be a good idea. Bacon's room in the Earl's house was cold and musty, and the chill developed into bronchitis and then pneumonia. Bacon may also have acquired a salmonella infection from the raw chicken meat.

Bacon's personal chaplain, William Rawley, recounted: "He died on the ninth day of April in the year 1626, in the early morning of the day then celebrated for our Saviour's resurrection, in the sixty-sixth year of his age, at the Earl of Arundel's house in Highgate, near London, to which place he casually repaired about a week before; God so ordaining that he should die there of a gentle fever, accidentally accompanied with a great cold, whereby the defluxion of rheum fell so plentifully upon his breast, that he died by suffocation."

Bacon is buried in the parish church of St. Michael's at St. Albans beneath a tomb topped by his seated statue.

CHRISTOPHER MARLOWE

Christopher Marlowe was about two months older than William Shakespeare, and the two were rivals until Marlowe's violent death at the age of twenty-nine. Born in Canterbury, Kent, probably on February 6, 1564, Marlowe sailed through the King's

School in Canterbury and Corpus Christi College in Cambridge
on scholarships, and then sallied forth to London to join the
Admiral's Men theatrical company.

Known to friends as Kit, he achieved early fame as a playwright with seven plays: *Dido, Queen of Carthage*; *Tamburlaine
the Great* (in two parts), *Doctor Faustus*; *The Jew of Malta*;
Edward II; and *The Massacre at Paris.* Through his friendship
with Sir Thomas Walsingham, Marlowe is also thought to have
worked as a spy, gathering damaging information about people
disloyal to Queen Elizabeth.

He also won a reputation for blasphemy and atheism, which
were serious crimes in Elizabethan England. One of his critics,
Thomas Beard, pulled no punches when he called Marlowe "a
poet of scurrility, who by giving too large a swinge to his own wit,
and suffering his lust to have the full reins,....denied God and his
son Christ and blasphemed the Trinity, affirming our Saviour to
be a deceiver and the holy Bible to be but vain and idle stories."

Despite his lack of religious conviction, Marlowe was able
to vividly portray the torments of eternal damnation in *Doctor Faustus*, when Mephistophilis answers Faustus's questions
about the location of hell by telling him:

Within the bowels of these elements,
Where we are tortur'd and remain forever:
Hell hath no limits, nor is circumscrib'd
In one self place; for where we are is hell,
And where hell is, there must we ever be.

Later Faustus contemplates his own consignment to this realm
of doomed souls:

Ah, Faustus,
Now hast thou but one bare hour to live,
And then thou must be damn'd perpetually!

O God,
If thou wilt not have mercy on my soul,
Yet for Christ's sake, whose blood hath ransom'd me,
Impose some end to my incessant pain:
Let Faustus live in hell a thousand years,
A hundred thousand, and at last be sav'd!
O, no end is limited to damned souls!
My God, my God, look not so fierce on me!
Adders and serpents, let me breathe a while!
Ugly hell, gape not! Come not, Lucifer!

Whether or not Marlowe himself feared ugly hell as Faustus did, he met his end suddenly in a brawl on May 30, 1593, in a tavern in Deptford, about three miles from London. The most commonly accepted story (painstakingly researched by Leslie Hotson for his 1925 book *The Death of Christopher Marlowe*) is that Marlowe was invited to the tavern for dinner by Ingram Frizer, a businessman with a shady reputation who also worked for Marlowe's friend Sir Thomas Walsingham. Marlowe and Frizer began to argue over who would pay the bill, and according to an account written in 1600 by William Vaughan, Marlowe "meant to stab with his poniard one named Ingram, that had invited him thither to a feast, and was then playing at tables, he quickly perceiving it, so avoided the thrust that withal drawing out his dagger for his defense, he stabbed Marlowe in the eye, in such sort that his brains coming out at the dagger's point, he shortly after died." The coroner's report confirms that Frizer killed Marlowe in self-defense.

Other stories circulated that Marlowe and Frizer were arguing over a woman whose favor they both sought, or that Marlowe's spy work was somehow related to his death. One tale even holds that Marlowe faked his own death in order to escape punishment for a charge of atheism that was pending against him.

His grave, unmarked, is in St. Nicholas Church, Deptford.

WILLIAM SHAKESPEARE

The private life of William Shakespeare, whose works are more widely known than those of any other author in the history of world (except for Agatha Christie and Jules Verne), remains cloaked in mystery. He was born sometime around April 23, 1564, to John Shakespeare, a glove-maker, and his wife, Mary Arden Shakespeare, in the Warwickshire town of Stratford-upon-Avon. He attended King Edward VI School in Stratford, and at the age of eighteen, married a young woman named Anne Hathaway. They had two daughters, Susanna and Judith, and a son, Hamnet, who died when he was nine.

Leaving his family in Stratford, Will headed for London sometime after 1585 and became part owner of a theatre company known first as the Lord Chamberlain's Men, and later, in a step up, as the King's Men. While living mostly in London, Shakespeare wrote numerous poems, including the famous *Sonnets* (1-154), and more than three dozen plays, most of which have become solid warhorses of the theatrical repertoire, among them the tragedies of *Hamlet, Othello, King Lear, Macbeth, Julius Caesar, Antony and Cleopatra,* and *Romeo and Juliet;* the comedies *Twelfth Night, A Midsummer Night's Dream, The Merchant of Venice, Much Ado About Nothing, The Taming of the Shrew, As You Like It,* and *The Merry Wives of Windsor;* and histories centered on several English kings: *King John, Richard II, Henry IV, Henry V, Henry VI, Richard III, and Henry VIII.*

Speculation about Shakespeare's religion, as well as his politics, his sexual orientation, his physical appearance, and the cause of his death remain just that: speculation. It has been variously suggested that Shakespeare was an Anglican, a secret Roman Catholic, and a nonbeliever—but no one knows. Similarly, he has been called a pro-Tudor conservative, an advocate of the rising bourgeoisie, and a proto-revolutionary—but no one knows. His sonnets suggest that he was in love with a "dark lady" or possibly a "lovely boy"—but no one knows. And whether Shakespeare really resembled the only known portrait of him, by Martin Droeshout (who probably never saw his subject in real life)—you guessed it: no one knows.

Death is a common occurrence in Shakespeare's works; the tragic heroes all meet their ends through flaws in their characters or in their perception of reality. Shakespeare's beliefs about death are ambiguous in his plays. In *Measure for Measure*, Claudio views death with horror:

> Ay, but to die, and go we know not where;
> To lie in cold obstruction, and to rot;
> This sensible warm motion to become
> A kneaded clod; and the delighted spirit
> To bathe in fiery floods or to reside
> In thrilling region of thick-ribbed ice;
> To be imprisoned in the viewless winds,
> And blown with restless violence round about
> The pendent world; or to be worse than worst
> Of those that lawless and incertain thought
> Imagine howling—'tis too horrible.
> The weariest and most loathed worldly life,
> That age, ache, penury, and imprisonment,
> Can lay on nature is a paradise
> To what we fear of death.

Lines from *Julius Caesar*, on the other hand, are more comforting—and more famous.

> Cowards die many times before their deaths;
> The valiant never taste of death but once.
> Of all the wonders that I yet have heard,
> It seems to me most strange that men should fear;
> Seeing that death, a necessary end,
> Will come when it will come.

Hamlet is torn between differing emotions in his famous soliloquy, "To be, or not to be," first welcoming death, but then being gripped by the fear of the unknown:

> To die, to sleep—
> No more, and by a sleep to say we end
> The heart-ache, and the thousand natural shocks
> That flesh is heir to; 'tis a consummation
> Devoutly to be wish'd: to die, to sleep!
> To sleep, perchance to dream, ay, there's the rub!
> For in that sleep of death what dreams may come
> When we have shuffled off this mortal coil
> Must give us pause.

Near the play's end, Hamlet reaches a philosophical acceptance of death. When his friend Horatio tries to forestall Hamlet's duel with Laertes, which he fears will end badly for his friend, Hamlet replies:

> Not a whit; we defy augury. There is a special providence
> in the fall of a sparrow. If it be now, 'tis not to come—if it
> be not to come, it will be now—if it be not now, yet it will
> come—the readiness is all.

Was Shakespeare himself ready? Apparently he had had enough of London life by the time he was forty-nine, and he retired to his home in Stratford, where he died three years later on April 23, 1616—his fifty-second birthday. There is no contemporary account of his last days, the earliest written version being fifty years later, when John Ward, vicar of Stratford from 1662 to 1681, noted in his diary what he had heard about Shakespeare's death: "Shakespeare, Drayton, and Ben Jonson had a merry meeting, and it seems drank too hard, for Shakespeare died of a fever there contracted."

This story is not beyond the realm of possibility: the poet Michael Drayton and the playwright Ben Jonson were friends of Shakespeare's and might have come to visit him in Stratford, possibly on the occasion of the marriage of his younger daughter, Judith. But it probably wasn't the drinking alone that did Shakespeare in; evidence suggests that he had been unwell for some while before his death, for he asked his lawyer, Francis Collins, to draw up a will in January of 1616. The document was not executed until March 25, 1616, less than a month before Shakespeare's death, and the signature is in a shaky hand. This is the famous will in which he left the bulk of his estate to his daughter Susanna, a lesser amount to Judith, and the grudging bequest of his "second-best bed" to his wife, Anne.

Shakespeare was buried two days after his death in a wooden coffin near the altar in Holy Trinity Church, Stratford, where he was a lay rector. Burial space was at a premium in the church, and in order to make room, older remains were sometimes moved to a charnel house underneath the church. To guard against this, some unknown person inscribed upon the gravestone the following bit of doggerel, possibly written by Shakespeare himself in allusion to the fate of poor Yorick's remains in *Hamlet*:

Good friend, for Jesus' sake forbear
To dig the dust enclosed here.

Blest be the man that spares these stones
And curst be he that moves my bones.

JOHN DONNE

Anyone who knows anything at all about John Donne knows that he wrote, "No man is an island, entire of itself; every man is a piece of the continent, a part of the main; if a clod be washed away by the sea, Europe is the less, as well as if a promontory were, as well as if a manor of thy friend's or of thine own were; any man's death diminishes me, because I am involved in mankind, and therefore never send to know for whom the bell tolls; it tolls for thee."

Poet, lawyer, member of Parliament, and Anglican clergyman, Donne was born in the area known as Bread Street, London, on January 22, 1572, to a Roman Catholic family. He was the son of a well-to-do ironmonger, who died when Donne was four. He attended both Oxford and Cambridge Universities, but as a Catholic he was prohibited from receiving a degree. He frittered away a small inheritance on women and frivolous pastimes, then went to the Continent, where he enlisted to fight against Spain.

He returned to England at age twenty-five, began to write poetry, studied law, launched a government career, was elected to Parliament, and was hired as secretary to Sir Thomas Egerton, Keeper of the Great Seal. He fell in love with Egerton's niece, Anne More, and because her Protestant family objected to her marriage to a Catholic, they were wed in a secret ceremony. Both

Donne and the priest who married them were briefly imprisoned. Donne and his wife had twelve children before her early death.

After his brother was jailed for Catholic loyalties and died in prison, Donne thought it might be prudent to convert to the Church of England. He did so and became a favorite of King James I, who insisted that Donne take holy orders in 1614. In 1621 he was named dean of St. Paul's Cathedral, a prestigious and lucrative post, which he held until his death.

His poetry, which uses fanciful metaphorical images known as "conceits" to convey both erotic and sacred concepts, was given the name "metaphysical" by John Dryden and later by Samuel Johnson. Most of Donne's love poems were written in the 1590s and published in two major volumes, *Satires* and *Songs and Sonnets*. The *Divine Poems* were published in 1607. In one of them, Donne scoffs at death:

> Death, be not proud, though some have called thee
> Mighty and dreadful, for thou art not so;
> For those whom thou think'st thou dost overthrow
> Die not, poor death, nor yet canst thou kill me.
> From rest and sleep, which but thy pictures be,
> Much pleasure; then from thee much more must flow,
> And soonest our best men with thee do go,
> Rest of their bones, and soul's delivery.
> Thou art slave to fate, chance, kings, and desperate men,
> And dost with poison, war, and sickness dwell,
> And poppy or charms can make us sleep as well
> And better than thy stroke; why swell'st thou then?
> One short sleep past, we wake eternally,
> And death shall be no more; death, thou shalt die.

"Death's Duel," a sermon preached in the presence of King Charles I only a month before Donne's death, took for its text Psalm 68,

Verse 20: "And unto God the Lord belong the issues from death."
From this, Donne took comfort in his belief in God's mercy:

...unto God the Lord belong the issues of death, that
is, the disposition and manner of our death: what kind
of issue and transmigration we shall have out of this
world, whether prepared or sudden, whether violent or
natural, whether in our perfect senses or shaken and
disordered by sickness, there is no condemnation to be
argued out of that, no Judgement to be made upon that,
for howsoever they die, precious in his sight is the death
of his saints, and with him are the issues of death, the
ways of our departing out of this life are in his hands.
And so in this sense of the words, this *exitus mortis*,
the issue of death, is *liberatio in morte*, a deliverance in
death; not that God will deliver us from dying, but that
he will have a care of us in the hour of death, of what
kind soever our passage be.

Donne was delivered in death on March 31, 1631, at the age of
fifty-nine. His fatal illness is thought to have been stomach cancer. According to one account, he had lain "fifteen days earnestly
expecting his hourly change." The bell tolled for him as he was buried in the old St. Paul's Cathedral, built between 1087 and 1314,
which stood on the site where the present St. Paul's was erected in
1666. Donne wrote his own Latin epitaph, which translates:

John Donne
Doctor of Divinity
after varied studies, pursued from early years
with perseverance and not without success,
entered into holy Orders
under the influence and pressure of the Holy Spirit
and by the advice and exhortation of King James,

in the year of his Jesus 1614 and of his age 42.
Having been invested with the Deanery of this church
on 27 November 1621,
he was stripped of it by death on the last day of March 1631.
He lies here in the dust but beholds Him
whose name is Rising.

BEN JONSON

Shakespeare's good friend Ben Jonson was the son of a prominent Protestant landowner who, not surprisingly, ran afoul of Catholic Queen "Bloody" Mary. As a result, she confiscated his land and imprisoned him. When Protestant Queen Elizabeth took the throne, she freed the elder Jonson, who started a new life as a Protestant clergyman. He died a month before Ben entered the world on June 11, 1572, in Westminster, London.

Growing up hearing tales of his father's tribulations, Ben wavered between the Church of England, in which he was raised, and Roman Catholicism. He went to Westminster School and expected to enroll in Cambridge University, but instead, his stepfather, a bricklayer, put him to work as an apprentice. As quickly as he could leave this trade, Ben joined the army, served on the Continent, and returned to England, where he joined the Admiral's Men theatrical company as an actor.

"Never a good actor," said one of his colleagues, "but an excellent instructor." Jonson began to write plays, most of them satires, and is now known as second only to his good friend, Will Shakespeare, among Elizabethan-Jacobean playwrights. His plays include *Every Man in His Humour*; *Volpone, or The Fox*; *The Alchemist*; *Bartholomew Fair*; and *Epicene, or The Silent Woman.*

Burly, blunt-spoken, quick to laugh and to anger, Jonson was described by his friend William Drummond as "a great lover and praiser of himself, jealous of every word and action of those about him, especially after drink . . . passionately kind and angry." In 1594, he married Ann Lewis, whom Drummond called "a shrew, but honest," and they had several children, three of whom died in early childhood.

A play Jonson co-wrote with Thomas Nashe, *The Isle of Dogs*, offended Queen Elizabeth, and he was arrested and held in prison, where he converted to Catholicism under the tutelage of a fellow prisoner who was a Jesuit priest. When he was released, he killed a fellow actor in a duel and was imprisoned again. He overcame these setbacks and was eventually named Poet Laureate of England by King James I.

Jonson rejoined the Church of England in 1610 because of his indignation over the assassination of the French Catholic King Henri IV, who had been tolerant of Protestants and was allegedly done away with on the orders of the pope. Nonetheless, Jonson remained interested in Roman Catholic doctrine and rituals for the rest of his life.

The quick-witted Jonson was very much a man of the world, and there is little evidence in his work that he spent much time thinking about death. But in his Epigram LXXX, "Of Life and Death," he wrote:

The ports of death are sins; of life, good deeds:
Through which our merit leads us to our meeds.
How willful blind is he then, that would stray,
And hath it in his powers, to make his way!
This world death's region is, the other life's:
And here, it should be one of our first strifes,

So to front death, as men might judge us past it.
For good men but see death, the wicked taste it.

He urged a *carpe diem* philosophy in this bit of doggerel:

Drink today, and drown all sorrow;
You shall perhaps not do it tomorrow;
Best, while you have it, use your breath;
There is no drinking after death.

And drink he did: his pension as Poet Laureate was raised by
King Charles I to £100 plus a tierce (about thirty-five gallons)
of wine per year. In 1626, Jonson suffered a stroke that left him
partially paralyzed. He had another stroke in 1628, and lingered
in failing health for another nine years, until his death on August
6, 1637, at the age of sixty-five.

Jonson was buried upright in the nave of Westminster Abbey
in a grave measured to his specifications: exactly eighteen inches
square, its small size possibly being an indication that he was short
of cash. The stone marker bears an inscription commissioned by
a friend as an afterthought: "O rare Ben Jonson." The stone does
not include the epitaph—with its allusion to Jonson's snail's pace
as a writer—that was reputedly begun by Jonson and finished by
his drinking pal Shakespeare during a merry evening in a tavern:

Here lies Ben Jonson
That was once one,
Who while he lived was a slow thing,
And now, being dead, is no thing.

JOHN MILTON

Some might think it smacked of hypocrisy for the author of
a monumental treatise condemning censorship to become the

official government censor for Oliver Cromwell's Commonwealth. But, as John Milton must have figured, a fellow has to make a living.

Like the earlier poet John Donne, Milton greeted the world in London's Bread Street. The son of John Milton, a prosperous composer of religious music, the younger John was born on December 9, 1608. A bright boy, he studied at St. Paul's School and then at Christ's College in Cambridge, earning an M.A. degree *cum laude*. While at Cambridge, he began to compose poems, among them "L'Allegro" and "Il Penseroso." He changed his mind about becoming an Anglican priest, and retired in a leisurely manner to his father's home in Buckinghamshire for six years of private study, immersing himself in Greek, Hebrew, Latin, French, Spanish, Italian, Old English, and Dutch.

When he was thirty, he embarked on a Grand Tour of the Netherlands, France, and Italy, where he met Galileo and was entertained by Cardinal Francesco Barberini, the pope's nephew and a noted arts patron. Returning to England, Milton took sides with the Puritans and Parliamentarians against the established episcopacy of the Church of England and the monarchy.

Milton married seventeen-year-old Mary Powell, who left him after a short time, provoking him to write a defense of divorce—the subsequent criticism of which led to his famous anti-censorship essay, *Areopagitica* (the name of a hill in Athens). He must have sweet-talked Mary, for she came back to him two years later—her impoverished parents in tow—bore four children, and then died in childbirth at the age of twenty-seven. By this time, the English Civil War had overthrown King Charles I, and Milton received a political payoff as Secretary for Foreign Tongues in Oliver Cromwell's Commonwealth. This was a job that required him to write pro-government propaganda and to act as censor of all printed materials. Opinions are divided as to how much actual censoring Milton ever did.

His eyesight began to fail—either retinal detachment or glaucoma is thought to be the cause—and by his mid-forties, Milton was completely blind. After the restoration of the monarchy in 1660, Milton was imprisoned until freed through the influence of the poet Andrew Marvell, who was a member of Parliament.

Milton retired to his home in Bunhill Row, Finsbury, and completed his masterpieces—*Paradise Lost, Paradise Regained*, and *Samson Agonistes*—composing in his head at night and dictating to his secretary the next day. He was married twice more: to Katherine Woodcock, who died in childbirth after two years, and then to Elizabeth Mynshull, his wife at the time of his death.

Although unquestionably a devout Christian, Milton never allied himself with any organized religious group, spurning not only Roman Catholics, but also the Church of England and dissenting nonconformist sects. He apparently felt some kinship with the Quakers, but did not attend any kind of religious services in his later years.

Religious affiliations aside, Milton's belief in the afterlife and the power of Christ's redemption shines through his verse. In *Paradise Lost*, he paints a vivid picture of Satan and hell, and in *Paradise Regained*, he reveals his trust in the salvation earned for mankind by Christ's death and resurrection.

His early poems, many composed to commemorate the death of friends, illustrate Milton's view of the life to come for the believing Christian. In one, he writes:

When Faith and Love, which parted from thee never,
Had ripen'd thy just soul to dwell with God,
Meekly thou didst resign this earthly load

Of Death, called Life; which us from Life doth sever.
Thy Works and Alms and all they good Endeavour
Stayed not behind, nor in the grave were trod;
But as Faith pointed with her golden rod,
Followed thee up to joy and bliss for ever.

And in *Lycidas*, an elegy for Edward King, a friend who drowned,
Milton imagines the heavenly kingdom in poetic imagery:

Weep no more, woeful Shepherds, weep no more,
For Lycidas your sorrow is not dead,
Sunk though he be beneath the watery floor,
So sinks the day-star in the Ocean bed,
And yet anon repairs his drooping head,
And tricks his beams, and with new-spangled Ore,
Flames in the forehead of the morning sky:
So Lycidas sunk low but mounted high,
Through the dear might of him that walk'd the waves.
…
In the blest Kingdoms meek of joy and love
There entertain him all the Saints above
In solemn troops, and sweet Societies
That sing, and singing in their glory move,
And wipe the tears forever from his eyes.

Milton lived simply. He drank wine sparingly, and each evening
after supper, about nine o'clock, he would smoke his pipe, drink
a glass of water, and retire. Despite his moderate habits, he suffered frequently from gout, the effects of which were apparent
in stiffened hands and finger-joints.

On Sunday evening, November 8, 1674, one month shy of
his sixty-sixth birthday, he had a severe gout attack, leading to
kidney failure, and—according to biographer Jonathan Richardson—Milton's life drew peacefully to a close "with so little

pain or emotion, that the time of his expiring was not perceiv'd by those in the room."

He was buried the next Thursday in the Church of St. Giles, Cripplegate, beside his father, and the funeral, wrote one biographer, was attended by "his learned and great Friends in London, not without a friendly concourse of the Vulgar."

MOLIÈRE

Jean-Baptiste Poquelin—better known by his stage name Molière—was born on January 15, 1622, to a prosperous Parisian family. His mother died when he was ten, and he and his father lived in the fashionable rue St. Honoré while Jean-Baptiste attended the academically rigorous Jesuit Collège de Clermont. After leaving school, he took up the royal appointment that his father had held before him—Keeper of the King's Carpet and Upholstery—and seemed destined for a cushy court career.

The theatre beckoned, however, even though it was regarded in polite society as a disreputable profession, and at age twenty-one, Jean-Baptiste joined the actress Madeleine Béjart to found the Illustre Théâtre—which went bankrupt within two years, leaving Jean-Baptiste with a pile of debts, for which he had to serve time in prison. After his release, he resumed his acting career, adopting the stage name of Molière—taken from the name of a village in the Midi—probably to avoid his creditors, as well as to spare his father the shame of having a son in the theatre.

Through the patronage of the Duc d'Orléans, brother of King Louis XIV, Molière won a command performance at the

Louvre before the king, for whom he performed a Pierre Corneille tragedy and one of his own farces, *The Doctor in Love*. He won the king's favor and was granted the use of two theatres, the Petit-Bourbon and the Palais-Royal, where he enjoyed great success. When he was forty, he married Armande Béjart, who he thought was his partner Madeleine's sister, although she was more likely her illegitimate daughter.

Although Molière preferred to write and perform tragedy, he found he could attract bigger audiences with comic satires spoofing the foibles of French professions and Parisian society (always exempting the monarchy from criticism). Among the most notable of the thirty-one comedies he wrote were *The Affected Ladies, School for Husbands, School for Wives, The Doctor in Spite of Himself, The Miser, The Would-Be Gentleman, The Misanthrope, Tartuffe or The Hypocrite*, and *The Imaginary Invalid*. Naturally they were roundly attacked by the professions he satirized, by the literary establishment, and especially by the Catholic Church. Despite his critics, Molière maintained a wide public following and always had the support of the king.

For many years, Molière suffered from pulmonary tuberculosis—probably acquired during his prison stint—but for him, illness and death were always subjects for satire, like almost everything else. In this scene from *The Imaginary Invalid*, the hypochondriac Argan pretends to be dead and instructs his maid Toinette to tell the bad news to his wife, Béline, in order to see how she will react:

TOINETTE: Your husband is dead.
BÉLINE: My husband is dead?
TOINETTE: Alas, the poor man is gone.
BÉLINE: You're sure?
TOINETTE: Oh, I'm sure. No one knows yet, and I was all alone when I found him. He died in my arms. Look how he's stretched out in that chair.

BÉLINE: Thank heavens! A great weight has been lifted from me. You are silly, Toinette, to grieve so over his death!

TOINETTE: Well, I thought I ought to cry.

BÉLINE: Nonsense, it's not worth the trouble. What loss is he to anyone, and what earthly purpose did he have when he was alive? A man who was nasty to everyone, rude, disgusting, always taking enemas or stuffing his stomach with nostrums, always sniveling, coughing, spitting—a tedious man, never having any fun, always in a bad temper, wearing out all his friends, and yelling at the servants day and night.

Toinette: That's quite a eulogy, Ma'am.

BÉLINE: You must help me carry out my plan, Toinette, and you can be sure that I will reward you. Now, don't let anyone know about this yet. We'll put him in bed and keep his death secret till I've finished what I have to do. There are some papers and some money that I want to get hold of—don't think I've given him the best years of my life for nothing! Come on, Toinette, help me look for the keys.

(*Argan rises*)

ARGAN: So, my dear wife, this is how you loved me!

TOINETTE: Uh-oh! The corpse isn't dead!

ARGAN: I am very happy to have seen you express your love in that beautiful tribute you gave me. You've certainly tipped me off to what I ought to do in the future—and spared me from doing some things that I might otherwise have done!

Molière's death, on February 17, 1673, at the age of fifty-one, was no laughing matter. He was, in fact, getting lots of laughs performing the comic role of Argan in *The Imaginary Invalid* when he was stricken with a tubercular seizure—coughing and hemorrhaging. Earlier that day, he had felt so weak that his wife urged him not to go on, but he insisted, reminding her of how many people's livelihoods depended on him. When the performance began, just after four in the afternoon, Molière seemed in top form to the audience, although his colleagues watching from the wings could tell that he was suffering. In the play's final scene, in which Argan ironically decides to become a physician himself, Molière had a sudden coughing attack, which he attempted to disguise with laughter. But then he began to hemorrhage and the curtain was rung down.

He was taken home and put to bed, requesting a "drugged pillow" to ease his pain. With more blood streaming from his mouth, he realized his time was near, and even though he had been a scoffer of religion, he asked for a priest to administer the last rites. His wife and an actor friend, Michel Baron, hurried to the nearby Church of St. Eustache, where two priests, tut-tutting at Molière's anti-clerical *Tartuffe*, declined to come to his aid. Another, more amenable priest was found, but he arrived too late. Molière was already dead in the arms of two nuns, whom he had for many years helped during their Lenten visits to Paris, and who, quite by chance, arrived at his door as he was dying.

French law prohibited actors from being buried in the consecrated ground of cemeteries, but Molière's widow appealed to King Louis XIV, who granted permission for him to be laid to rest in the dark of night in a plot reserved for unbaptized infants. In 1792, after the Revolution, his remains were transferred to the National Museum of French Monuments, and in 1817 to the Père Lachaise Cemetery.

BLAISE PASCAL

Blaise Pascal must have been a pretty glum fellow. Chronically ill most of his life, he rejected most medical treatment, saying, "Sickness is the natural state of Christians." This dour French philosopher-scientist was born on June 19, 1623, in Clermont-Ferrand, but after the death of his mother when he was three, he moved with his father, a tax collector, and two sisters to Paris.

A home-schooled child prodigy, Pascal became not only a religious thinker, but also a physicist, mathematician, and inventor who devised a mechanical calculator, made important discoveries about fluids, and developed a probability theory that influenced economics and social sciences.

Pascal got religion for the first time at the age of twenty-three, when two Jansenist doctors treated his father for a broken hip. The family fell under the doctors' spell and became eager adherents of the teachings of Cornelius Jansen, a theologian with Calvinist tendencies, who preached a doctrine of the total depravity of mankind and the predestined salvation of only a select few.

After a time, Pascal drifted away from the church and led a worldly life until he was thirty-one, when he got religion for a second time. He had a mystical vision on the night of November 23, 1654, possibly the result of banging his head in a carriage accident. During the next eight years, he practiced a more orthodox Catholicism and began writing *Pensées* (*Thoughts*), his monumental defense of the Christian faith. In it, he posited his famous "wager," a logical justification for belief in God. A simplified approximation of the wager is: If you erroneously believe God exists, when death comes, you lose nothing. But if you correctly believe in God, you gain eternal bliss. On the other hand, if you are correct in disbelieving in God, you gain nothing at death. But if you are wrong in your disbelief, you suffer eternal damnation. The smart money would obviously be on believing.

Suffering frequently from severe headaches and digestive disorders, Pascal accepted his afflictions as a sign of God's grace. In the *Pensées*, he wrote: "Thus I extend my arms to my

Savior who, having been foretold for 4,000 years, came to suffer and die for me on earth in the time and under the circumstances that were foretold, and, by his grace, I await death in peace, in hope of being eternally united with him; and I live meanwhile joyously, both in the blessings that he gives me, and in the evil that he sends for my benefit and teaches me to endure by his example."

In 1662, Pascal's health grew worse, and he finally sought admission to a hospital for the incurable, but his doctor pronounced him too ill to move from his home. He began to have convulsions on August 18 and was given the last rites by the Reverend Paul Beurrier, the *curé* of Pascal's parish church, St. Étienne-du-Mont. Pascal died the next morning at the age of thirty-nine, having uttered his last words, "May God never abandon me." An autopsy disclosed disease of the stomach and other internal organs, as well as brain lesions. Although never precisely determined, the cause of death was probably a combination of stomach cancer and tuberculosis.

A funeral mass was offered on August 22 at St. Étienne-du-Mont, the shrine of Saint Geneviève, a patron saint of Paris. Beurrier officiated, and following the mass, Pascal's body was interred in a tomb behind the high altar.

The Enlightenment

JONATHAN SWIFT

Illness and death haunted Jonathan Swift throughout his multi-faceted life. Widely hailed as the foremost satirist in the English language, Swift is remembered for *Gulliver's Travels*, *A Modest Proposal*, *A Journal to Stella*, *Drapier's Letters*, *The Battle of the Books*, *An Argument Against Abolishing Christianity*, and *A Tale of a Tub*.

He was born on November 30, 1667, his father having died a month earlier. His mother moved to England, leaving young Jonathan in the care of an influential uncle. Swift received his B.A. degree in 1686 from Trinity College in Dublin, and then joined his mother in London, where he became secretary to Sir John Temple. While in England, he also earned an M.A. from Oxford.

Swift suffered from Ménière's disease, causing him to have bouts of severe vertigo and progressive deafness. Seeking escape from the pressures of London, he returned to Ireland and was ordained a minister in the Church of Ireland. He was given a small parish in Kilroot, where he spent two years preaching, gardening, doing house repairs, and writing. After leaving Kilroot, he shuttled back and forth for many years between Ireland and England, in various positions as a secretary to politicians, an

adviser to the Tory government, and a church official. At the age
of forty-five, he accepted the prestigious position of dean of St.
Patrick's Cathedral, Dublin, where he remained until his death.

Although he never married (so far as is known), Swift was
romantically and enigmatically involved with two women
named Esther. One was Esther Johnson, whom he referred to
as Stella, who was an object of lifelong infatuation (and whom
he may have secretly married). The other was Esther Vanhom-
righ, whom he called Vanessa. The exact nature of his relationships with them is still a subject of conjecture, but there is no
doubt that he was inconsolably grief-stricken when each one
died: Vanessa in 1723, at age thirty-five, and Stella in 1728, at
age forty-seven.

Death figured increasingly in Swift's life after this. He was
able to keep his sense of humor about it, and he had fun imagin-
ing his own demise in *Verses on the Death of Dr. Swift*:

> The time is not remote, when I
> Must by the course of nature die;
> When, I foresee, my special friends
> Will try to find their private ends.
> Though it is hardly understood
> Which way my death can do them good,
> Yet thus, methinks, I hear 'em speak:
> "See, how the Dean begins to break!
> Poor gentleman, he droops apace:
> You plainly find it in his face.
> That old vertigo in his head
> Will never leave him till he's dead.
> Besides, his memory decays;
> He recollects not what he says;
> He cannot call his friends to mind;
> Forgets the place where last he dined;
> Plies you with stories o'er and o'er;

He told them fifty times before.
How does he fancy we can sit
To hear his out-of-fashion wit?
...
Behold the fatal day arrive!
"How is the Dean?"— "He's just alive."
Now the departing prayer is read.
"He hardly breathes"—"The Dean is dead."
...
My female friends, whose tender hearts
Have better learned to act their parts,
Receive the news in doleful dumps:
"The Dean is dead (and what is trumps?)"

After two of his closest friends, John Gay and John Arbuthnot, died, Swift began to show signs of mental illness. At the age of seventy-four, he suffered a stroke, losing the ability to speak. He once foresaw such a disability: "I shall be like a tree and die at the top." As it turns out, he did. He was legally declared of "unsound mind," and guardians were appointed to oversee his affairs. Shamefully, some of his servants went so far as to charge curious gawkers a fee to get a glimpse of the Dean in his sadly impaired condition. Swift died on October 19, 1745, at the age of seventy-seven.

He was buried in St. Patrick's Cathedral, next to Esther Johnson. Most of his estate of twelve thousand pounds was left to establish a hospital for the mentally ill. He left his own Latin epitaph, which is translated:

Here is laid the Body
of Jonathan Swift, Doctor of Sacred Theology,
Dean of this Cathedral Church,
where ferocious Indignation
can no longer

lacerate his Heart.
Go forth, Voyager,
and copy, if you can,
this vigorous (to the best of his ability)
Champion of Liberty.

ALEXANDER POPE

Born to a Roman Catholic family in Protestant England, denied a formal education, and sickly from childhood, Alexander Pope overcame those odds and achieved fame, wealth, and literary prominence as a poet, satirist, and translator. Son of a well-to-do linen merchant, he was born in London on May 21, 1688, and had a scattered education, learning a little Greek and Latin as a private pupil of various schoolmasters and Catholic priests. He suffered from Pott's disease, a form of tuberculosis that affects the spine, which left him hunchbacked and only four feet six inches in height. He relished his poor health, and in one poem refers to "this long disease, my life."

Through his father's friends, Pope was introduced into London literary society as a prodigy and began a life devoted almost exclusively to writing—"poetry his only business," as he said, "and idleness his only pleasure." An acerbic wit who made many enemies with his caustic comments, he was a master of the heroic couplet, evidenced in such works as his *Essay on Criticism* and *Essay on Man. The Rape of the Lock*, a mock-heroic poem, is regarded as a witty classic, satirizing pretentious society. *The Dunciad*, which excoriated many of England's leading literary lights, including the Poet Laureate, Colley Cibber, was dedicated to Pope's good friend, Jonathan Swift.

Among the aphorisms for which Pope is remembered are "The proper study of Mankind is Man"; "To err is human, to forgive divine"; "A little learning is a dangerous thing"; and "An honest man's the noblest work of God." Pope's translations of *The Iliad* and *The Odyssey* earned him eight thousand pounds on their publications—a fortune in those days, and an edition of Shakespeare added to his wealth. He purchased a home in Twickenham, near London, where he and his mother lived. Pope's continued barbed comments earned him the nickname "Wasp of Twickenham."

Pope never married, but he is alleged to have maintained a long-lasting love affair with a childhood friend named Martha Blount, to whom he willed the use of his estate during her lifetime. He also wrote witty letters to a number of other female friends.

With lifelong maladies, Pope must have been constantly aware of the imminence of death. When he was only twenty-four, he wrote "The Dying Christian to His Soul," a reverie in which he considers what it might be like to die:

I.

Vital spark of heavenly flame!
Quit, oh quit this mortal frame:
Trembling, hoping, lingering, flying,
Oh the pain, the bliss of dying!
Cease, fond Nature, cease thy strife,
And let me languish into life.

II.

Hark! they whisper; Angels say,
Sister Spirit, come away.
What is this absorbs me quite?

Steals my sense, shuts my sight,
Drowns my spirits, draws my breath?
Tell me, my Soul, can this be Death?

III.
The world recedes; it disappears!
Heaven opens on my eyes! my ears
With sounds seraphic ring;
Lend, lend your wings! I mount! I fly!
O Grave! where is thy Victory?
O Death! where is thy Sting?

His worsening illness brought Pope respiratory problems, frequent fevers, eye inflammations, and abdominal pains. On May 29, 1744, Pope felt so ill that he called for a priest to administer the last rites. The next day, his physician visited him and told him he was much improved. Pope disdained the diagnosis: "Here am I," he said, "dying of a hundred good symptoms." And indeed he was right: he did expire, surrounded by friends, that evening about eleven o'clock, at the age of fifty-six. The precise nature of his final illness is not known, but was probably congestive heart failure.

Pope left specific instructions for his burial in his will: "I resign my Soul to its Creator in all humble Hope of its future Happiness, as in the Disposal of a Being infinitely Good. As to my Body, my Will is, That it be buried near the Monument of my dear Parents at Twickenham . . . and that it be carried to the Grave by six of the poorest Men of the Parish, to each of whom I order a Suit of Grey coarse Cloth, as Mourning."

Even though he was nominally a Roman Catholic, Pope was buried as he wished in Twickenham's Anglican Church of St. Mary the Virgin. His friend William Warburton later added a Latin inscription to the tomb which translates as the epitome of faint praise: "He wrote nothing inept."

VOLTAIRE

Few corpses get to ride to their funerals sitting up in a carriage, looking as if they were alive, as Voltaire did. The man known as Voltaire was born François-Marie Arouet on November 21, 1694, to a minor government official and his aristocratic wife. The fourth of five children, he attended the Jesuit Collège Louis-le-Grand (formerly the Collège de Clermont), the same school attended by Molière, who, along with Jean Racine and Pierre Corneille, was one of his idols.

At his father's insistence, François-Marie tried his hand at law school and as secretary to a diplomat, but gave up these jobs in favor of writing plays. He wrote some fifty or more in his lifetime, along with two thousand histories, philosophical tracts, and scientific articles—and an estimated twenty thousand letters. His most famous work is *Candide, or The Optimist,* a satire of the philosophy of Leibniz and others who believed "this is the best of all possible worlds."

As a pen name, he used Voltaire, which is an anagram of the Latinized spelling of his surname (AROVET), plus the letters "LI," an abbreviation for "le jeune," French for "the younger." Voltaire was noted as a hedonist, a skeptic, and a champion of empirical science, freedom of religion and expression, and separation of Church and State. An avowed enemy of hypocrisy, he was frequently at odds with the king and government officials, with *haute* society, and with Catholic clergy. Voltaire's iconoclastic opinions involved him in several disputes with prominent dignitaries, sometimes requiring him to flee Paris. During one such exile, he spent three years in England, where he became well acquainted with Jonathan Swift, Alexander Pope, and John Gay.

Voltaire had romantic attachments to two women, first to Emilie du Chatelet, a married aristocrat who was also a distinguished mathematician, in whose home he lived for fifteen years; and later in his life to his widowed niece, Marie Louise Denis.

Voltaire was a fierce critic of organized religion, but believed in a supreme being, in the tradition of Deism. "It is perfectly evident to my mind," he wrote, "that there exists a necessary, eternal, supreme, and intelligent being. This is no matter of faith, but of reason." On one occasion, when fellow Deist Benjamin Franklin visited him in Paris and asked Voltaire to bless his grandson, Voltaire's blessing was "God and liberty." He is also famous for saying, "If God did not exist, it would be necessary to invent him."

Voltaire's death at age eighty-three was preceded by several months of painful illness, resulting from prostate cancer. In February of 1778, he was living in Paris, and his friend Madame du Deffand, who had a noted salon, reported that he frequently suffered bladder pain, hemorrhoids, and vertigo. He suffered for many weeks from bouts of slow, painful urination, alternating with incontinence. He was also severely constipated, his doctor reporting a "complete cessation of peristaltic movement."

Knowing that he was dying, church officials tried to persuade him to recant his anti-ecclesiastical statements. On February 10, an abbé named Gaultier visited Voltaire and gave him absolution for his sins—although Voltaire refused to accept Communion, claiming he was coughing blood.

By April he was in increasing pain, agitated, and unable to sleep, but he continued to involve himself in the absentee management of his estate at Ferney and in Parisian literary business. He was working on revisions of his play *Irene*, for the Comédie-Française, and on a new dictionary he was urging the Académie Française to publish. On May 7, Voltaire attended a meeting about the dictionary, but was not well enough to return for another on May 9. On May 10, he developed a high fever and summoned his doctor, Théodore Tronchin, who gave him an opiate to relieve his distress. Voltaire overdosed and was in a stupor for several days.

On the morning of May 30, Gaultier and another priest came to his bedside to exhort him once more. They asked him if he believed in the divinity of Christ. Voltaire replied, "In the name of God, don't mention that man to me again—and let me die in peace." Asked to renounce Satan, Voltaire observed, "This is not the time to make any more enemies." He expired at eleven o'clock on the evening of May 30, 1778.

Despite the absolution he had earlier received from Abbé Gaultier, the Church refused him a Catholic burial. Voltaire's nephew, Alexandre Mignot, Abbé of Scellières, near Troyes, was determined that his uncle would be laid to rest in con-secrated ground. It was decided to transport Voltaire to the Scellières abbey, where he could be buried in a Catholic ritual. In a bizarre plot to circumvent interference by church authori-ties during the journey, Voltaire's corpse was embalmed and then dressed in his usual clothing, and he was propped up in a carriage, as though he were still alive. The subterfuge worked and Voltaire reached his destination, where a funeral mass and Christian burial were accorded to him on June 2. The following day, the Bishop of Troyes heard what was afoot and issued an order forbidding church participation in Voltaire's funeral, but it was too late—he was already safely six feet underground. Thirteen years later, French revolutionaries honored Voltaire by moving his remains to Paris, where he was interred in the Panthéon.

BENJAMIN FRANKLIN

Benjamin Franklin would have rated several pages in *Who's Who*, if only it had been published in his day. He was an author and epigrammatist, a successful newspaper editor, a skilled printer, a prosperous entrepreneur, an innovative postmaster, an accomplished musician, a respected scientist, a prolific inventor, a dedicated public servant, a wily diplomat, and the only Founding Father to have signed all four of the documents establishing the United States of America: the Declaration of Independence, the Treaty of Paris, the Treaty of Alliance with France, and the Constitution.

Born on January 17, 1706, in Boston to a soap- and candlemaker named Josiah and his second wife, a staunch Puritan named Abiah, young Benjamin attended Boston Latin School until the age of thirteen. At seventeen, he ran away from home and found work as a printer's devil in Philadelphia. Largely self-taught, without the benefit of higher education, he nonetheless later founded the University of Pennsylvania and received honorary doctorates from Harvard, Yale, Oxford, and St. Andrews universities.

Franklin published several newspapers, including the *Pennsylvania Gazette*, and became wealthy from the annual publication of *Poor Richard's Almanack*, in which he dished out such adages as "Early to bed, early to rise, makes a man healthy, wealthy, and wise." He invented the lighting rod, bifocals, the

Franklin stove, the odometer, and a glass musical instrument he called an "armonica." He played the violin, the harp, and the guitar, and composed classical music. His experiments with lightning and electrical current gained international scientific acclaim. He established America's first subscription library, which survives today as a research institute: the Library Company of Philadelphia. He served in numerous government posts, including Philadelphia city councilman, justice of the peace, member of the Pennsylvania Assembly, delegate to the Continental Congress and the Constitutional Convention, governor of Pennsylvania, first postmaster general of the United States, and first ambassador to France.

Whew! And if all that wasn't enough, he also founded the American Philosophical Society and the first hospital in colonial America.

Franklin and his common-law wife, Deborah Read, had two children, but only their daughter, Sarah, lived to adulthood. They also raised William, Franklin's illegitimate son. Always one with an eye for the ladies, Franklin had a reputation for dalliance during his lengthy sojourns in Europe—but the truth, alas, is probably that these relationships were platonic.

Franklin, the child of Puritan parents, thought of himself as a Christian, but he did not attend church services, and his religious beliefs were those of a Deist. In reply to an inquiry, he wrote:

Here is my Creed: I believe in one God, creator of the universe. That he governs it by his providence. That he ought to be worshipped. That the most acceptable service we can render to him, is doing good to his other children. That the soul of man is immortal, and will be treated with justice in another life respecting its conduct in this. As to Jesus of Nazareth, I think the system of morals and his religion as he left them to us, the best the world ever saw, or is likely to see; but I have some doubts as to his divinity: though it is a question I do not dogmatize upon, having never studied it, and think it needless to busy myself with it now, when I expect soon an opportunity of knowing the truth with less trouble.

The afterlife, for Franklin, would be a jolly party, as he expressed in a letter to his sister-in-law after her husband's death: "Our friend and we are invited abroad on a party of pleasure—that is to last forever. His chair was first ready and he is gone before us. We could not all conveniently start together, and why should you and I be grieved at this, since we are soon to follow, and we know where to find him."

In his final years, Franklin suffered numerous ailments: lung disease, gout, psoriasis. A hearty eater and drinker during his prime, he observed in old age, "People who live long, who will drink the cup of life to the very bottom, must expect to meet with some of the usual dregs." When he was seventy-six, he developed kidney stones that caused him pain and impaired his mobility for the rest of his life.

On the occasion of George Washington's inauguration in 1789, Franklin wrote to him: "For my own personal ease, I should have died two years ago. But though those years have been spent in excruciating pain, I am pleased that I have lived them, since they have brought me to see the present situation."

In April 1790, while living in Philadelphia at the home of his daughter, Sarah Bache, Franklin developed an abscess in his left lung—caused by an infection that would be called pleurisy today. He told a visitor, "The pains will soon go away. Besides… what are the pains of a moment compared with the pleasures of eternity?"

Franklin's physician, Dr. John Jones, gave this account of his last days to the *Pennsylvania Gazette*:

About sixteen days before his death, he was seized with a feverish indisposition, without any particular symptoms attending it until the third or fourth day, when he complained of a pain in his left breast, which increased until it became extremely acute, attended with a cough and laborious breathing. In this frame of body and mind he continued till five days before his death, when his pain and difficulty breathing entirely left him, and his family were flattering themselves with the hopes of a recovery, when an imposthumation [abscess], which had formed itself in his lungs, suddenly burst, and discharged a great quantity of matter, which he continued to throw up while he had sufficient strength to do it, but, as that failed, the organs of respiration became gradually oppressed—a calm lethargic state succeeded—and on the 17th instant, about 11 o'clock at night, he quietly expired, closing a long and useful life of eighty-four years and three months.

After the abscess burst, Franklin's daughter suggested shifting his position in bed to breathe more easily. "A dying man can do nothing easily," said Franklin, in what are regarded as his last words.

Approximately twenty thousand people attended his funeral, including the clergy of nearly every religious group in Philadelphia. He was interred in the Anglican Christ Church burial ground.

When he was only twenty-two and immersed in the publishing business, Franklin wrote an epitaph for himself:

The body of B. Franklin printer; like the cover of an old book, its contents torn out, and stript of its lettering and gilding, lies here, food for worms. But the work shall not be wholly lost: for it will, as he believed, appear once more, in a new & more perfect edition, corrected and amended by the Author.

Franklin's actual grave, however, as he specified in his will, is a plain marble slab, six feet long and four feet wide, with the simple inscription: "Benjamin and Deborah Franklin."

SAMUEL JOHNSON

Although Samuel Johnson was afflicted with lifelong poor health from the day of his birth, he knew, as he later said, it does a man "no good to whine." Dr. Johnson, as he is usually known thanks to his biographer, James Boswell, was born September 18, 1709, in Lichfield, Staffordshire, England, the son of an impecunious bookseller. As an infant, Samuel suffered from scrofula, an infection of the lymph nodes that causes chronic swelling in the neck. An unsuccessful operation left him with permanent scars on his face, neck, and body.

He attended Lichfield Grammar School, where he excelled in Latin, and then, owing to a small inheritance, was able to enroll in Pembroke College, Oxford. By this time Johnson had developed what is now known as Tourette syndrome, causing him to have lifelong nervous tics. He also suffered from depression and poor eyesight, especially in his left eye— as well as severe hypochondria (with more cause than most). His money soon ran out, and he was forced to leave university without a degree, but years later was awarded honorary doctorates from Oxford University and Trinity College in Dublin.

He taught school for a while, then wound up in Birmingham, where he eked out a living as a writer. When he was twenty-five, he married a widow, Elizabeth Porter, who was twenty years his senior and had a comfortable income. After trying unsuccessfully to operate a boarding school (one of his few pupils was the future actor David Garrick), Johnson made his way to London and found steady work on *The Gentleman's Magazine.*

He continued to scramble for a living, writing a series of essays known as *The Rambler* and a play called *Irene.* These labors were generally ill-paid, and no doubt inspired his famous comment, "No man but a blockhead ever wrote, except for money." He hoped to make some with his *Dictionary of the English Language*, on which he had been working for nine years. Published in 1755, it remained for 150 years the standard English lexicon.

His other major works include a mythical fable called *Rasselas, Prince of Abyssinia*; an edition of Shakespeare's plays; *A Journey to the Western Islands of Scotland*; and *The Lives of the Poets.* Johnson's wife died in 1752, when he was forty-two.

At the age of fifty-two, Johnson began receiving an annual stipend of £300 from King George III, which eased his constant financial struggles. Along with several of his impecunious friends, he lived for more than fifteen years in comfortable rooms over a brewery owned by a friend, Henry Thrale, whose wife nursed Johnson through his various ailments. They included frequent gout, testicular cancer, chronic pulmonary fibrosis, hypertension, coronary disease, constant depression that he feared was a symptom of madness, and what Boswell described as "horrible melancholia, with perpetual irritation, fretfulness, and impatience; and with a dejection, gloom, and despair, which made existence misery."

Through it all, Johnson remained a devout, conservative Anglican in his religious beliefs. In answer to a question from

Boswell about how death should be approached, Johnson said, "It matters not how a man dies, but how he lives. The act of dying is not of importance, it lasts so short a time. A man knows it must be so, and submits. It will do him no good to whine."

Despite his faith, Johnson was worried about his soul's ultimate fate. He told a friend: "No rational man can die without uneasy apprehension. His hope of salvation must be founded on the terms on which it is promised that the mediation of our Saviour shall be applied to us, namely, obedience; and where obedience has failed, then repentance. But no man can be sure that his obedience and repentance will obtain salvation."

Johnson suffered a stroke on June 17, 1783, which caused him to lose his ability to speak for a few days. He then underwent surgery for his gout and was confined to his room for four months. Defiant of his illness, Johnson vowed to fight it: "I will be conquered; I will not capitulate!" But his health continued to go downhill during the next year, and by early December of 1784, he was near death. His physician, Thomas Warren, asked him if he felt any better. "No, sir; you cannot conceive with what acceleration I advance toward death."

A number of friends, including the novelist Fanny Burney, visited him in his final days. One who sat with him during his last night said, "No man could appear more collected, more devout, or less terrified at the thoughts of the approaching minute." On the afternoon of December 13, 1784, Johnson fell into a coma and died at seven o'clock that evening, at the age of seventy-five.

Johnson's funeral in Westminster Abbey created a controversy among his friends. Although he was buried near Shakespeare and his old pupil Garrick, he was not accorded the honor of a cathedral service—an omission that his friends thought disrespectful—and, to make matters worse, Johnson's old friend, the Reverend John Taylor, who conducted the simple burial rites, was accused of doing so in an "unfeeling manner." Johnson's executor, Sir Joshua Reynolds, explained that a grander funeral, with lights and music, would have been too expensive.

THOMAS PAINE

Thomas Paine, whose radical pamphlet *Common Sense* was a catalyst for the American Revolution, was a johnny-come-lately to the colonies, arriving on the very eve of hostilities in late 1774. Before that, he led a varied life, which began with his birth in Thetford, Norfolk, England, January 29, 1737, to a Quaker corset-maker father and an Anglican mother. He was apprenticed to his father for a time, then broke loose to set up his own shop as a stay-maker. He married a young woman named Mary Lambert, who died with their newborn in childbirth.

Paine tackled other jobs in various English locales, including customs officer, schoolteacher, and tobacconist. He was married again, to his landlord's daughter, Elizabeth Ollive, from whom he separated four years later. Armed with a letter of introduction from Benjamin Franklin, whom he had met in England, Paine emigrated to America.

In Philadelphia, the versatile Paine became editor of *Pennsylvania Magazine*, and also worked as a designer and inventor, executing plans for a bridge, a smokeless candle, and a steam engine. He penned a pamphlet, *Common Sense*, issued in 1776 and endorsing revolt against the British. One of the most famous documents in American history, it brewed controversy from the outset; even some revolutionaries thought the views expressed in *Common Sense* were far from sensible. John Adams called it a "poor, ignorant, malicious, shortsighted, crapulous mass." Undeterred, Paine followed this with *The American Crisis*— famous for the line "These are the times that try men's souls." Feeling insufficiently appreciated after the Revolution, Paine nagged the state of New York to reward him for his services to the new nation, and the state grudgingly granted him a farm near New Rochelle.

Thereafter, Paine regarded himself as a revolutionary missionary to the world. First he went back to England, where his agitation resulted in his expulsion. Then he fled to France and became active in the French Revolution, issuing a new manifesto called *The Rights of Man*. Unfortunately, he aligned himself with the wrong camp, incurring the wrath of Maximilien Robespierre, who imprisoned him for several months. Paine believed George Washington had conspired in causing his incarceration, and he wrote scurrilous attacks on the American leader while seeking solace in frequent and generous doses of brandy. In 1794, Paine issued *The Age of Reason*, a free-thinking attack on religion.

Unpopular in Europe, he returned to the United States, but there he was reviled for his views and largely ignored by the public that had once adulated him. He lived in a succession of seedy rooming houses, and continued to write and to drink more heavily.

For all his anti-religious views, Paine was not an atheist. Although he castigated churches as "human inventions, set up to terrify and enslave mankind, and monopolize power and profit," he also wrote in *The Age of Reason*: "I believe in one God, and no more; and I hope for happiness beyond this life. I believe in the equality of man; and I believe that religious duties consist in doing justice, loving mercy, and endeavoring to make our fellow-creatures happy." Although he never called himself a Deist, his views were similar to those held by other Deists, like his friend Franklin.

The circumstances of Paine's death, on June 8, 1809, in the home of a longtime friend, Marguerite de Bonneville, in New York's Greenwich Village, are still marked by controversy. He had been ill for some time, possibly from alcoholism, and certainly from the effects of a stroke he had suffered in 1806, tumbling down a flight of twenty stairs and temporarily losing the ability to speak or use his hands. He also suffered from some sort of palsy, which may have been Parkinson's disease. He was bedridden for several weeks before his death, coughing blood and plagued by bedsores that wore his flesh away.

During his final days, Paine had numerous visitors urging him to embrace Christianity, each of whom conveyed his own version of Paine's state of mind. A Methodist minister warned Paine that unless he repented, he would be eternally damned. Paine, weak with illness, rose in his bed and ordered the clergyman to leave the room. Another cleric asked Paine if he wished to believe that Jesus was the son of God. Paine's reply was, "I have no wish to believe on that subject."

A Catholic priest, Joseph Fenwick (later Bishop of Boston), was asked by Paine to visit him on his sickbed. Fenwick recalled:

> We found him just getting out of his slumber. A more wretched being in appearance I never beheld. He was lying in a bed besmeared with filth; his look was that of a man greatly tortured in mind; his eyes haggard, his countenance forbidding, and his whole appearance that of one whose better days had been one continued scene of debauch. His only nourishment at this time was milk punch. He had partaken recently of it, as the sides and

corners of his mouth exhibited traces of it, as well as of blood, which had also followed in the track and left its mark on the pillow. Immediately upon making known the object of our visit, Paine interrupted by saying: "That's enough, sir; that's enough, I see what you would be about. I wish to hear no more from you, sir. My mind is made up on that subject. I look upon the whole of the Christian scheme to be a tissue of absurdities and lies, and Jesus Christ to be nothing more than a cunning knave and impostor. Away with you and your God, too; leave the room instantly; all that you have uttered are lies—filthy lies; and if I had a little more time I would prove it, as I did about your impostor, Jesus Christ."

Other sources reported Paine's last words as an echo of the Biblical David's Psalm: "My God, my God, why have you forsaken me?" A friend recounted: "On the eighth of June, 1809, about nine in the morning, he placidly, and almost without a struggle, died, as he had lived, a Deist." Paine was seventy-two.

Some accounts maintain that Paine died in a drunken delirium, anguished by torment and fear. Others claim that he repented and had a deathbed conversion to Christianity. But most evidence suggests that he held on to his anti-ecclesiastical principles to the very end.

Only seven people attended his funeral, and he was refused burial in a Quaker cemetery, as he had wished, so he was laid to rest at his farm in New Rochelle. His obituary in the *New York Citizen* said, "He had lived long, did some good and much harm."

Ten years later, the radical journalist William Cobbett dug up Paine's earthly remains and brought them to England, intending to rebury them beneath a memorial monument. Cobbett died, however, before the monument could be built, and the bag of Paine's moldy bones disappeared.

JOHANN WOLFGANG VON GOETHE

Now best known for his lofty tragic play retelling the German legend of Faust, but renowned in his lifetime for a novel about a love-smitten suicide, Johann Wolfgang von Goethe began his long life on August 28, 1749, in Frankfurt, then a free imperial city of the Holy Roman Empire, now part of Germany. His family was well-to-do, and young Johann received lessons in riding, fencing, and dancing, as well as a privately tutored education in Greek, Latin, Hebrew, English, French, and Italian.

He studied law, but felt drawn to theatre and poetry. At age twenty, he suffered a serious year-long illness, which was probably a stubborn urinary infection, before going to Strasbourg for further legal study. He then opened a small—and unsuccessful—legal practice. When he was only twenty-five, and heartbroken by an unhappy romance, he published a blockbuster novel, *The Sorrows of Young Werther*, about a young man heartbroken by an unhappy romance—but who, instead of writing a novel, shoots himself. A bestseller throughout Europe, it caused a number of copycat suicides and brought Goethe worldwide notoriety, allowing him to give up the practice of law. He was invited to Weimar by his patron, the Duke of Saxe-Weimar, and he made his home there for the rest of his life, managing the court theatre and continuing to write plays and poetry, as well as scientific treatises on botany, anatomy, and color theory.

When he was thirty-nine, Goethe began an eighteen-year affair with a young woman named Christiane Vulpius, with whom he had several children (only one of whom survived to adulthood), and whom he finally married in 1806. In 1808, he published Part I of *Faust*, which he continued to revise throughout his lifetime. Part II was finished in 1832, the year he died, and published posthumously.

Raised a Lutheran, Goethe as a young man described his faith as "not anti-Christian, nor un-Christian, but most certainly non-Christian." His religious beliefs later in life were hard to pin down. Friedrich Nietzsche characterized Goethe's creed as "a joyous and trusting fatalism" that has "faith that only in its totality does all redeem and affirm itself." At various times, Goethe identified with pantheism, humanism, and various esoteric mystical medieval philosophies. He sometimes spoke in veiled abstractions, as when he said, "Death is a commingling of eternity with time; in the death of a good man, eternity is seen looking through time."

Despite intermittent ailments, especially urinary infections, gout, and intestinal disorders, for which he received continuing treatment, Goethe lived to the ripe old age of eighty-two. The cause of his death has been variously attributed to a heart attack, cholera, or, most likely, a chest cold that developed into pneumonia. Theatre historian Alfred Bates provides this account:

On Friday, March 16th, 1832, Goethe awoke with a chill, from which he gradually recovered, and was so much better by Monday that he designed to begin his regular work on the following day. But in the middle of the night he woke up with a deathly coldness, which extended from his hands over his body, and which it took many hours to overcome. It then appeared that the lungs were attacked and that there was no possible hope of recovery. Goethe did not anticipate death. He sat fully clothed in his arm-chair, spoke confidently of his recovery, and of the walks he would take in the fine April days. On the morning of the 22nd his strength gradually left him, and he sat slumbering in his arm-chair, holding his daughter-in-law Ottilie's hand. His last words were an order to a servant to open another shutter to let in more light. After this he traced with his forefinger letters in the air. At half-past eleven in the forenoon he drew himself, without any sign of pain, into the left corner of his arm-chair, and went so peacefully to sleep that it was long before the watchers knew that his spirit was fled.

Goethe was buried in the ducal vault at Weimar's Historical Cemetery, next to the remains of his friend and colleague, the author Friedrich Schiller.

The Romantic Era

WILLIAM WORDSWORTH

The fountainhead of English Romanticism—a poetic movement that included Coleridge, Southey, Keats, Shelley, and Byron—William Wordsworth sowed a few radical wild oats when he was young, but settled into a more mundane regimen in his middle years. He was born April 7, 1770, in Cockermouth, Cumbria, in the Lake District of England. Orphaned with his four siblings at an early age, young William attended Hawkshead Grammar School and then won a position at St. John's College in Cambridge, where he had a lackluster career and graduated without honors. He journeyed to France, where he became caught up in the spirit of the Revolution, and began a brief love affair with Annette Vallon, with whom he had a daughter named Caroline.

On his return to England, he took up residence at Dove Cottage in Grasmere, with his solicitous sister Dorothy, and wrote copious amounts of poetry extolling nature and the common man. When he was thirty-two, he married Mary Hutchinson, with whom he had five children, two of whom died in childhood. Wordsworth landed a job as an official distributor of postage stamps in his district, a sinecure that gave him a comfortable living. With both his wife and his sister, he moved to a larger home in nearby Rydal, called Rydal Mount. He continued to write poetry and received many honors, including an honorary doctorate from Oxford and an appointment as Britain's Poet Laureate.

In his youth, Wordsworth's religious views were grounded in a virtually pantheistic belief in the universal presence in nature of an ethereal God, the spirit of love, and in his conviction of the goodness of all mankind. He also had a mystical side, in which he experienced sudden flashes of insight. In "Lines Composed A Few Miles Above Tintern Abbey," written when he was twenty-eight, he says:

> I have learned
> To look on Nature not as in the hour
> Of thoughtless youth; but hearing oftentimes
> The still, sad music of humanity,
> Nor harsh nor grating, though of ample power
> To chasten and subdue. And I have felt
> A presence that disturbs me with the joy
> Of elevated thoughts, a sense sublime,
> Of something far more deeply interfused,
> Whose dwelling is the light of setting suns,
> And the round ocean and the living air,
> And the blue sky, and in the mind of man:
> A motion and a spirit, that impels
> All thinking things, all objects of all thought,
> And rolls through all things.

In the ode "Intimations of Immortality," completed when he was thirty-four, he characterizes the spiritual realm from which human life emerged:

> The Soul that rises with us, our life's Star,
> Hath had elsewhere its setting,
> And cometh from afar:

Not in entire forgetfulness,
And not in utter nakedness,
But trailing clouds of glory do we come
From God, who is our home.

At the age of forty, in his essay "Upon Epitaphs," he suggested that ". . . without the consciousness of a principle of Immortality in the human soul, Man could never have had awakened in him the desire to live in the remembrance of his fellows."

By the time he wrote the final version of *The Prelude*, an autobiographical poem published after his death by his widow, his views had modified to more closely reflect Christian orthodoxy. In words that suggest belief in the conventional idea of immortality, he speaks, for example, of:

Faith in life endless, the sustaining thought
Of human Being, Eternity and God.

Whatever Wordsworth may have ultimately thought about the afterlife, he was able to discover it for himself at the age of eighty, when a cold turned into pleurisy. The lung infection worsened, and he died at Rydal Mount on April 23, 1850. He was buried in St. Oswald's Churchyard in Grasmere, and a monument to his memory was erected in Poets' Corner of Westminster Abbey.

SAMUEL TAYLOR COLERIDGE

When Samuel Taylor Coleridge sought inspiration, the three poetic Muses—Calliope, Erato, and Euterpe—didn't stand a chance against opium, laudanum, and brandy. One of the founders of the English Romantic movement in poetry, Coleridge was born on October 21, 1772, in the village of Ottery St. Mary in Devonshire, youngest of ten children of an Anglican vicar and his second wife. Samuel's father died when he was eight, and he

was sent to Christ's Hospital, a charity school in London. There he met Charles Lamb, who would become a lifelong friend. Coleridge later attended Jesus College in Cambridge, where he won prizes for his poetry and accumulated large debts, but received no degree.

Rejected by the object of his affection, Mary Evans, he joined the Royal Dragoons under the false name Simon Tomkyn Comberbache. He was discharged on grounds of "insanity"—more likely depression caused by bipolar disorder—and returned to Cambridge, but never finished his studies. He befriended fellow poets Robert Southey and William Wordsworth, launched his own career as a writer, and married Southey's wife's sister, Sarah Fricker. It was an unhappy marriage, and they spent much time apart before finally separating permanently.

In 1798 Coleridge and Wordsworth jointly published *Lyrical Ballads*, which is regarded as the genesis of the Romantic movement in literature. It included Coleridge's most famous poem, "The Rime of the Ancient Mariner," which, along with other hallucinatory poems like "Kubla Khan," "Christabel," and "The Pains of Sleep," are generally thought to have been written under the influence of drugs. Coleridge's other principal writings are a major work of criticism called *Biographia Literaria*, commentaries on Kant and Shakespeare, numerous translations, and essays on political theory. Coleridge coined the term "willing suspension of disbelief," still much cited in literary criticism.

In addition to his severe mental depression, Coleridge suffered from lifelong heart and lung disorders, stemming from childhood rheumatic fever. Treatment with laudanum led to his addiction to opium. Always plagued by financial problems, he lived for a time in the Lake District and then on the island of Malta.

Seeking a cure for his addiction, he moved into rooms in the home of a physician friend in Highgate, north of London, where he planned to stay a few weeks. He remained a bit longer—for eighteen years, entertaining literary lights like Carlyle and Emerson, and, despite efforts to kick his addictions, continuing to indulge in opium and brandy until he died. He started many grand projects, but finished few of them, often chiding himself for "indolence."

His eldest son, Hartley, was a ne'er-do-well who was expelled from Oxford for drunkenness. One day in 1822, he asked his father if he could borrow some money. Soft-hearted Coleridge agreed, and Hartley was to return that evening to collect it. Instead he skipped town, and although he later carved out a lack-luster career as a schoolmaster and a critic, Coleridge never saw him again.

At various times in his life, Coleridge espoused Unitarianism, pantheism, neo-Platonism, and other philosophical systems, but in his later years, he returned to the Christian orthodoxy of his youth. Just a few days before his death, he wrote in a letter to his godchild, Adam Steinmetz Kinnaird:

> The greatest of all blessings, as it is the most ennobling of all privileges, is to be indeed a Christian. . . . And I, thus on the brink of the grave, solemnly bear witness to you, that the Almighty Redeemer, most gracious in his promises to them that truly seek Him, is faithful to perform what He has promised; and has reserved, under all pains and infirmities, the peace that passeth all understanding, with the supporting assurances of a reconciled God, who will not withdraw His Spirit from the conflict, and in His own good time will deliver me from the evil one.

Heart and lung failure, aggravated by drugs and drink, was the cause of Coleridge's death on July 25, 1834, at the age of sixty-one. An autopsy disclosed he had an enlarged heart.

His friend, Charles Lamb, delivered the eulogy at his funeral, saying: "When I heard of the death of Coleridge, it was without grief. It seemed to me that he long had been on the confines of the next world,—that he had a hunger for eternity."

Coleridge was buried in Old Highgate Chapel, London, now part of St. Michael's Church. His epitaph, which he wrote in the last year of his life, reads:

Stop, Christian Passer-by!–Stop, child of God,
And read with gentle breast. Beneath this sod
A poet lies, or that which once seem'd he.–
O, lift one thought in prayer for S.T.C.;
That he who many a year with toil of breath
Found death in life, may here find life in death!
Mercy for praise–to be forgiven for fame
He ask'd, and hoped, through Christ.
Do thou the same.

A bust in Coleridge's memory was erected in Poets' Corner of Westminster Abbey in 1885, near the memorials for his friends Wordsworth and Southey.

JANE AUSTEN

Jane Austen, who has been called the Stephen Colbert of her generation, was a sharp observer and deft satirist of society's foibles. She is known for six novels, only four of which were published during her lifetime—and those were anonymous, attributed merely to "A Lady."

Born December 16, 1775, in Steventon, Hampshire, England, she was the daughter of an Anglican rector and part-time farmer and his wife, who came from a prominent family. Jane had six brothers and an older sister, Cassandra, who was her lifelong confidante. The two of them were privately educated together in Oxford and later at home, learning French, spelling, music, drama—and dancing, which Jane took great delight in as an adult. From age twelve, Jane began writing poems, plays, and stories.

The Austen family moved to Bath, where Jane received a marriage proposal from a well-to-do landowner named Harris Bigg-Wither. She accepted, but on the following day changed her mind. As she later observed, "Anything is to be endured rather than marrying without Affection." She never came so close to marrying again.

After her father's death, Jane, Cassandra, and their mother moved to Worthing in Sussex, then to Southampton, and finally to a house provided for them by Jane's brother Edward in Chawton, East Hampshire. With the help of her brother Henry, who acted as her agent, Jane published *Sense and Sensibility*, *Pride and Prejudice*, and *Mansfield Park*. They were well received, and their fans included the prince regent, who discovered the author's identity and made it known that she had "permission" to dedicate her next novel to him. Austen, who despised the future King George IV's vanity and licentiousness, bit her tongue and honored him with the dedication of *Emma*, the final novel published during her lifetime.

Jane Austen remained a devout Christian throughout her life. Her religion was of a rational and cheerful kind, with practical emphasis on living morally in the here and now, and with scant speculation about the afterlife. In her religion, as in her novels, illness and death were treated lightly and without sentimentality. She often composed prayers for her private devotions, one of which reads:

> Look with Mercy on the Sins we have this day committed, and in Mercy make us feel them deeply, that our Repentance may be sincere, and our resolutions steadfast of endeavouring against the commission of such in future. Teach us to understand the sinfulness of our own Hearts, and bring to our knowledge every fault of Temper and every evil Habit in which we have indulged to the discomfort of our fellow-creatures, and the danger of our own Souls. May we now, and on each return of night, consider how the past day has been spent by us, and what have been our prevailing Thoughts, Words, and Actions during it, and how far we can acquit ourselves of Evil. Have we thought irreverently of Thee, have we disobeyed thy Commandments, have we neglected any known Duty, or willingly given pain to any human being? – Incline us to ask our Hearts these questions Oh! God, and save us from deceiving ourselves by Pride or Vanity.

In early 1816, Austen began to suffer from skin discoloration, exhaustion, recurrent fever, bilious attacks, and rheumatic pains. In typical fashion, she first ignored and then made light of her illness, while she continued to write and to participate in the usual family activities. Undiagnosed at the time, her trouble may have been Addison's disease, an insufficiency of adrenalin. Other experts who have studied her symptoms believe she suffered from lymphoma, a form of blood cancer. More recent theories suggest she had bovine tuberculosis, acquired from drinking unpasteurized milk, possibly aggravated by a recurrence of an illness related to the typhus she had had as a child.

Whatever it was that ailed her, she finally went to Winchester for treatment, but to no avail. It was there that she died, at dawn on Friday July 18, 1817, at the age of forty-one, her head cradled on a pillow in Cassandra's lap.

Austen's brother Henry arranged for her burial in the north aisle of the nave of Winchester Cathedral. The inscription on her tombstone by her brother James reads in part:

> *She departed this Life . . . after a long illness supported with the patience and the hopes of a Christian. The benevolence of her heart, the sweetness of her temper, and the extraordinary endowments of her mind obtained the regard of all who knew her and the warmest love of her intimate connections. Their grief is in proportion to their affection, they know their loss to be irreparable, but in their deepest affliction they are consoled by a firm though humble hope that her charity, devotion, faith and purity have rendered her soul acceptable in the sight of her REDEEMER.*

Almost as an afterthought, James later added a brass plaque that briefly acknowledged that Jane was a writer:

> *Known to many by her writings, endeared to her family by the varied charms of her character and ennobled by her Christian faith and piety.... "She openeth her mouth with wisdom and in her tongue is the law of kindness."*

Henry arranged for the posthumous publications of *Persuasion* and *Northanger Abbey*—which, for the first time, identified Jane Austen as the author. All of her novels have remained in print since their first publication.

LORD BYRON

"Mad, bad, and dangerous to know" was the description of Lord Byron by Lady Caroline Lamb, who, as one of his many mistresses, would have had an expert opinion. Flamboyant, sexually voracious, and immensely popular as a poet—a virtual rock star with the literary public—Byron had a brief, tumultuous life, and is regarded as the embodiment of Romanticism.

He was born George Byron on January 22, 1788, in London, to a fortune-hunting ne'er-do-well, Captain "Mad Jack" Byron, and his wife, Catherine Gordon, whose family was Scottish aristocracy. "Mad Jack," who died when George was three, had taken the name Gordon in order to claim his wife's estate, and his son was known by that name for a while. But when he was ten, George inherited his great-uncle's title as sixth Baron Byron of Rochdale, and thereafter was known simply as Lord Byron.

Afflicted with a clubfoot from birth, he moved with his mother to Scotland, where he attended Aberdeen Grammar School, and then was enrolled in Harrow and at Trinity College, Cambridge, where he ran up large debts while earning an M.A. He was known as something of a dandy, and, despite his disability, excelled at boxing, swimming, and horseback riding.

He began to publish his writings, and he was prolific in turning out lyric verse, satire, dramas, long narratives, odes, and voluminous correspondence, much of it in verse. His most notable works include the satirical *English Bards and Scotch Reviewers*; heroic narratives like *Don Juan*, *Childe Harold's*

Pilgrimage, and *The Corsair*; and hundreds of lyric and narrative poems such as "She Walks in Beauty," "The Prisoner of Chillon," and "The Destruction of Sennacherib."

Byron's infamous bisexual life titillated his countrymen. He was seduced when he was eleven by the family maid and seemed to take the experience to heart. At Cambridge, he had a number of liaisons with younger men and boys, and he continued such attachments throughout his life. He married Annabella Milbanke, had a daughter named Ada, and divorced after a year of marriage. Thereafter he had a succession of mistresses, including Lady Caroline Lamb, Lady Frances Webster, and Clair Clairmont, with whom he had a daughter. Byron also had an affair with his own half-sister, Augusta.

Largely to escape censure for his sexual proclivities, Byron went to the Continent, living for a while in Italy. There he became caught up in the Greek struggle for independence from the Ottoman Turks. He traveled to Greece, where he put money into refitting the Greek Navy for an assault on the Turks that he was planning to lead until his untimely death interrupted his plan.

In matters of religion, Byron remained influenced by the Presbyterian Calvinism of his youth, and he maintained a great affection for the Bible. He was a freethinker, however, and his own beliefs probably tended toward Deism tinged with nihilism.

Death for Byron was a release into an unconscious state from the sorrows of life. In an early poem called "Euthanasia," he wrote:

> 'Ay, but to die and go,' alas!
> Where all have gone, and all must go!
> To be the nothing that I was
> Ere born to life and living woe!
>
> Count o'er the joys thine hours have seen,
> Count o'er thy days from anguish free,

And know, whatever thou hast been,
'Tis something better not to be.

Byron escaped that living woe in 1824. On April 9, in
Missolonghi, Greece, while out riding, he was soaked by heavy
rains and developed fever and rheumatic pains, which a physician treated with castor oil and by blood-letting—attaching a
dozen leeches to his head. As a result of this treatment, Byron
was infected with sepsis and lapsed into a coma on Easter Sunday, April 18. His utterances were limited to fragments of Italian and English. He regained consciousness Sunday night long
enough to say, "Now I shall go to sleep." He died during an
electrical storm at six o'clock the next evening, April 19, at the
age of thirty-six.

Byron's body was embalmed by the Greeks, who allegedly
kept his heart as a token, and shipped the rest of him to London,
where it arrived on June 29 and lay in state for two days in a
house on Great George Street. Westminster Abbey refused to allow
his burial there, owing to his "questionable morality," and on Friday, July 16, 1824, Lord Byron was interred in the family vault
beneath the chancel of St. Mary Magdalene's Church, Hucknall,
Nottinghamshire. Almost a century and a half later, in 1969, a
memorial was placed in Poets' Corner in Westminster Abbey.

The Greeks proclaimed Byron a national hero, and his death
galvanized them against the Turks, eliciting support from the
British, French, and Russians, who destroyed the Turkish fleet
in 1827, assuring Greek independence.

PERCY BYSSHE SHELLEY

"Mad Shelley" was the nickname given to Percy Bysshe Shelley by his college mates at Oxford, owing to his absentminded
behavior, violent temper, interest in alchemy, espousal of free
love, and vocal promotion of atheism. It was a pamphlet entitled

"The Necessity of Atheism" that resulted in his expulsion from Oxford only a year after arriving there.

Born on August 4, 1792, in Warnham, Sussex, England, the son of a member of Parliament, Percy was sent to Eton College and then to University College, Oxford. After being expelled, he was estranged from his family and eloped to Scotland with sixteen-year-old Harriet Westbrook, who bore him three children before committing suicide when he abandoned her five years into their marriage. Shelley then married Mary Godwin, later the author of *Frankenstein*, with whom he had three more children.

Percy and Mary moved permanently to Italy, where they befriended Lord Byron, and where Shelley wrote most of his poetical works. He is known for his hundreds of lyrical poems, including "Ode to the West Wind" ("If Winter comes, can Spring be far behind?"), "To a Skylark" ("Hail to thee, blithe Spirit"), "The Cloud" ("I bring fresh showers for thirsting flowers"), "Ozymandias," and "Epipsychidion"; longer poems such as "Julian and Maddalo," "The Revolt of Islam," "Letter to Maria Gisborne," and "The Triumph of Life"; and verse dramas, *The Cenci*, *Prometheus Unbound*, and *Hellas*.

"Adonais," Shelley's elegy on the death of John Keats, expresses Shelley's belief, despite his professed atheism, in a kind of pantheistic monism, in which human life, like all creation, springs from and returns to the eternal oneness of the universe:

Dust to the dust! But the pure spirit shall flow
Back to the burning fountain whence it came,
A portion of the Eternal, which must glow
Through time and change, unquenchably the same,
Whilst thy cold embers choke the sordid hearth of shame.
…
The One remains, the many change and pass;
Heaven's light forever shines, Earth's shadows fly;
Life, like a dome of many-coloured glass,
Stains the white radiance of Eternity,
Until Death tramples it to fragments.—Die,
If thou wouldst be with that which thou dost seek!

Shelley died in 1822, a month before he would have turned thirty, when his boat went down in a storm off the coast of Italy. He and his friend Edward Williams had been visiting Byron in Pisa and were returning from the port of Livorno to Lerici, where Mary Shelley and Edward's wife, Jane (with whom Shelley was having an affair), were waiting for them. They set out in a small sailboat Shelley had bought from Byron, accompanied by an Italian sailor-boy, about six o'clock in the evening of July 8 to travel a distance of about twenty miles. The boat, which Byron had named "Don Juan," but Shelley preferred to call "Ariel," made it as far as Via Reggio when a sudden, violent storm arose. When it had cleared, the "Ariel" had vanished. The bodies of the three occupants were found ten days later, washed up several miles from the point of the storm.

Initially, Shelley's friends assumed that the boat had gone down in the strong winds, but the boat's structural damage suggested it might have been rammed by another vessel. A tale later emerged that an Italian seaman had made a death-bed confession—that he had been on the crew of a fishing vessel that collided intentionally with Shelley's boat in order to steal a large sum of money mistakenly believed to be on board, in the possession of Lord Byron. This was the story believed by Shelley's friend Edward Trelawny, who found the bodies, identifying Shelley by a copy of Keats's poems in his pocket. He first buried Shelley in the sand, where the body remained for a month, and then on August 15 cremated him on the beach in the ancient Greek fashion. He snatched Shelley's heart from the fire and sent it to Mary. The remainder of his ashes were interred in the Protestant Cemetery in Rome.

The English public was largely unmoved by Shelley's death. One newspaper reported: "Shelley, the writer of some infidel poetry, has been drowned; now he knows whether there is a God or not."

JOHN KEATS

It was a cruel twist of irony that John Keats— a poet licensed to practice medicine—succumbed to an incurable disease in the prime of his youth. Keats, the eldest son of a stable keeper, was born in Finsbury, London, on October 31, 1795. Both parents died early; his father when Keats was eight, and his mother when he was fifteen. The Keats children were raised by a guardian named Richard Abbey, who was a tea merchant. John was sent to Mr. Clarke's School in Enfield and then apprenticed to a surgeon—while translating Virgil's *Aeneid* in his spare time. He interned in Guy's and St. Thomas's Hospitals and received an apothecary's license, enabling him to practice as a physician and surgeon.

Poetry was his true gift, however, and he became friends with Shelley, Wordsworth, and Leigh Hunt while pursuing his writing. His first volume of verse was followed by a wealth of lyrical poems that earned him a place, as he predicted, "among the English poets." His most notable works include "Ode on a Grecian Urn" ("Beauty is truth, truth beauty"), "On First Looking into Chapman's Homer" ("Silent, upon a peak in Darien"), "La Belle Dame Sans Merci" ("And no birds sing"), "The Eve of St. Agnes," "Lamia," and such longer works as "Hyperion," "Otho the Great," and "Endymion" ("A thing of beauty is a joy forever").

On a seaside holiday to Hastings in 1817, Keats struck up an acquaintance with an alluring twenty-two-year-old woman named Isabella Jones, who may or may not have had a husband lurking in the background, and with whom Keats may or may not have had a torrid love affair. This connection, whatever its nature, ended abruptly in the following year, when Keats met Fanny Brawne, an eighteen-year-old girl who lived next door to him in London. He became infatuated with her in a consuming, but unconsummated, passion.

At about the same time Keats began suffering from the effects of pulmonary tuberculosis, which had claimed his brother Tom's life. Keats, already weakened with a sore throat and stomach trouble from dosing himself with mercury—a dangerous and controversial treatment for various ailments, including syphillis and gonorrhea—may have acquired tuberculosis from nursing his ailing brother. From then until the end of his life, Keats suffered from worsening sore throats, gastric upset, coughs, loss of hair, and frequent hemorrhages. In February of 1820, he experienced two severe lung hemorrhages and, at his doctor's suggestion, moved from the damp English climate to Italy, accompanied by his friend, the painter Joseph Severn. In the same year he published "Ode to a Nightingale," in which he wrote:

> Darkling I listen; and, for many a time
> I have been half in love with easeful Death,
> Call'd him soft names in many a mused rhyme,
> To take into the air my quiet breath;
> Now more than ever seems it rich to die,
> To cease upon the midnight with no pain,
> While thou art pouring forth thy soul abroad
> In such an ecstasy!

Keats was more explicit about his wish for—and fear of—death in a letter to his friend Charles Armitage Brown:

> I wish for death every day and night to deliver me from these pains, and then I wish death away, for death would destroy even those pains, which are better than nothing. Land and sea, weakness and decline, are great separators, but Death is the great Divorcer forever. . . . Is there another life? Shall I awake and find this all a dream? There must be, we cannot be created for this sort of suffering.

Keats and Severn settled in the Piazza di Spagna, Rome, where Keats was attended by English expatriate Dr. James Clarke. At eleven o'clock on the night of February 23, 1821, in his room overlooking a Bernini fountain, Keats called to Severn, "Lift me up, for I am dying. I shall die easy. Don't be frightened. Thank God it has come." A few moments later he was gone, at the age of twenty-five. He was buried four days later in Rome's Protestant cemetery.

Shelley gives this account of Keats's passing in the introduction of his elegy "Adonais":

The savage criticism of his *Endymion*, which appeared in the *Quarterly Review*, produced the most violent effect on his susceptible mind; the agitation thus originated ended in the rupture of a blood-vessel in the lungs; a rapid consumption ensued, and the succeeding acknowledgements from more candid critics of the true greatness of his powers were ineffectual to heal the wound thus wantonly inflicted.

Byron commented that Keats was "snuffed out by an article."

Shelley described Keats's burial place as:

. . . the romantic and lonely cemetery of the Protestants in that city [Rome], under the pyramid which is the tomb of Cestius, and the massy walls and towers, now mouldering and desolate, which formed the circuit of ancient Rome. The cemetery is an open space among the ruins, covered in winter with violets and daisies. It might make one in love with death, to think that one should be buried in so sweet a place.

Keats had asked Severn to inscribe on his tomb a line paraphrased from *Philaster* by Beaumont and Fletcher: "Here lies one whose name was writ in water." Severn embellished it considerably:

This Grave
contains all that was Mortal
of a Young English Poet
Who
on his Death Bed
in the Bitterness of his Heart
at the Malicious Power of his Enemies
Desired
these Words to be engraved upon his Tomb Stone
Here lies One whose Name was writ in Water.

MARY SHELLEY

Mary Shelley wrote the work for which she is famous on a dare when she was only nineteen. It was conceived in a "can-you-top-this?" challenge around a campfire with her husband, Percy Bysshe Shelley; Lord Byron; and John Polidori, Byron's physician, each of whom vowed to write a Gothic horror story. Byron and Percy never finished theirs. Polidori wrote *The Vampyre*, which later inspired Bram Stoker's *Dracula*. Mary wanted her story to be one "which would speak to the mysterious fears of our nature and awake thrilling horror—one to make the reader dread to look round, to curdle the blood, and quicken the beatings of the heart." The result was a novel, *Frankenstein; or, the Modern Prometheus*. It remains one of the most enduring pieces of fiction ever written, and its monster, as portrayed on the screen by Boris Karloff, is indelibly etched in the memories of terrified filmgoers.

Mary, born on August 30, 1797, in Somerstown, London, was the daughter of two free-thinking, iconoclastic, atheist political philosophers: William Godwin, and his feminist wife, Mary Wollstonecraft, who died when infant Mary was only eleven days old. Raised by her father, she became infatuated with one of his disciples, the young poet Shelley, who was already married. The two fled to Europe to escape society's censure of their adulterous affair. She married Shelley after his first wife committed suicide.

After Shelley drowned in Italy, Mary returned to London, where she spent the rest of her life raising her son, also named Percy, and continuing to write novels, essays, biographies, and travel journals. Her writings include *Rambles in Germany and Italy* and the novels *Valperga*, *Perkin Warbeck*, *The Last Man*, *Lodore*, and *Falkner*.

The daughter of two atheists and the wife of another, Mary Shelley was very likely one herself, although her views on religion and death are not really known. *The Last Man* is an apocalyptic novel about a plague that kills every human being except the protagonist Verney, who is an autobiographical stand-in for Mary herself. He faces his solitary life on earth alternating acceptance of death with fear of it:

> And now I do not fear death. I should be well pleased to close my eyes, never more to open them again. And yet I fear it; even as I fear all things; for in any state of being linked by the chain of memory with this, happiness would not return—even in Paradise, I must feel that your love was less enduring than the mortal beatings of my fragile heart, every pulse of which knells audibly,
>
> The funeral note
> Of love, deep buried, without resurrection.
>
> No—no—me miserable; for love extinct there is no resurrection!

In another place, Verney says, "Death will perpetually cross my path, and I will meet him as a benefactor."

Mary wrote in her diary: "At the age of twenty-six I am in the condition of an aged person—all my old friends are gone ... & my heart fails when I think by how few ties I hold to the world."

By her early forties, Mary was suffering frequent headaches and partial paralysis, probably early symptoms of the brain tumor that ultimately killed her. She died on February 1, 1851, at the age of fifty-three, at her home on Chester Square in London, where she lived with her son and his wife.

Mary had asked to be buried with her parents in St. Pancras churchyard, but her son regarded that as a dreary site and opted instead to exhume her parents and inter them all at St. Peter's in Bournemouth. A year after Mary's death, her son opened her desk and found a parcel containing some ashes and the heart of her husband, who had died in Greece in 1822.

The Victorian Era

JOHN HENRY NEWMAN

Calvinist Evangelical, then Anglican priest, and finally Roman Catholic cardinal, John Henry Newman was born in London February 21, 1801, with a silver spoon clamped firmly in his mouth. His father was a London banker, and his mother was descended from a distinguished family of French Huguenots. At age seven, John Henry was sent to Great Ealing School, and at fifteen he became an Evangelical Christian. He graduated without honors from Trinity College in Oxford. Despite his poor academic showing, he became a fellow of Oriel College, Oxford's intellectual center. Shortly thereafter, he abandoned Evangelicalism and was ordained a priest in the Church of England in 1825.

Newman was active in the Oxford Movement, a group of high-church Anglicans who advocated more Catholic doctrines and rituals. This led to Newman's conversion to Roman Catholicism and his ordination as a Catholic priest in 1845. He settled in Edgbaston, an upscale Birmingham neighborhood, where he established the Oratory of St. Philip Neri, a church in which J. R. R. Tolkien was later a parishioner. In 1879, Newman was made a cardinal by Pope Leo XIII.

Newman's writings include *The Idea of a University*, *Apologia Pro Vita Sua*, *The Dream of Gerontius*, *An Essay in Aid of a Grammar of Assent*, and the hymn "Lead, Kindly Light."

In *The Dream of Gerontius*, inspired by Dante's *Divine Comedy*, Newman paints a vivid picture of the afterlife. The narrator is an elderly man, facing imminent death:

> JESU, MARIA—I am near to death,
> And Thou art calling me; I know it now.
> Not by the token of this faltering breath,
> This chill at heart, this dampness on my brow,—
> (Jesu, have mercy! Mary, pray for me!)
> 'Tis this new feeling, never felt before,
> (Be with me, Lord, in my extremity!)
> That I am going, that I am no more.
> 'Tis this strange innermost abandonment,
> (Lover of souls! great God! I look to Thee,)
> This emptying out of each constituent
> And natural force, by which I come to be.
> Pray for me, O my friends; a visitant
> Is knocking his dire summons at my door,
> The like of whom, to scare me and to daunt,
> Has never, never come to me before;
> 'Tis death,—O loving friends, your prayers!— 'tis he!

After death, Gerontius's soul is pained by the sight of God, and he begs to spend time in Purgatory until he is properly prepared to be in the divine presence. The poem ends with an angel's assurance that Gerontius will soon be purified and worthy to meet God:

> Softly and gently, dearly-ransomed soul,
>   In my most loving arms I now enfold thee,
> And, o'er the penal waters, as they roll,
>   I poise thee, and I lower thee, and hold thee.
>
> And carefully I dip thee in the lake,
>   And thou, without a sob or a resistance,

Dost through the flood thy rapid passage take,
  Sinking deep, deeper, into the dim distance.

Angels, to whom the willing task is given,
  Shall tend, and nurse, and lull thee, as thou liest;
And Masses on the earth, and prayers in heaven,
  Shall aid thee at the Throne of the Most Highest.

Farewell, but not forever! brother dear,
  Be brave and patient on thy bed of sorrow;
Swiftly shall pass thy night of trial here,
  And I will come and wake thee on the morrow.

Newman's death from pneumonia at the age of eighty-nine was chronicled in the *Times* of London on Tuesday, August 12, 1890:

> We have to record, with feelings of the most sincere regret, the death of His Eminence Cardinal Newman. He died last evening at the Oratory, Edgbaston, in his 90th year, after less than three days' illness. . . . On Saturday night the Cardinal had an attack of shivering, followed by a sharp rise of temperature, and the symptoms indicative of pneumonia rapidly supervened and became acute. . . . During the day Cardinal Newman, though rapidly becoming worse, was able to speak to those about him, and in the afternoon, at his request, the Rev. W. Neville recited with him the Breviary. Yesterday morning he fell into an unconscious condition. . . . The rite of extreme unction was performed by the Rev. Austin Mills. Owing to the patient's comatose condition the Viaticum was not administered. . . . Bishop Illsley visited the Cardinal early in the afternoon and made the "commendation of his soul" in the presence of the Oratory Fathers. There was an appointment on the part of the doctors to meet for

consultation at 8 o'clock last evening. At that time it was seen that life was fast ebbing away, and both medical men remained until 12 minutes to 9, when Cardinal Newman breathed his last. He died in the presence of the Fathers of the Congregation, and there is every reason to believe that his death was painless.

Eight days later he was buried, as he had instructed, in the cemetery at Rednal Hill, Birmingham, in the same grave as his friend and fellow priest, Ambrose St. John, with whom he had shared a house for thirty-two years. Newman was beatified in 2010 by Pope Benedict XVI.

RALPH WALDO EMERSON

"The Sage of Concord," Ralph Waldo Emerson, spent his final years unable to remember his own name. Until that unhappy turn of events, he was a highly regarded intellectual, known as the Father of Transcendentalism, a philosophy that holds that a divine spirit dwells in everything that exists, and that each person's own moral sense is the standard that should dictate conduct. Emerson came by these beliefs through Unitarianism, his father being a minister of that denomination in Boston, where Waldo—as he later liked to call himself—was born on May 25, 1803. His father died when he was seven, and Waldo was sent to Boston Latin School and thereafter to Harvard College, from which he graduated at age eighteen. He taught school for several years, then attended Harvard Divinity School.

Ailing with chronic tuberculosis, which caused him chest pains, visual problems, and muscle weakness, Emerson became a "snowbird" and went south to St. Augustine, Florida, when he was twenty-three. He remained there for several months and met Prince Achille Murat, Napoleon Bonaparte's nephew. The two had many philosophical discussions that Emerson later credited with helping to form his own views.

Emerson returned to Boston, married Ellen Tucker, and accepted a position as junior pastor of Boston's Second (Unitarian) Church. His wife died less than two years later. Emerson resigned his pastorate in a dispute with church officials about the nature of communion, a commemoration that he said was "not suitable" to him. He took an extended journey to Europe, where he met John Stuart Mill, William Wordsworth, Samuel Taylor Coleridge, and Thomas Carlyle.

On his return to the United States, he moved in with his mother in Concord, Massachusetts. In 1835, he married for the second time, to Lydia Jackson—whom he insisted on calling Lidian, because the name sounded better ending with a consonant preceding "Emerson." With his wife and his mother, he moved into the Concord home where he would live until it burned in 1872. He and Lidian had four children, one of whom died in childhood of scarlet fever.

Emerson made his living from lecture fees and from a settlement of his first wife's estate, although he had to sue her family to get it. Among Emerson's notable works were several collections of essays, on such topics as "Nature," "The American Scholar," "Self-Reliance," and "The Over-Soul," and numerous poems, of which the most famous is "Concord Hymn," with the well-worn line "the shot heard round the world."

Tuberculosis haunted Emerson throughout his life. Not only did he suffer from it as a young man, but also two of his brothers, his first wife, and his close friend Henry David Thoreau all died of it at early ages.

Emerson's religious beliefs were rooted in Unitarianism, but developed into the vaguely pantheistic notions associated with Transcendentalism. "Trust thyself" was his motto. In 1837, Emerson delivered a lengthy graduation address at his old alma mater, Harvard Divinity School, and so outraged the establishment by denying the divinity of Christ and comparing him to a "demigod" like Osiris or Apollo, that he was condemned as an atheist and not invited back to Harvard for thirty years.

Immortality of the soul was a nebulous topic for Emerson, as can be seen from his comments in his essay on "Worship" from *Conduct of Life:*

> Of immortality, the soul, when well employed, is incurious. It asks no questions of the Supreme Power. . . . Higher than the question of our duration is the question of our deserving. Immortality will come to such as are fit for it, and he who would be a great soul in future, must be a great soul now. It is a doctrine too great to rest on any legend, that is, on any man's experience but our own. It must be proved, if at all, from our own activity and designs, which imply an interminable future for their play. . . . You must do your work, before you shall be released. And as far as it is a question of fact respecting the government of the Universe, Marcus Antoninus summed the whole in a word, "It is pleasant to die, if there be gods; and sad to live, if there be none."

Poor health began to affect Emerson in his sixties, and he greatly reduced his activities. He began to suffer memory loss that eventually resulted in his not being able to recall his own name. When asked how he was, he would reply, "Quite well. I've lost my mental faculties, but I am perfectly well." The lung problems that had plagued him in his youth caught up with him, and on April 21, 1882, he was diagnosed with pneumonia and died six days later at the age of seventy-eight.

He is buried in what is now known as Authors Ridge, in Sleepy Hollow Cemetery, Concord, where his friends Thoreau and Nathaniel Hawthorne had earlier been laid to rest.

NATHANIEL HAWTHORNE

At Nathaniel Hawthorne's funeral, his friend Ralph Waldo Emerson spoke of "the painful solitude of the man, which I suppose could no longer be endured, and he died of it." Shunning social life almost to the point of being a recluse, Hawthorne grappled with his family legacy of strict Puritanism in all his stories and novels, the most famous of which are *Twice-Told Tales*, *The Scarlet Letter*, and *The House of Seven Gables*.

The Puritan family into which he was born on July 4, 1804, in Salem, Massachusetts, had a long history; one of Nathaniel's ancestors was a judge in the Salem witch trials of 1692. When Nathaniel was four, his father, a sea-captain, died of yellow fever in Surinam, and his mother and an uncle saw to Nathaniel's education, sending him to Bowdoin College. Among his college friends were the poet Henry Wadsworth Longfellow and Franklin Pierce, a future U.S. president of modest achievement.

As early as age seventeen, Hawthorne knew he wanted to be an author, and for several years after college he lived with his mother and wrote stories. He published *Twice-Told Tales* and then took a job in the Boston Custom House. He married Sophia Peabody, a shy girl who shared Hawthorne's antisocial tendencies, and they moved to Concord, where they rented a house from Emerson and embraced his Transcendental philosophy.

Among Hawthorne's friends and associates were Margaret Fuller, Henry David Thoreau, Oliver Wendell Holmes Sr., and Herman Melville.

The Hawthornes then moved to Salem, where Nathaniel worked briefly in the Salem Custom House, and over the next few years they lived in various other Massachusetts towns. His old classmate Franklin Pierce asked Hawthorne to write a biography for his presidential campaign, and when he was elected, he rewarded Hawthorne with the lucrative post of United States consul in Liverpool, England. He remained in the job for seven years, also traveling throughout Europe and completing his last novel, *The Marble Faun*.

Always torn between his family's Puritanism and the Transcendental ideas he was first exposed to during a youthful stay at the experimental commune Brook Farm, Hawthorne adhered precariously to orthodox beliefs, at least in his concept of life after death. In *Mosses from an Old Manse*, he expressed an approving view of immortality:

> I recline upon the still unwithered grass, and whisper to myself:—"Oh, perfect day!—Oh, beautiful world!— Oh, beneficent God!" And it is the promise of a blessed Eternity; for our Creator would never have made such lovely days, and have given us the deep hearts to enjoy them, above and beyond all thought, unless we were meant to be immortal. The sunshine is the golden pledge thereof. It beams through the gates of Paradise and shows us glimpses far inward.

On his return to the United States from Europe, Hawthorne's health began to fail, but he refused to consult a doctor, and so the true nature of his illness is unknown. It is speculated that it might have been some form of cancer, possibly a brain tumor. In May of 1864, he set out with his friend, former President Pierce, on a trip to the hills of New Hampshire, which he hoped might help restore his health. But on May 19, the second night out, in Plymouth, New Hampshire, Hawthorne died unexpectedly in his sleep at the age of fifty-nine.

Emerson, Longfellow, and Louisa May Alcott were among the mourners as he was interred in the Sleepy Hollow Cemetery at Concord.

ELIZABETH BARRETT BROWNING

Half of the world's most famous poetic love affair, Elizabeth Barrett Moulton Barrett, was born on March 6, 1806, in Durham, England, the eldest of twelve children. Barrett was part of her given name as well as the family name, as a result of her grandfather's desire to perpetuate the name among his heirs. Both her tyrannical father and her mother came from wealthy families with large land holdings dependent on slave labor in Jamaica. The Moulton Barretts moved to Hope End, a secluded part of Herefordshire, where Elizabeth grew up, reading the classics and writing poetry at an early age. The family had business reverses and lost much of its wealth, then moved to London to a house at 50 Wimpole Street.

When she was fifteen, Elizabeth began suffering from a life-long undiagnosed illness, which affected both her lungs and her spine and eventually led to her dependence upon laudanum and morphine. Her poetic output was prolific, including a translation of Aeschylus's *Prometheus Bound* when she was twenty-seven.

By the 1840s, Elizabeth B. Barrett was a well-known literary name. A friend of Wordsworth, Coleridge, Carlyle, and Tennyson, she was Tennyson's rival for appointment as England's Poet Laureate on the death of Wordsworth in 1850.

In 1844, Robert Browning, a poet six years her junior, was so dazzled by her work that he wrote to her, "I love your verses with all my heart, dear Miss Barrett." This infatuation blossomed into a love affair, vigorously opposed by Elizabeth's father, and memorialized in the famous 1930 play by Rudolf Besier, *The Barretts of Wimpole Street.* After a secret courtship, Elizabeth and Robert were married on September 12, 1846, at St. Marylebone Parish Church, after which Elizabeth returned alone to her father's home. One week later, on the pretext of walking her dog, Elizabeth left the house, taking her dog and her maid with her, and went with Browning to Paris for a honeymoon. Regarding Browning as a grasping gold-digger, Elizabeth's father promptly disinherited her—as he did each of his three children who married during his lifetime.

The Brownings remained on the Continent for the rest of Elizabeth's life, living on their literary earnings and occasional financial aid from friends. They resided in Paris and in various Italian cities—Rome, Siena, Lucca, and, for fourteen years, in Florence. Literary luminaries including William Makepeace Thackeray, Margaret Fuller, Harriet Beecher Stowe, John Ruskin, and George Sand were among their acquaintances.

Devoutly Christian in her faith, Elizabeth was influenced by both Dante's *Inferno* and Milton's *Paradise Lost*, and once observed that "Christ's religion is essentially poetry—poetry glorified." She was also interested in spiritualism and dabbled in Mesmerism and Swedenborgianism. One of Browning's pet names for her was "my little Portuguese," and this undoubtedly was the inspiration for her *Sonnets from the Portuguese.* In one of the sonnets, she exhibits not only her love for Browning, but also her confident Christian faith:

How do I love thee? Let me count the ways.
I love thee to the depth and breadth and height
My soul can reach, when feeling out of sight
For the ends of being and ideal grace.
I love thee to the level of every day's
Most quiet need, by sun and candle-light.
I love thee freely, as men strive for right;
I love thee purely, as they turn from praise.
I love thee with the passion put to use
In my old griefs, and with my childhood's faith.
I love thee with a love I seemed to lose
With my lost saints. I love thee with the breath,
Smiles, tears, of all my life; and, if God choose,
I shall but love thee better after death.

In 1860, Elizabeth's old lung disease began to plague her again, and her health steadily deteriorated, increasing her dependence on morphine. Although the exact nature of her illness is not known, later medical experts have speculated that the symptoms might have indicated hypokalemic periodic paralysis, a genetic disorder of body chemistry.

On June 29, 1861, at the age of fifty-five, Elizabeth Barrett Browning died at home in Casa Guidi in Florence, in the arms of her husband, who later wrote, "Then came what my heart will keep till I see her again and longer—the most perfect expression of her love to me within my whole knowledge of her. Always smilingly, happily, and with a face like a girl's, and in a few minutes she died in my arms, her head on my cheek. . . . There was no lingering, nor acute pain, nor consciousness of separation, but God took her to himself as you would lift a sleeping child from a dark uneasy bed into your arms and the light. Thank God. . . . Her last word was—'Beautiful'."

She was buried in the Protestant Cemetery of Florence.

HENRY WADSWORTH LONGFELLOW

Henry Wadsworth Longfellow's literary reputation took a nosedive in the years following his death. Although no longer a favorite of the literati, during his lifetime he was among the most acclaimed and financially successful poets who ever lived. In an era when poetry could actually make money, he was famous on both sides of the Atlantic, admired by Queen Victoria, and one of his volumes sold ten thousand copies in a single day in England. His annual income in 1868 was close to a million dollars in today's values.

This literary lion was born on February 27, 1807, in Portland, Maine (then part of Massachusetts), to Stephen and Zilpah Longfellow. His father was a lawyer, state legislator, and trustee of Maine's Bowdoin College, to which young Henry was admitted at age fourteen. Gifted in languages, he was named Bowdoin's first professor of modern European languages, teaching French, Italian, and Spanish; writing poetry; and turning out several textbooks. In 1834, he accepted a similar position at Harvard.

He and his wife, Mary, celebrated his appointment with a trip to Europe, where she died of complications of a miscarriage. Profoundly grieved, Longfellow returned to Cambridge and plunged into his work: teaching, chairing the department, and continuing to write poetry—which made him an international celebrity. His often-quoted poems, memorized by millions of schoolchildren, include *Evangeline* ("This is the forest primeval"), *The Song of Hiawatha* ("By the shore of Gitche

Gumee/By the shining Big-Sea-Water"), *The Courtship of Miles Standish* ("Why don't you speak for yourself, John?"), *Tales of A Wayside Inn* (which includes "Paul Revere's Ride"), and hundreds of lyric poems such as "The Day is Done" ("And the night shall be filled with music"), "The Wreck of the Hesperus," "The Village Blacksmith" ("Under a spreading chestnut-tree"), "The Children's Hour," "The Arrow and the Song" ("I shot an arrow into the air") and "Excelsior."

In 1843, he married Fanny Appleton, whom he had courted for seven years, and they had five children. At the age of forty-seven, Longfellow resigned his burdensome academic job at Harvard and devoted himself full-time to poetry and literary celebrity. He continued to live in Cambridge for the rest of his life, traveling on occasion to Europe. His circle of friends and acquaintances included his Bowdoin classmate Nathaniel Hawthorne; Ralph Waldo Emerson; Oliver Wendell Holmes; James Russell Lowell; Walt Whitman; Alfred, Lord Tennyson; John Ruskin; William Gladstone; and Oscar Wilde.

Longfellow's wife, Fanny, died tragically in 1861. The family story is that she was melting sealing wax when her clothing caught fire, and she died of burns the next day. There is some evidence, however, that the fire was caused by the Longfellows' five-year-old daughter playing with matches. Longfellow himself, in trying to save Fanny, was badly burned on the lower part of his face, and to hide the scars he grew the beard that is seen in his famous portraits. After Fanny's death, Longfellow confined himself largely to translations, including his monumental version of Dante's *Divine Comedy*.

Longfellow's religious views were uncertain, sometimes veering toward Unitarianism and on other occasions taking a more orthodox Christian tone. One view of life after death is found in his poem "Resignation," an elegy for his one-year-old daughter:

We see but dimly through the mists and vapors;
    Amid these earthly damps
What seem to us but sad, funereal tapers
    May be heaven's distant lamps.
There is no Death! What seems so is transition;
    This life of mortal breath
Is but a suburb of the life elysian,
    Whose portal we call Death.

Longfellow was plagued throughout his life by poor health. He suffered constant pain from neuralgia, his eyesight was bad, and in his later years he was afflicted with rheumatism. Resigned to constant ailments, he wrote to his friend Charles Sumner, "I do not believe anyone *can* be perfectly well, who has a brain and a heart." On one occasion, a woman admirer knocked on the door of his house in Cambridge, and, unaware that she was greeted by Longfellow himself, asked, "Is this the house where Longfellow was born?" Longfellow told her it was not. She then asked if he had died here. "Not yet," he replied.

Death did come in March of 1882, when Longfellow took to his bed with a severe stomach pain, now known to be peritonitis, which he treated for several days with opium. He died on Friday, March 24, at the age of seventy-five, surrounded by members of his family.

He was buried beside both of his wives in Mount Auburn Cemetery, Cambridge. He left an estate of more than eight million dollars in current values.

EDGAR ALLAN POE

Macabre twists and turns marked Edgar Allan Poe's life, his works, and, especially, his death. Born January 19, 1809, in Boston, Massachusetts, to two actors who were appearing in

King Lear, he was named Edgar after a character in that play who feigns madness, and he was orphaned by the age of two.

Raised by a prosperous foster family named Allan, who gave him his middle name, he lived in Richmond, Virginia, then briefly in Britain. After returning to Virginia with the Allans, he enrolled in the University of Virginia to study languages, but lasted there only one year, withdrawing to try his luck as a writer and odd-job worker in Boston. He enlisted in the Army, rose to the rank of sergeant major, and then secured an early discharge to enroll in the U.S. Military Academy at West Point. Meanwhile, he had published his first book of poetry, including the ill-received "Tamerlane." Disinherited after quarrelling with his foster father, Poe purposely contrived his expulsion from West Point and published another volume of poetry.

He worked in Boston, New York, Philadelphia, and Baltimore, in various writing and editorial jobs, and when he was twenty-seven, he married his thirteen-year-old cousin, Virginia Clemm. Virginia developed tuberculosis, lingered with it for several years, and died of it when she was twenty-four.

Poe continued to publish gothic poems, literary criticism, and fiction replete with murder, mayhem, and supernatural happenings. "The Raven," with its haunting line, "Quoth the Raven 'Nevermore'"—a poem for which Poe was paid only ten dollars—made him famous as an erratic literary figure. While popular with the public, he was never well compensated for his work, and he never won the esteem of the literary establishment—Ralph Waldo Emerson called him "the jingle man." In addition to "The Raven," his most famous poems include "Annabel Lee" ("It was many and many a year ago/

In a kingdom by the sea"), "The Bells," "The City in the Sea," "Eldorado," "To Helen" ("To the glory that was Greece/And the grandeur that was Rome"), and "Ulalume." Among his macabre stories were "The Black Cat," "The Cask of Amontillado," "The Murders in the Rue Morgue," "The Fall of the House of Usher," "The Gold-Bug," "The Tell-Tale Heart," and "The Pit and the Pendulum."

Although reputedly a drunkard and a drug addict (thanks to a malicious biography by a grudge-bearing rival named Rufus Griswold), there is little evidence that Poe used drugs, other than medicinal opiates that were common as pain-relievers, and his consumption of alcohol was fairly moderate, except for occasional binges.

Although depictions of death permeate his work, Poe apparently devoted little thought to an afterlife. Baptized and raised an Episcopalian and married by a Presbyterian minister, Poe was a knowledgeable student of the Bible and a card-playing crony of the Jesuit priests at St. John's College in the Bronx ("they smoked, drank, and played cards like gentlemen and never mentioned religion"). His own religious views, however, were hard to pin down, although he provides some hints about them in *Eureka*, an abstruse prose-poem subtitled "Essay on the Material and Spiritual Universe." He enigmatically writes:

> No thinking being exists who, at some luminous point of his life of thought, has not felt himself lost amid the surges of futile efforts at understanding or believing that anything exists *greater than his own soul.* . . . each soul is, in part, its own God—its own Creator . . . God— the material *and* spiritual God—*now* exists solely in the diffused Matter and Spirit of the Universe; and . . . the regathering of this diffused Matter and Spirit will be but the reconstitution of the *purely* Spiritual and

Individual God. . . . [M]yriads of individual Intelligences [will] become blended—when the bright stars become blended—into One . . . the sense of individual identity will be gradually merged in the general consciousness — . . . Man, for example, ceasing imperceptibly to feel himself Man, will at length attain that awfully triumphant epoch when he shall recognize his existence as that of Jehovah.

Poe's bizarre death is the subject of great controversy. On September 27, 1849, having proposed to Sarah Royster Shelton, his widowed childhood sweetheart, and having set an October wedding date, Poe boarded a steamer from Richmond to Baltimore, where he intended to take a train to New York to conduct some business. On Wednesday afternoon, October 3, he was found, dazed and delirious, with "lusterless and vacant eyes," outside a polling place in Baltimore, wearing a rumpled, stained, ill-fitting bombazine suit, worn-down shoes, and an old straw hat—clearly not his own clothes.

He was taken to Washington Medical College Hospital, where he remained in a room with barred windows in an area reserved for drunkards. Semi-comatose for four days, under the care of Dr. John J. Moran, Poe was never lucid enough to account for his lost six days. Moran reported that Poe frequently called out the name "Reynolds," but no one knew what he meant. At five o'clock on the morning of October 7, after murmuring, "It's all over...write 'Eddie is no more,'" and "Lord, help my poor soul," Poe died at the age of forty.

The precise cause of death remains a mystery. No medical records exist. Obituaries mentioned "congestion of the brain" and "cerebral inflammation." Subsequent speculation has pointed to delirium tremens, epilepsy, encephalitis, syphilis, cholera, influenza, diabetes, apoplexy, rabies, lead or mercury poisoning, hypoglycemia, drug overdose, and suicide. One theory is that Poe was fatally beaten by political thugs after being coerced into a vote-rigging scheme, in which he was drugged and forced to cast fraudulent votes at multiple polling places.

Poe's funeral was at four o'clock in the afternoon on a cold and gloomy Monday, October 8, at Baltimore's Westminster Hall and Burying Ground. In attendance were a handful of friends, including college classmate Zaccheus Collins Lee, first cousin Elizabeth Herring and her husband, and former schoolmaster Joseph Clarke. The officiant was the Reverend W. T. D. Clemm, a Methodist minister and cousin of Poe's late wife, who did not bother with a sermon because there were so few people present. Poe's uncle, Henry Herring, provided a cheaply made mahogany coffin that had no handles, no nameplate, no lining, and no cushion for his head. The graveside service lasted three minutes, and Poe was laid to rest beneath a marker that read simply "No. 80."

His old nemesis, Griswold, wrote a mean-spirited obituary in the *New-York Daily Tribune*, averring that Poe's death "will startle many, but few will be grieved by it" inasmuch as he had "few or no friends."

Poe was given a new burial and monument in 1875, in a ceremony attended by Walt Whitman, with a poetic tribute sent by Alfred, Lord Tennyson, which read:

Fate that once denied him,
And envy that once decried him,
And malice that belied him,
Now cenotaph his fame.

Every year from the 1930s until 2009, in the early morning hours of January 19, Poe's birthday, a mysterious figure dressed in black was observed at the original site of Poe's grave. Known as the "Poe Toaster," the figure would drink a glass of cognac and leave three red roses and the unfinished Martell cognac bottle on the stone marker.

ALFRED, LORD TENNYSON

England's Poet Laureate from 1850 until his death in 1892—the longest term ever served—Alfred Tennyson achieved fame, wealth, and even a peerage with his poetry. Born August 6, 1809, in Somersby, Lincolnshire, to an Anglican vicar who suffered from depression and alcoholism, and his wife, whose father was also a vicar, Alfred was the fourth of twelve children. He was taught classics by his father, then attended King Edward VI Grammar School and Trinity College, Cambridge. His father's death forced him to leave the university without a degree, and he returned to live with his mother, two brothers, and a sister, who stayed on in the Lincolnshire vicarage as guests of his father's successor. After six years, to their great distress, the Tennysons were turned out of the vicarage and went to live in High Beach, a tiny hamlet in Epping Forest.

During this period, Tennyson published several volumes of verse, including *The Lady of Shalott.* He became engaged to his childhood sweetheart, Emily Sellwood, but they were unable to marry until Tennyson's financial fortunes improved ten years later. Tennyson was deeply grieved by the death of his close friend (and his sister's fiancé), Arthur Hallam, an event that inspired Tennyson's most profound statement about life and death, *In Memoriam A. H. H.*

As Poet Laureate, Tennyson enjoyed such success that by the 1850s, he was earning the equivalent of more than a million dollars a year—enabling him to buy a country home in Surrey and a retreat on the Isle of Wight. He maintained friendships with Elizabeth Barrett Browning, Thomas Carlyle, Samuel Taylor Coleridge, Charles Dickens, and Prime Minister William Gladstone, who conferred a baronetcy on him.

Tennyson's most famous works include "Locksley Hall," "The Idylls of the King," "Morte d'Arthur," "Ulysses," "Tithonus," "Maud," "Tiresias," "The Lotos-Eaters," "Enoch Arden," and "The Charge of the Light Brigade." His poems are the source of many phrases in common use today, such as, "In the spring a young man's fancy lightly turns to thoughts of love," "Nature, red in tooth and claw," "'Tis better to have loved and lost / Than never to have loved at all," "Theirs not to reason why, / Theirs but to do and die," "My strength is as the strength of ten, / Because my heart is pure," and "To strive, to seek, to find, and not to yield."

Although his poetry often seems to embody orthodox Christian theology, Tennyson himself was harder to pin down in his beliefs. Toward the end of his life, he categorized himself variously as an agnostic, a pantheist, and a follower of the free-thinking philosophies of both Giordano Bruno and Baruch Spinoza. In *In Memoriam A. H. H.*, Tennyson wants to believe in a life hereafter:

Strong Son of God, Immortal Love,
   Whom we, that have not seen thy face,
   By faith, and faith alone, embrace
Believing where we cannot prove;

Thine are these orbs of light and shade;
   Thou madest Life in man and brute;
   Thou madest Death; and lo, thy foot
Is on the skull which thou hast made.

Thou wilt not leave us in the dust;
   Thou madest man, he knows not why,

He thinks he was not made to die;
And thou hast made him: thou art just.

But Tennyson was bothered by doubts, which he tried to transform into belief:

There lives more faith in honest doubt,
Believe me, than in half the creeds.

No matter how much he struggled with faith, he kept his hope that life would continue after death, as expressed in the famous lines from "Crossing the Bar":

For tho' from out our bourne of Time and Place
The flood may bear me far,
I hope to see my Pilot face to face
When I have crost the bar.

In September of 1892, at Aldworth, his country home in Surrey, Tennyson came down with severe bronchitis that developed into influenza. He became pale and weak, and though his condition worsened, his mind remained lucid until the end. On the night of October 6, a few hours before his death, he was reading Shakespeare's *Cymbeline.* With the volume clasped in his hands, and with the moonlight bathing his face in what an attendant described as "an unearthly majestic beauty," Lord Tennyson crossed the bar at the age of eighty-three.

He was buried with much pomp six days later in Westminster Abbey, in a funeral attended by thousands of mourners and bedecked with flowers, including a wreath from Queen Victoria. Music included a choral version of "Crossing the Bar," set to music by the Abbey organist, and "The Silent Voices," Tennyson's last poem, which had been set to music by his wife. Other musical offerings were the hymn "Holy, Holy, Holy" and Handel's "Dead

March" from *Saul*. The officiant was Tennyson's friend, the Reverend George Granville Bradley, the dean of the Abbey. Tennyson was laid to rest between John Dryden and Robert Browning.

MARGARET FULLER

Margaret Fuller's life was filled with feminist firsts. The Betty Friedan of her day, she was the first American to write a book about women's equality, the first editor of the Transcendental journal *The Dial*, the first woman journalist on Horace Greeley's *New-York Daily Tribune*, the first fulltime female book reviewer, and the first woman war correspondent.

She was born May 23, 1810, in Cambridgeport, Massachusetts, to Timothy Fuller, a lawyer who later served in the U.S. House of Representatives, and his wife, Margaret. Her father began a rigorous education for her, and by age eight she was reading Virgil's *Aeneid* in Latin, and by age ten she was translating Cicero's works. Short and plump, with a spinal curvature, acne scars, and a myopic squint, Margaret attended several schools in the Boston area and made plans for a literary career. Her father's death when she was twenty-five forced her to take up teaching to help support the family.

She met Ralph Waldo Emerson and was accepted into the Transcendentalist circle. Her acquaintances included Henry David Thoreau, Bronson Alcott, Oliver Wendell Holmes, and Nathaniel Hawthorne. She began a series of "Conversations" for women intellectuals that established her as a leader in the Transcendental movement. She wrote books, contributed literary criticism and translations to various journals, and became known as "the best read person in New England."

Fuller was indirectly involved in a messy scandal involving Edgar Allan Poe, who was romantically linked to a married woman, also a poet and a friend of Fuller's. She asked Fuller to visit Poe to retrieve some letters she had written to him. A furious Poe dismissed Fuller as a "busybody."

The *New-York Daily Tribune* sent Fuller to Europe as a foreign correspondent in 1846. During her travels, she met George Sand, Thomas Carlyle, Matthew Arnold, William Wordsworth, Robert and Elizabeth Barrett Browning, and the Italian revolutionary Giuseppe Mazzini. She also met and ultimately married the Italian Marchese Giovanni Angelo Ossoli, a revolutionary supporter, with whom she had a son, named Angelo. As the *Tribune*'s war correspondent, she covered the Italian revolution of 1848–1849 from the battlefronts and began to write a book-length history of Italy.

After the revolutionaries were defeated, she decided to return to the United States, hoping to secure publication of her book. With Ossoli and two-year-old Angelo, she set sail for New York on May 17, 1850, on the American merchant freighter *Elizabeth.* While at sea, the captain died of smallpox, and the ship's command was taken over by the inexperienced first mate. On July 19, at 3:30 a.m., less than a hundred yards from Fire Island, New York, the ship slammed into a sandbar. Badly damaged, it took twelve hours to sink, as onlookers waded out to scavenge the cargo that floated ashore, but neglected to render aid to the stranded passengers. Some survived by swimming to shore—but not Margaret and her family. Julia Ward Howe, author of "The Battle Hymn of the Republic," gives this account of Fuller's final hours in her 1883 biography:

The commanding officer made one last appeal to Margaret before leaving his post. To stay, he told her, was certain and speedy death, as the ship must soon break up. He promised to take her child with him. . . . Margaret still refused to be parted from child or husband. The crew were then told to "save themselves," and all but four jumped overboard. The commander and several of the seamen reached the shore in safety, though not without wounds and bruises.

By three o'clock in the afternoon the breaking-up was well in progress. Cabin and stern disappeared beneath the waves, and the forecastle filled with water. The little group now took refuge on the deck, and stood about the foremast. The deck now parted from the hull, and rose and fell with the sweep of the waves. The final crash must come in a few minutes. The steward now took Angelo in his arms, promising to save him or die. At this very moment the foremast fell, and with it disappeared the deck and those who stood on it. The steward and the child were washed ashore soon after, dead, though not yet cold.... Margaret, last seen at the foot of the mast, in her white nightdress, with her long hair hanging about her shoulders, is thought to have sunk at once. Two others, cook and carpenter, were able to save themselves by swimming, and might, alas! have saved her, had she been minded to make the attempt.

What strain of the heroic in her mind overcame the natural instinct to do and dare all upon the chance of saving her own life, and those so dear to her, we shall never know. No doubt the separation involved in any such attempt appeared to her an abandonment of her husband and child.

Resting in this idea, she could more easily nerve herself to perish with them than to part from them. She and the babe were feeble creatures to be thrown upon the mercy of the waves, even with the promised aid. Her husband, young and strong, was faithful unto death, and would not leave her. Both of them, with fervent belief, regarded death as the entrance to another life, and surely, upon its very threshold, sought to do their best.

Although her body was never recovered, Fuller undoubtedly perished in the sea, at the age of forty. The manuscript of her Italian history was also lost. Through Howe's efforts, a memorial to Fuller was erected on the beach at Fire Island in 1901. In Mount Auburn Cemetery, Cambridge, Massachusetts, is a cenotaph, under which Angelo is buried, with an inscription in tribute to Fuller:

By birth a child of New England
By adoption a citizen of Rome
By genius belonging to the world.

CHARLES DICKENS

A literary star in both England and America, wealthy from his writings and his lectures, Charles Dickens began life in bleak poverty, as poor as Little Dorrit. He was born in Portsmouth, England, on February 7, 1812, the second of eight children, to John Dickens, a Cratchit-esque clerk and his wife, Elizabeth. When Charles was ten, the family moved to Camden Town, then an impoverished section of London, and two years later, Charles's father was in debtors' prison. Forced to leave school, Charles worked as a bootblack in a rat-infested factory. An inheritance gave the family a brief respite from poverty, and Charles started school again—only to be forced to quit once more and go to work as an office boy when he was fifteen.

He began to freelance as a reporter in the law courts and to submit sketches to various papers under the pen name "Boz," a nonsensical childhood nickname for his brother. He married Catherine Hogarth, daughter of a music critic and newspaper editor, and they had ten children before separating permanently after twenty-two years of marriage. Their separation followed Dickens's infatuation with an eighteen-year-old actress named Ellen Ternan, with whom he began a lifelong affair.

Dickens's first novel, *The Posthumous Papers of the Pickwick Club*, was published from 1836 to 1837 in installments, as most of his works were, and became immensely popular. He followed this with *Oliver Twist, The Life and Adventures of Nicholas Nickleby, The Old Curiosity Shop*, and *Barnaby Rudge.* Soon he was an international celebrity, and he lectured in America, from Virginia to Missouri, on a visit that yielded fees equivalent to a million and a half dollars in today's money. The American travels also provided material for two more books, the snarky *American Notes for General Circulation* and *The Life and Adventures of Martin Chuzzlewit.*

His timeless classic, *A Christmas Carol*, and his generally acknowledged masterpiece, *David Copperfield*, followed—but after the death of both his father and a daughter and his separation from his wife, Dickens's mood turned darker with *Bleak House, Hard Times*, and *Little Dorrit.* He came out of the doldrums and produced two more first-rate novels, *A Tale of Two Cities* and *Great Expectations.*

In 1865, Dickens was in a train wreck in which seven carriages plunged off a bridge. His was one of the only carriages that stayed on the track, and he never fully recovered from the trauma of that crash. It may have contributed to the first of several small strokes that drained his energy, and he may have also been suffering from what is known today as bipolar disorder.

Dickens's views of death and the afterlife were based on the vaguest sort of Christianity, perhaps also influenced by his interest in Unitarianism and by the theology of the Baptist chapel that he attended in his youth. Although he disdained organized religion, he wrote a devotional book for his children, *The Life of Our Lord*, not published until 1934. He wrote of heaven as a place "where we hope to go, and all to meet each other after we are dead, and there be happy always together."

He was never explicit in expressing such views in his novels. The death of little Nell in *The Old Curiosity Shop* is treated with religious reverence, but holds out no promise of an afterlife. In a scene of which Oscar Wilde said, "One must have a heart of stone to read the death of little Nell without laughing," Dickens wrote:

> For she was dead. There, upon her little bed, she lay at rest. The solemn stillness was no marvel now.
>
> She was dead. No sleep so beautiful and calm, so free from trace of pain, so fair to look upon. She seemed a creature fresh from the hand of God, and waiting for the breath of life; not one who had lived and suffered death.
>
> Her couch was dressed with here and there some winter berries and some leaves, gathered in a spot she had been used to favour. 'When I die, put near me something that has loved the light, and had the sky above it always.' Those were her words.
>
> She was dead. Dear, gentle, patient, noble Nell was dead. Her little bird—a poor, slight thing the pressure of a finger would have crushed—was stirring nimbly in its cage; and the strong heart of its child mistress was mute and motionless forever.

Dickens's own death came at age fifty-eight, on June 9, 1870, twenty-four hours after a having paralytic stroke at Gadshill, his home in Kent. He had worked a few hours on *The Mystery of Edwin Drood*, the novel he never finished. Then he relaxed by smoking a cigar in his new conservatory, and after that wrote some letters in the library. Then he joined his sister-in-law, Georgina Hogarth, for an early dinner. Here is Dickens's friend John Forster's account of what happened next:

. . . before dinner, which was ordered at six o'clock with the intention of walking afterwards in the lanes, he wrote some letters, and dinner was begun before Miss Hogarth saw, with alarm, a singular expression of trouble and pain in his face. "For an hour," he then told her, "he had been very ill"; but he wished dinner to go on. These were the only really coherent words uttered by him. They were followed by some, that fell from him disconnectedly, of quite other matters . . . but at these latter he had risen, and his sister-in-law's help alone prevented him from falling where he stood. Her effort then was to get him on the sofa, but after a slight struggle he sank heavily on his left side. "On the ground" were the last words he spoke. It was now a little over ten minutes past six o'clock. His two daughters came that night with Mr. F. Beard, who had also been telegraphed for, and whom they met at the station. His eldest son arrived early next morning, and was joined in the evening (too late) by his younger son from Cambridge. All possible medical aid had been summoned. The surgeon of the neighbourhood was there from the first, and a physician from London was in attendance as well as Mr. Beard. But human help was unavailing. There was effusion on the brain; and though stertorous breathing continued all night, and until ten minutes past six o'clock on the evening of Thursday, 9 June, there had never been a gleam of hope during the twenty-four hours.

Contrary to his wishes to be buried in Kent in Rochester Cathedral "in an inexpensive, unostentatious, and strictly private manner," Dickens instead was laid to rest in Westminster Abbey. To avoid a public display, his grave in Poets' Corner, between those of George Frederick Handel and Richard Brinsley Sheridan, was dug at night. The following morning at nine-thirty, three coaches and a hearse arrived for the interment, attended by only twelve mourners. The funeral service, from the Book of Common Prayer, was read by the dean, the Reverend Arthur Penrhyn Stanley, in the silent and nearly empty Abbey. The grave was then left open for two days, as thousands of people came to pay respects and throw flowers into it. It is marked by a stone inscribed with Dickens's name in "plain, English letters," as he instructed.

ROBERT BROWNING

Robert Browning led a relatively obscure life as an unsung poet until after the death of his more famous wife. Born to a well-to-do bank clerk and his pianist wife, a Nonconformist evangelical, on May 7, 1812, in the London suburb of Camberwell, Robert was tutored at home with lessons in Greek, Hebrew, Latin, French, Italian, and Spanish, as well as the English poets. When he was fourteen, Robert persuaded his devoutly religious mother to buy him a copy of "Mr. Shelley's atheistic poem," *Queen Mab*.

The aspiring poet began to write lyric poems and tragic dramas that were published privately by his family. Among his works of this period was *Sordello*, a long, convoluted, obscure poem about a thirteenth-century Lombard troubador. Browning continued to live with his parents until his marriage at the age of thirty-four to Elizabeth Barrett, a well-known poet.

The Brownings moved to Italy, where they had a son, Robert Barrett Browning, nicknamed Pen, and they remained on the Continent until Elizabeth's death in 1861. Browning then returned to England, where he lived for a time with his son and also with his younger sister. Only then did his works begin to gain acceptance with the British public.

Among the most notable are his many short narrative poems that he called dramatic lyrics, dramatic romances, and monologues, such as "The Pied Piper of Hamelin," "How They Brought the Good News from Ghent to Aix," "The Lost Leader," "My Last Duchess," "Soliloquy of the Spanish Cloister," "Rabbi Ben Ezra" ("Grow old along with me, / The best is yet to be") and "Home Thoughts From Abroad"—with the famous line "Oh, to be in England / Now that April's there!" *The Ring and the Book*, a 21,000-line dramatic poem in blank verse about an Italian murder case, was a bestseller. His drama *Pippa Passes* contains one of his most famous lyrical poems, which ends, "God's in his heaven, / All's right with the world."

An interesting sidelight about *Pippa Passes* is Browning's unwitting use in it of the word *twat*, a vulgar term for female genitalia. He wrote:

> Then owls and bats,
> Cowls and twats,
> Monks and nuns, in a cloister's moods,
> Adjourn to the oak-stump pantry!

Browning naïvely thought the word meant a nun's headdress, based on his misunderstanding of a bawdy satirical poem of 1660 called "Vanity of Vanities," in which these lines appear:

> They talk't of his having a Cardinall's Hat,
> They'd send him as soon as an Old Nun's Twat...

Whether the sunny optimism expressed in much of Browning's work is a true reflection of the poet's religious beliefs is open to question. Most of his works are dramatic in nature, and the thoughts expressed in them are in the mouths of different characters. A professed atheist in his youth, Browning turned in later life to a vague Christianity tempered with skepticism. Once he was asked whether he was a Christian and is said to have answered with a thunderous "NO!" His most naked feelings about death are seen in "Prospice," a poem written shortly after Elizabeth's death, in which he contemplates his own demise and hopes to face it heroically:

> Fear death?—to feel the fog in my throat,
>   The mist in my face,
> When the snows begin, and the blasts denote
>   I am nearing the place,
> The power of the night, the press of the storm,
>   The post of the foe;
> Where he stands, the Arch Fear in a visible form,
>   Yet the strong man must go:
> For the journey is done and the summit attained,
>   And the barriers fall,
> Though a battle's to fight ere the guerdon be gained,
>   The reward of it all.
> I was ever a fighter, so—one fight more,
>   The best and the last!
> I would hate that death bandaged my eyes, and forebore,
>   And bade me creep past.
> No! let me taste the whole of it, fare like my peers,
>   The heroes of old,
> Bear the brunt, in a minute pay glad life's arrears
>   Of pain, darkness and cold.
> For sudden the worst turns the best to the brave,
>   The black minute's at end,

And the elements' rage, the fiend-voices that rave,
    Shall dwindle, shall blend,
Shall change, shall become first a peace out of pain,
    Then a light, then thy breast,
O thou soul of my soul! I shall clasp thee again,
    And with God be the rest!

Browning was on holiday at his son's home in Venice, Ca' Rezzonico, a restored baroque palace, when he came down with a severe case of bronchitis. The damp Venetian air worsened the disease, which, after two weeks, proved too much for his heart to withstand, and he died on December 12, 1889, at the age of seventy-seven.

In reporting his death, one British paper noted, "To many readers, indeed, Robert Browning is simply the name of a poet who wrote 'Sordello'—a work which nobody but himself professed to understand."

Browning's wish to be buried next to his wife was thwarted, since the English Cemetery in Florence, where she was interred, had since been closed to new burials. Instead he was laid to rest in Poets' Corner, Westminster Abbey, on December 31, a bleak, foggy day. The church was filled with mourners, and a wreath from Lord Tennyson was placed atop the polished pine coffin. A bevy of clergy were in attendance, including the dean and canons of the Abbey and the Archbishop of Canterbury. Music included the hymns "We All Go to Our Place," "Meditation," and "O God, Our Help in Ages Past"; a poem by Browning's wife, "He Giveth His Beloved Sleep," which had been set to music; and Handel's "Dead March" from *Saul*.

CHARLOTTE BRONTË

Charlotte Brontë, one of three literary sisters, was born on April 21, 1816, in Thornton, Yorkshire, to Maria and the Reverend

Patrick Brontë—a surname the clergyman had invented to replace the Irish and less elegant-sounding Prunty. Charlotte had four younger sisters, two of whom died of tuberculosis in childhood while enrolled at the Clergy Daughters School. Charlotte and her sister Emily  were also students at the same school, but withdrew after their sisters' deaths and attended the nearby Roe Head School, as did the youngest daughter, Anne.

After working in several positions as a governess, Charlotte established a school with her two sisters—rather unsuccessfully, as not one student enrolled. All three sisters had a literary bent, and all three achieved publication of novels in 1847, under assumed masculine names: Charlotte, as Currer Bell, published *Jane Eyre*; Emily, as Ellis Bell, *Wuthering Heights*; and Anne, as Acton Bell, *Agnes Grey*.

Within the next two years, both Emily and Anne died of tuberculosis, a disease that some years later also killed their only brother, Bramwell, who was beset by alcoholism as well. Charlotte continued to write and became known in literary circles. In 1854, Charlotte accepted a proposal of marriage from Arthur Bell Nicholls, a curate at her father's church, who had first proposed nine years earlier.

As the daughter and wife of Anglican clergymen of the "low-church," evangelical variety, Charlotte seemingly maintained adherence to the Church of England, but her skepticism simmered just below the surface. In *Jane Eyre*, the heroine has her doubts about the ultimate fate of her dying friend, Helen Burns. Languishing on her deathbed, Helen engages Jane in consideration of the afterlife:

"By dying young, I shall escape great sufferings. I had not qualities or talents to make my way very well in the world: I should have been continually at fault."

"But where are you going to, Helen? Can you see? Do you know?"

"I believe; I have faith: I am going to God."

"Where is God? What is God?"

"My Maker and yours, who will never destroy what he created. I rely implicitly on his power, and confide wholly in his goodness: I count the hours till that eventful one arrives which shall restore me to him, reveal him to me."

"You are sure, then, Helen, that there is such a place as heaven; and that our souls can get to it when we die?"

"I am sure there is a future state; I believe God is good; I can resign my immortal part to him without any misgivings. God is my father; God is my friend: I love him; I believe he loves me."

"And shall I see you again, Helen, when I die?"

"You will come to the same region of happiness; be received by the same mighty, universal Parent, no doubt, dear Jane."

Again I questioned; but this time only in thought. "Where is that region? Does it exist?"

Jane harbored doubts; perhaps Charlotte did, too.

Soon after her marriage, Charlotte became pregnant, but at the same time, her health began to fail. Her friend and biographer, Elizabeth Gaskell, gives this account of her final days in March of 1855:

Soon after her return [from visiting friends nearby], she was attacked by new sensations of perpetual nausea, and ever-recurring faintness. After this state of things had lasted for some time, she yielded to Mr. Nicholls' wish that a doctor should be sent for. He came, and assigned a natural cause for her miserable indisposition; a little patience, and all would go right. She, who was ever patient in illness, tried hard to bear up and bear on. But the dreadful sickness increased and increased, till the very sight of food occasioned nausea....

"I dare say I shall be glad some time," she would say; "but I am so ill–so weary." Then she took to her bed, too weak to sit up. Long days and longer nights went by; still the same relentless nausea and faintness, and still borne on in patient trust. About the third week in March there was a change; a low wandering delirium came on; and in it she begged constantly for food and even for stimulants. She swallowed eagerly now; but it was too late. Wakening for an instant from this stupor of intelligence, she saw her husband's woe-worn face, and caught the sound of some murmured words of prayer that God would spare her. "Oh!" she whispered forth, "I am not going to die, am I? He will not separate us, we have been so happy."

Early on Saturday morning, March 31st, the solemn tolling of Haworth church-bell spoke forth the fact of her death to the villagers who had known her from a child, and whose hearts shivered within them as they thought of the two sitting desolate and alone in the old grey house.

The precise cause of Charlotte's death, at the age of thirty-eight, was officially listed as phthisis (pulmonary tuberculosis), but it has been speculated that the proximate cause was dehydration as a result of excessive vomiting in extreme morning sickness during her pregnancy. There is also evidence to suggest that she had contracted typhus, as well as pneumonia.

Charlotte Brontë was buried in the family vault at the Church of St. Michael and All Angels in Haworth. Her father, who survived his wife and all six children by several years, published her early novel *The Professor* posthumously.

HENRY DAVID THOREAU

If anyone ever heard a different drummer, it was Henry David Thoreau. He was born as David Henry on July 12, 1817, in Concord, Massachusetts, a town near Boston, where he lived virtually all his life. His father, a pencil manufacturer, sent David to Harvard, where he graduated in the top half of his class. He taught school briefly, but gave it up and went to work in his father's pencil factory. Since everyone called him Henry, Thoreau began to style himself as Henry David after graduating from Harvard.

His friend, neighbor, mentor, and fellow Transcendentalist, Ralph Waldo Emerson, invited Thoreau to live in his house, where he did odd jobs for his upkeep. He became friends with the Transcendentalist circle that included Emerson's wife, Lidian, Margaret Fuller, Nathaniel Hawthorne, Bronson Alcott, and Louisa May Alcott.

Hawthorne said of Thoreau's appearance that he was "as ugly as sin, long-nosed, queer-mouthed, and with uncouth and rustic, though courteous manners, corresponding very well with such an exterior. But his ugliness is of an honest and agreeable fashion, and becomes him much better than beauty." For years he had a beard that grew around his neck, which he insisted women found attractive. Louisa Alcott, however, said that Thoreau's facial hair would "assuredly deflect amorous advances and preserve the man's virtue in perpetuity." It apparently did exactly that, and Thoreau never married. He stayed with Emerson about two years, and then went back to the pencils and a room in his parents' home.

Finding little quiet or privacy to write, Thoreau persuaded Emerson to let him build a cabin, which he made from an old chicken coop, on a piece of land at Walden Pond. He remained there for two years, writing and developing his simple philosophy of nature. His principal writings are two books, *A Week on the Concord and Merrimack Rivers* and *Walden, or Life in the Woods*, and an essay, *Civil Disobedience.* In them, he explains his version of Transcendentalism, which emphasizes reverence for nature, a preference for a life of great simplicity ("Beware of all enterprises that require new clothes"), resistance to civil authority and its taxing power, and opposition to commercial development, waste, pretension, and slavery. *Walden* became a classic.

Like all Transcendentalists, Thoreau emphasized the importance of life in the present and gave little thought to the possibility of an afterlife. He wrote in his journal: "Take time by the forelock. Now or never! You must live in the present, launch yourself on every wave, find your eternity in each moment. Fools stand on their island opportunities and look toward another land. There is no other land; there is no other life but this, or the like of this."

Thoreau developed tuberculosis when he was eighteen, and he suffered periodically from it the rest of his life. One night in 1859, he decided to count the rings on some tree stumps during a rainstorm, and he developed a severe case of bronchitis, from which he never fully recovered. Over the next three years, he suffered continual pulmonary problems and was at last confined to his bed. Aware that he was not long for the world, his aunt asked him if he had made his peace with God. Thoreau replied, "I did not know we had ever quarreled." He was serene in facing the prospect of his death. "For joy I could embrace the earth," he wrote in his journal. "I shall delight to be buried in it." As death approached, Thoreau was heard to say, "Now comes good sailing," followed by two cryptic words: "moose" and "Indian."

He died on May 6, 1862, at age forty-four. At his funeral, Bronson Alcott read selections from his work, and Emerson delivered a eulogy in which he said, "The country knows not yet, or in the least part, how great a son it has lost. . . . His soul was made for the noblest society; he had in a short life exhausted the capabilities of this world; wherever there is knowledge, wherever there is virtue, wherever there is beauty, he will find a home."

Originally buried in his mother's family plot, Thoreau was later moved to Authors Ridge in the Sleepy Hollow Cemetery in Concord.

WALT WHITMAN

"Bacchus-browed, bearded like a satyr, and rank" was Bronson Alcott's description of the poet Walt Whitman when they met in 1855. It was a description in keeping with Whitman's undisciplined, boisterous, free-wheeling, and possibly unwashed poetic persona.

Born in West Hills, Long Island, New York, on May 31, 1819, the second of eight children, Walter Whitman Jr. was known as "Walt" from infancy. He moved with his family to Brooklyn when he was four, left public school when he was eleven, and then worked as an apprentice on several newspapers. He tried teaching, but returned to newspaper work and held various jobs as a reporter and as editor of the *Brooklyn Eagle* and the *Brooklyn Daily Times.*

The publication of *Leaves of Grass*, his constantly evolving collection of poems, brought acclaim from the literary establishment, including Thoreau and Emerson, who wrote to congratulate him on the "beginning of a great career." Whitman imprudently quoted Emerson's letter without permission in a subsequent edition of *Leaves of Grass*—which infuriated the Sage of Concord.

Whitman moved to Washington, D.C., and worked as a nurse during the Civil War. At war's end, he stayed on in Washington with clerical jobs at the Departments of the Interior and Justice. His real career was the constant tweaking and reissuing of *Leaves of Grass*, which included such strikingly innovative poems as "I Hear America Singing," "Song of Myself," "I Sing the Body Electric," "Out of the Cradle Endlessly Rocking," "O Captain! My Captain!" and "When Lilacs Last in the Dooryard Bloom'd"— the last two about the assassination of Abraham Lincoln.

Many of his poems have imagery that is graphically sexual, creating a raffish reputation for Whitman. He never married and never had any permanent relationship with anyone of either sex. He had close friendships with several younger men, but despite rampant speculation, there is no solid evidence that these were sexual in nature. He claimed on occasion to have fathered six illegitimate children, but there is no proof that this was so.

When he was fifty-three, Whitman suffered the first of several "whacks"—his name for strokes—that left him progressively more paralyzed for almost two decades. He moved to Camden, New Jersey, to be near his brother, and lived there the rest of his life.

Whitman professed no formal religion, but his thinking was obviously influenced by the Deism of Jefferson and Franklin.

For Whitman, the soul was immortal and in a state of constant development, and his poems often speak of death as a natural and sometimes welcome end to life. In "When Lilacs Last in the Courtyard Bloom'd," one section is a "death carol," in which Whitman writes:

> *Come lovely and soothing death,*
> *Undulate round the world, serenely arriving, arriving,*
> *In the day, in the night, to all, to each,*
> *Sooner or later delicate death.*

In "Great Are the Myths," Whitman also welcomes death:

> Great is Death—sure as Life holds all parts together,
>   Death holds all parts together,
> Death has just as much purport as Life has,
> Do you enjoy what Life confers? you shall enjoy what
>   Death confers,
> I do not understand the realities of Death, but I know
>   they are great…

And in "Whispers of Heavenly Death," Whitman conveys the unfathomable mystery of what is to come:

> Darest thou now O Soul,
> Walk out with me toward the Unknown Region,
> Where neither ground is for the feet nor any path to follow?
>
> No map there, nor guide,
> Nor voice sounding, nor touch of human hand,
> Nor face with blooming flesh, nor lips, nor eyes, are in that land.

Confined to his home in Camden in his last years, Whitman died there at 6:43 p.m. on March 26, 1892, at the age of seventy-two.

The *New York Times* of March 27 had this detailed account of his last hours:

> He began to sink at 4:30, and grew gradually weaker until the end. As soon as his attendants noticed that he was failing, they sent a messenger for his physician, Dr. McAllister, who arrived at the house at 5:45 o'clock [sic]. He immediately saw that his patient was dying and that he could do nothing for him.
>
> The end was very peaceful. The aged poet when asked by the physician if he felt any pain answered in an almost inaudible voice, "No."
>
> About twenty minutes before his death he said to his attendant, Warren Fitzsinger: "Warren, shift," meaning that he should turn him over. These were his last words and they were uttered so low as to be hardly distinguished. [Other accounts say that Whitman's words were actually "Hold me up, Warren, I want to shit."] His heart continued to beat for ten minutes after there was any noticeable aspiration. He remained conscious until the last, but, owing to his extremely weak condition, he was unable to converse with his few faithful friends who were gathered around him in his last hours....
>
> Mr. Whitman had been in bed since the 17th day of last December, when he was taken sick with pneumonia, by which his death was indirectly caused. After several weeks of suffering, his physicians, Dr. Daniel Longacre of this city and Dr. McAllister of Camden, pronounced him cured. The disease, however, left him so weak that it was impossible to predict when he might die from the failing of his vital powers.... At times he took no nourishment at all for several days, and at other times he ate heartily and seemed to enjoy his food, which consisted mainly of milk punch, toast, eggs, champagne, oysters, and occasionally bits of meats.

An autopsy was performed by Professor Henry W. Cattell of the University of Pennsylvania, who found that the cause of Whitman's death was "pleurisy of the left side, consumption of the right lung, general miliary tubercular abscesses, involving the bones, and pachymeningitis" (thickening of the membrane around the brain). The right lung was found to be completely useless, and the left lung was down to one-eighth capacity.

Whitman was laid out in a simple gray wool suit in a casket of English quartered oak with oxidized trimmings and interior lining of corded silk. A silver plate on the lid bore the simple inscription in old English text: "Walt Whitman." The funeral at 3:00 p.m. on March 29, attended by mourners estimated in the thousands, featured remarks by Robert G. Ingersoll, "the Great Agnostic." No clergyman was on the program. Whitman's remains were placed in a recently completed tomb in Harleigh Cemetery, on the outskirts of Camden, in a spot Whitman had chosen. The tomb is a substantial structure, built of massive rough granite blocks, some of them weighing over seven tons.

HERMAN MELVILLE

Herman Melville, author of *Moby Dick*, hailed today as one of the greatest novels ever written, died in obscurity, forgotten by so many that one columnist remarked that the very few who did remember him thought that he had died years earlier. The *New York Times* reported, "There has died and been buried in this city . . . a man who is so little known . . . that only one newspaper contained an obituary account of him, and this was but of three or four lines."

As for *Moby Dick,* it was a failure when it first appeared, selling fewer than three thousand copies and earning Melville only a little over $1,000 in lifetime royalties.

Born to a socially prominent family in New York City on August 1, 1819, Melville led an unexpectedly adventurous early life following his education at the Albany Academy and Columbia Preparatory School. Melville's father was forced into bankruptcy, and Herman worked in his brother's store and also taught school—but not for long.

When he was eighteen, he shipped out for Liverpool as a cabin boy on a merchant ship. He returned to New York and had several teaching jobs, but then the sea called again, and he sailed as a crew member on the *Acushnet* for the South Seas. He jumped ship in the Marquesas Islands and was held captive by a band of cannibals. He then signed on aboard an Australian ship and shortly led a mutiny of the unpaid crew. Jailed in Tahiti, he escaped and returned to the United States. He shipped out again aboard a whaling vessel to Hawaii, where he joined the crew of the frigate *United States* and eventually returned to Boston.

Melville began a literary career, using his seagoing adventures to write the novels *Typee* and *Omoo,* which were bestsellers. He married Elizabeth Shaw, daughter of the chief justice of Massachusetts, and they had four children. Melville continued to write successful novels and stories for various journals.

In 1851, he published *Moby Dick,* first in England and two years later in the United States. With few exceptions—such as praise from Nathaniel Hawthorne—it was poorly received. "An ill-compounded mixture of romance and matter-of-fact," said the London *Athenaeum.* Its failure reversed Melville's fortunes as a writer. He traveled to Europe and then, in desperate need of income, embarked upon American lecture tours talking about the charms of Roman statuary.

Through the influence of his wife's family, he landed a low-paying job as a customs collector and held on to it for nineteen years. He suffered from bouts of depression, worsened by the deaths of both his sons, and his wife's family urged her to have him committed to a mental institution, which she refused to do. He retired when his wife received an inheritance that was sufficient to support them, and he continued to dabble, unsuccessfully, at writing.

Although Melville was a nominal member of the Unitarian church, he remained skeptical of all religions. He wrote: "I have no objection to any person's religion, be it what it may, so long as that person does not kill or insult any other person, because that other person don't believe it also. But when a man's religion becomes really frantic; when it is a positive torment to him; and, in fine, makes this earth of ours an uncomfortable inn to lodge in; then I think it high time to take that individual aside and argue the point with him."

The critic Alfred Kazin said that, like Abraham Lincoln, Melville was a "tortured soul who wanted to believe in God in the face of annihilation." He seems to have had a residual belief in the survival of the soul, as suggested by Ishmael, the narrator of *Moby Dick*, who says:

Yes, there is death in this business of whaling—a speechlessly quick chaotic bundling of a man into Eternity. But what then? Methinks we have hugely mistaken this matter of Life and Death. Methinks that what they call my shadow here on earth is my true substance. Methinks that in looking at things spiritual, we are too much like oysters observing the sun through the water, and thinking that thick water the thinnest of air. Methinks my body is but the lees of my better being. In fact take my body who will, take it I say, it is not me.

Melville died in his home in New York City shortly after midnight on September 28, 1891, at the age of seventy-two, of a heart attack that his death certificate described as "cardiac dilation." He was buried in Woodlawn Cemetery in the Bronx (where the songwriter Irving Berlin was also later interred).

Billy Budd, Melville's other highly acclaimed work, was published posthumously in 1924.

GEORGE ELIOT

Mary Ann Evans had a face that, if it would not stop a clock, would at least give it pause. Even the prim and proper Henry James reported to his father, "She is magnificently ugly—deliciously hideous. She has a low forehead, a dull gray eye, a vast pendulous nose, a huge mouth full of uneven teeth." She herself likened her appearance to a "withered cabbage in a flower garden." To be fair, James admitted, "In this vast ugliness resides a most powerful beauty which, in a very few minutes steals forth and charms the mind, so that you end as I ended, in falling in love with her . . . yes, literally in love with this horse-faced bluestocking."

Whether or not her horsey looks influenced her decision, when she launched her career as a writer, she changed her name to George Eliot (she said it was because a woman's name made people think of "silly" romances). Born on a farm estate in Warwickshire on November 22, 1819, she was the author of *Middlemarch*, which Martin Amis and Julian Barnes agree is the greatest novel in the English language. Mary Ann's father, the manager of the estate and a devout low-church Anglican, sent her to various schools until she was sixteen, when her mother died and she came home to help run the household. She moved with her father to Coventry and stayed there until his death when she was thirty.

She then traveled to Switzerland with the Charles Bray family, freethinkers whom she had met in Coventry and who greatly influenced her rejection of Christianity. She settled in London and began to write for various journals. As an increasingly accepted member of the literary establishment, she met and fell in love with the philosopher George Henry Lewes, who, inconveniently, was already married to a woman who refused to divorce him. Mary Ann and Lewes, shunned by friends and family for their adultery, lived openly together for twenty-five years until his death in 1878.

In 1854, using the pen name George Eliot, she published her first novel, *Adam Bede*, which was a success. Her other major novels followed: *The Mill on the Floss*, *Silas Marner*, *Romola*, *Middlemarch*, and *Daniel Deronda*.

Although she had been raised as an Anglican and continued to attend church until her father's death, after the 1840s, George Eliot was not a believer in a traditional concept of God or any personal afterlife. She was quoted as saying, "God, Immortality, Duty: how inconceivable the first, how unbelievable the second, and yet how peremptory and absolute the third."

Two years after Lewes's death, George Eliot married John Cross, an American banker who was twenty years her junior, and they honeymooned in Venice—where Cross jumped or fell from a hotel balcony into the Grand Canal. Rumors circulated that he wanted to die rather than make love to his ugly old wife. He didn't get his wish, however, for he survived and the couple returned to London, where George Eliot fell ill with a throat infection. The doctors said it was laryngitis and nothing to worry about. But coupled with the kidney disease from which she had suffered for several years, this infection led to her death on December 22, 1880, at the age of sixty-one.

Because of her rejection of Christianity, Eliot was denied burial in Westminster Abbey and was instead laid to rest in London's Highgate Cemetery in a section filled with agnostics, next to Lewes, and not far from where Karl Marx was interred three years later. In 1980, a memorial stone was erected in Poets' Corner of Westminster Abbey.

FYODOR DOSTOYEVSKY

Four years of hard labor in Siberia might not be considered a lucky break by most people—but for Fyodor Dostoyevsky, it was a welcome lifesaver. Minutes before he was to be executed by a firing squad, the tsar commuted his sentence to imprisonment. After serving his term, Dostoyevsky returned to Moscow, full of religious fervor and with a sharpened desire to be a writer.

The son of an army doctor, young Fyodor had set out to be an army engineer—but his interest in literature, social reform, and religion kept distracting him. Born in Moscow on October 30, 1821, he was well schooled in the classics at home and at boarding schools, and then graduated from St. Petersburg's Army Engineering College. He resigned his army position when he was twenty-three and began to write, publishing his first novel, *Poor Folk*, followed shortly by *The Double.*

Dostoyevsky's interest in social reform led him to join a group of utopian socialists whose activities were considered treasonous by the tsar. This involvement led to his arrest and sentence to death. His prison experiences formed the basis of *The House of the Dead* and two other novels.

Dostoyevsky married a young widow, Maria Isaev, and worked as a journalist for several publications. Maria died after seven years of marriage, and a distraught Dostoyevsky began to gamble heavily, which left him broke most of the time. But he kept cranking out novels and reached a watershed in his development with *Notes from the Underground*, followed shortly by *Crime and Punishment*, *The Idiot*, and *The Possessed*. At last, Dostoyevsky was recognized as one of Russia's preeminent authors.

When he was forty-six, he married his twenty-two-year-old secretary, Anna Snitkina, with whom he had four children. Anna helped Dostoyevsky shake his gambling habit, which had drained his finances, and he devoted himself to his final masterpiece, *The Brothers Karamazov*, published in 1879.

Dostoyevsky's religious views pervaded much of his writing. Nominally Russian Orthodox, with a profound hatred of Roman Catholicism, he did not attend regular services, and referred to himself on some occasions as a Deist. Despite the imprecision of his views, he was devoted to Jesus Christ, to the theological concept of the trinity, and to a firm belief in personal immortality. Although it is in the voice of one of his characters, Dostoyevsky probably agreed with this notion from *The Brothers Karamazov*: "If there is no immortality, then there is no virtue. If you destroyed the belief in immortality, then love and every living force that inspires the world would also die."

Troubled by epilepsy from the age of nine, Dostoyevsky also developed pulmonary problems, for which he received periodic treatment at European spas. An inveterate smoker who rolled his own cigarettes, he was diagnosed with early-stage emphysema in August of 1879. Seventeen months later, in January of 1881, at his home in St. Petersburg, he began hemorrhaging from his throat and lungs, which his wife attributed to his agitation while searching for a lost penholder. A second and a third hemorrhage followed within days, and on the afternoon of January 28, Dostoeyvsky told his children farewell, and died that evening at the age of fifty-nine.

Among the last words he murmured were this quotation from the Book of Matthew: "But John stopped him, saying, I have need to be baptized of thee, and comest thou to me? And Jesus answering said unto him, Suffer it to be so now: for thus it becometh us to fulfill all righteousness."

Throngs of admirers—some accounts said almost a hundred thousand—attended Dostoyevsky's funeral at Alexander Nevsky Monastery in St. Petersburg. He was buried on the monastery grounds, in Trinity Cemetery, where the composer Tchaikovsky was later interred. Dostoyevsky's tombstone is inscribed with this New Testament passage from the Book of John: "Verily, verily, I say unto you, except a corn of wheat fall into the ground and die, it abideth alone: but if it die, it bringeth forth much fruit."

LEO TOLSTOY

Suffering from malaria and typhoid fever, but mostly from a fractious marriage to Sonya Behrs, an ailing Leo Tolstoy complained, "My illness is Sonya." He died, in fact, trying desperately to get away from her.

Author of two acknowledged masterpieces, *War and Peace* and *Anna Karenina*, Tolstoy holds a place of honor among the world's great novelists. Born September 9, 1828, on his family's estate in Russia's Tula province, he was the youngest of four boys, sons of a minor Russian nobleman, from whom they inherited the title of Count. Leo's mother died when he was two, his father just seven years later, and he was raised by an aunt. He was educated primarily at home by French and German tutors, then enrolled briefly at the University of Kazan, where his carefree partying resulted in his withdrawal without a degree.

He tried farming on the family estate, where he frolicked with the female serfs, then had a stint as a junior officer in the army, during which he fought in the Crimean War and also published an autobiographical memoir called *Childhood*. After leaving the army, he devoted himself to writing, and published a second autobiographical work, *Boyhood*, and a short novel called *The Cossacks*. He became a well-known literary figure, an anarchist, and a gambler—losing all of his money during a spree in Paris. Chastened, he returned to live on the family estate, married Sonya, a doctor's daughter, and devoted himself to becoming a serious writer, when he wasn't busy siring thirteen children. *War and Peace* was published in installments during the 1860s, and Tolstoy's reputation was secure. He followed that with *Anna Karenina* during the 1870s.

Sonya assisted him with both of these major works, but she was not sympathetic to his spiritual conversion in the late 1870s. He turned first to the Russian Orthodox Church, but regarded it as shallow and corrupt, and consequently developed his own personal, mystical, ascetic religion, based on strict adherence to the teachings of Jesus Christ. Tolstoy also renounced meat, alcohol, and tobacco, and he endeavored to give away most of his belongings—an act of extreme charity to which Sonya vigorously objected. He mollified her by signing over all his royalties on previous works to her, but the two of them remained at odds for the rest of his life.

Tolstoy directly confronted the prospect of death through the title character in the novella *The Death of Ivan Ilyich*, a judge who is dying of an incurable illness. At the moment of death, he expresses repentance for a hedonistic life, in which he had no thought for others, and his pity for his wife and children. Having purged his soul, Ilyich also loses the fear of death that had plagued him:

And suddenly it grew clear to him that what had been oppressing him and would not leave him was all dropping away at once from two sides, from ten sides, and from all sides. He was sorry for them, he must act so as not to hurt them: release them and free himself from these sufferings. "How good and how simple!" he thought. "And the pain?" he asked himself. "What has become of it? Where are you, pain?"

He turned his attention to it.

"Yes, here it is. Well, what of it? Let the pain be."

"And death . . . where is it?"

He sought his former accustomed fear of death and did not find it. "Where is it? What death?" There was no fear because there was no death.

In place of death there was light.

"So that's what it is!" he suddenly exclaimed aloud. "What joy!"

To him all this happened in a single instant, and the meaning of that instant did not change. For those present his agony continued for another two hours. Something rattled in his throat, his emaciated body twitched, then the gasping and rattle became less and less frequent.

"It is finished!" said someone near him. He heard these words and repeated them in his soul.

"Death is finished," he said to himself. "It is no more!"

He drew in a breath, stopped in the midst of a sigh, stretched out, and died.

Tolstoy endured poor health for the last years of his life. Besides depression, malaria, typhoid fever, and other, age-related ailments, he suffered from a form of psychologically induced epilepsy, which resulted in hallucinations, fainting, fever, delirium, and amnesia. In a letter to his friend and editor Vladimir Chertkov a few months before his final illness, Tolstoy seemed to welcome the prospect of his own death. He wrote:

"It is getting closer and closer—the sure unfolding of the blessed mystery, which we've been groping towards. This closing-in of death cannot but draw me towards it and fill me with happiness."

At his estate, Yasnaya Polyana, about 120 miles from Moscow, on the night of November 10, 1910, he woke to find Sonya rifling through his papers. What she was looking for is not clear—probably either a new will or a diary that she wished to publish against Tolstoy's wishes. Whatever it was, her meddling infuriated Tolstoy, who decided to leave home at once. He awakened his youngest daughter, Alexandra, and accompanied by the family physician, Dr. Dushan Makovitsky, they fled the house in the wee hours, traveling in a third-class railway compartment to avoid recognition. They stopped to rest the next night at a monastery, but fearing Sonya was hot on their trail, they sneaked away at four o'clock in the morning to continue their journey by train to Novocherkassk.

Exhausted and chilled, Tolstoy developed a fever and was taken off the train at the village of Astapovo to rest in the stationmaster's home. His condition worsened into pneumonia, and friends and medical personnel were summoned to his side. When the press got wind that he was there, the town filled with journalists eager for news of the ailing literary master. They were housed in a railway car, since Astapovo had nary a hotel.

Tolstoy lapsed into labored breathing, paroxysms of pain, and a persistent bout of hiccups. He repeatedly urged his doctors and friends to keep Sonya from visiting him, as it would be "calamitous" for him. Sonya arrived on November 19, but doctors refused to let her see him. She insisted, however, and at two o'clock in the morning on November 20, she was allowed into his room. At six o'clock, Tolstoy died, at the age of eighty-two.

The funeral was a hastily assembled ceremony two days later at Yasnaya Polyana. Thousands of people showed up for the simple occasion—Tolstoy's coffin was placed in a room containing a bookcase, a portrait of his brother, and a statue of Buddha. For two and a half hours, the assembled crowd filed past the coffin to pay their respects, as two choirs outside alternated in singing "Eternal Memory," a Slavonic church chant. Tolstoy's body was then carried to a wooded knoll on the estate and laid to rest in a simple grave with no stone and only a mound of earth to mark it.

EMILY DICKINSON

Emily Dickinson was a confirmed homebody. Born December 10, 1830, in Amherst, Massachusetts, she lived there all her life, seldom even leaving her house after her late thirties. She lived with her parents and younger sister, Lavinia, and became a virtual recluse. Her father was a lawyer and, briefly, a United States congressman.

Emily attended the Amherst Academy, receiving a firm grounding in Latin, English and classical literature, mathematics, and the natural sciences. She then went on to Mount Holyoke Female Seminary (later College), but stayed only one year. She read deeply, and found inspiration in Shakespeare, the Book of Revelation, Donne, Wordsworth, Keats, Emerson, and the Brownings. Raised a strict Calvinist, she strayed from orthodox beliefs and, as an adult, in keeping with her eremitic life, did not attend church.

She began to write poetry—short, pithy, trenchant verses—on a regular basis, although with little thought to having it published. No more than a dozen of her poems saw print during her lifetime. The first collected volume appeared four years after her death, cobbled together by two well-intentioned, but ill-advised, friends who took the liberty of "correcting" her distinctively idiosyncratic punctuation and syntax.

Dickinson never married or had any overt romantic relationship, although she corresponded with several male friends with whom she had great intellectual affinity. She was deeply affected by the deaths of several of her loved ones. A young lawyer who befriended the family died of tuberculosis in his twenties. When Dickinson was forty-three, her father died of a stroke, and a simple funeral was held in the family home; she observed the ceremony from her room, behind a door that was slightly ajar. Her mother, to whom she was never close, died eight years later, and Emily's favorite nephew died the following year of typhoid. She wrote: "The Dyings have been too deep for me."

Death and thoughts of immortality permeated both her life and her poetry. Having lived for fifteen years in her youth adjacent to the town cemetery, she was perhaps understandably haunted by what she called the "deepening menace" of death and a fear of immortality. In a letter to a friend, she called the thought of eternity "dreadful" and "dark." In one poem, she calls death the "vermin's will," and in another, she refers to it in terms of the spirit putting on an "overcoat of clay."

Dickinson donned her clay overcoat on May 15, 1886, at the age of fifty-five. She had been in poor health for more than two years, suffering from nausea, severe headaches, and fainting spells. It has been suggested that she had what would today be called bipolar disorder. Diagnosis was difficult, since her visits to her Amherst physician, Dr. Otis F. Bigelow, consisted of her walking slowly past the open door of his examining room while he remained inside observing her. She never allowed him to even take her pulse. "Now what besides mumps could be diagnosed that way!" the understandably frustrated Bigelow complained.

Emily was confined to her bed for the last seven months of her life. On the day of her death, her brother Austin recorded in his diary: "She ceased to breathe that terrible breathing just before the whistles sounded for six [p.m.]."

Her death was attributed to Bright's disease, or nephritis, a kidney ailment, but later scholars believe the actual cause was heart failure, induced by severe hypertension.

Clad in a white dress and lying in a white coffin at her funeral in the family home, Dickinson was said to look far younger than her years—"Not a gray hair or a wrinkle," as a friend reported, "and perfect peace on the beautiful brow." A minister led a prayer, and a friend read Emily Brontë's poem on immortality that begins:

No coward soul is mine
No trembler in the world's storm-troubled sphere
I see Heaven's glories shine

And Faith shines equal arming me from Fear

and ends exultantly with:

There is not room for Death
Nor atom that his might could render void
Since thou art Being and Breath
And what thou art may never be destroyed.

The honorary pallbearers, including the president and several professors of Amherst College, carried her coffin only to the back door, where it was taken by six Irish laborers who had worked on the Dickinson property. Following her instructions, they carried her body around her flower garden, through the barn, and across a field of buttercups to West Cemetery, where she was interred in the family plot in a grave lined with evergreen boughs. The original grave marker carried only her initials, but years later her niece replaced it with a marble stone that read "Called Back"—the title of a popular novel, and the only words in a letter she wrote to her cousins during her final illness.

LOUISA MAY ALCOTT

Louisa May Alcott, the daughter of Bronson Alcott, the Transcendentalist teacher and writer, was born on her father's thirty-third birthday, November 29, 1832, in Germantown, Pennsylvania. By strange coincidence, she died on the day of his funeral, March 6, 1888, in Boston. Her father's association with the Transcendental movement provided young Louisa with an education by such redoubtable figures as Ralph Waldo Emerson, Henry David Thoreau, Margaret Fuller, and Nathaniel Hawthorne, as well as her supremely redoubtable father himself. Financial setbacks for the Alcott family forced Louisa to take up work in her twenties as a seamstress, a governess, a domestic helper, and an occasional teacher.

She also began to write and found success with some early sketches, such as *Transcendental Wild Oats* and *Flower Fables*. Sometimes she wrote under the pen names Flora Fairfield and A. M. Barnard. She served briefly as a nurse in a Union hospital during the Civil War, and her experiences gave her another book, *Hospital Sketches*. Major success came to her after the war with the publication of *Little Women*, loosely based on her own childhood, followed by further episodes in the fictional March family saga in *Little Men*, *Eight Cousins*, and *Jo's Boys*.

Alcott never married, although she is said to have had a romantic attachment (whatever that may mean) to Ladislas Wisinewski, a young Pole she met in Switzerland during a European sojourn. In her journal, she refers to him as "Laddie" and

"Laurie," a name she later used for a character in *Little Women*. She writes that he was "very gay and agreeable, and being ill and much younger we petted him. He played beautifully, and was very anxious to learn English, so we taught him that and he taught us French." She must have nursed him back to good health, for later she notes: "Laurie very interesting and good. Pleasant walks and talks with him in the château garden and about Vevey. A lovely sail on the lake, and much fun giving English and receiving French lessons." Alcott deleted from the journal many of her comments about Laddie.

She enigmatically explained her spinsterhood in a comment that raises curiosity rather than dispelling it: "I am more than half-persuaded that I am a man's soul put by some freak of nature into a woman's body . . . because I have fallen in love with so many pretty girls and never once the least bit with any man."

Alcott's views on life and death were formed by her Transcendentalist background, which emphasized the here and now with little thought devoted to the possibility of an afterlife. As a young woman in Boston, she occasionally attended Unitarian services. In her diaries, she spoke of religious feelings and belief in a higher power, but she never affiliated with any organized religion.

As Alcott entered her fifties, she suffered from a variety of ailments, including frequent vertigo, headaches, rheumatism, muscular and skeletal pain, skin rash, dyspepsia, constipation, and what the *New York Times* referred to as "nervous prostration."

She was under treatment at a rest home near Boston and came to visit her father a few days before his death. On the ride back home, according to the *Times*, she caught a cold that settled at the base of her brain and developed into cerebral-spinal meningitis. Her death on March 6, 1888, at the age of fifty-five, was thought to have been partly caused by mercuric poisoning from a medication she had received years earlier as treatment for typhus. Later medical studies, however, suggest that she suffered and possibly died from systemic lupus erythe-matosus, an autoimmune disease that can cause tissue damage in many parts of the body.

Alcott is buried in the Sleepy Hollow Cemetery, in Concord, Massachusetts, in the section known as Authors' Ridge, where Emerson, Thoreau, and Hawthorne also lie.

MARK TWAIN

Waggish old Mark Twain could be irreverent about death: "I do not fear death. I had been dead for bil-lions and billions of years before I was born, and had not suffered the slightest inconvenience from it." Or, putting on his serious hat, he could be philosophical: "Death, the refuge, the solace, the best and kindliest and most prized friend and benefactor of the erring, the forsaken, the old and weary and broken of heart."

Before facing that inevitability, he filled his life with mad-cap adventures, irreverent challenges to conventional behav-ior, and several literary masterpieces. Author of major classics that include *The Adventures of Tom Sawyer, Life on the Mis-sissippi, The Prince and the Pauper, A Connecticut Yankee in King Arthur's Court*, and his most highly revered work, *The Adventures of Huckleberry Finn*, Twain began his career as a printer's devil in Hannibal, Missouri, not far from where he was born—in Florida, Missouri, on November 30, 1835, as Samuel Langhorne Clemens.

The sixth of seven children, he completed only the sixth grade before going to work at age eleven after his father died. At eighteen, Sam went east, and as he recalled, "I became a newspaperman; I hated to do it, but I couldn't find honest employment." He worked on newspapers in New York and Philadelphia before returning to Missouri to embark on a career as a riverboat pilot on the Mississippi.

The Civil War soon put a stop to river traffic, and Sam joined his brother in Nevada, tried his hand (unsuccessfully) at silver mining, then went to work for a series of newspapers in Nevada and California. He also began to publish stories using the pen name "Mark Twain," derived from a riverboat phrase that means two fathoms, or twelve feet, in depth.

Twain went to Hawaii, Europe, and the Holy Land as a newspaper correspondent. On one trip, he met his future brother-in-law, Charles Langdon, who showed him a picture of his sister, Olivia, and Twain fell in love literally at first sight. They courted for two years before marrying and settling first in Buffalo, New York, and then Hartford, Connecticut, in a twenty-five-room house that cost $45,000—close to a million dollars in today's money. By this time, Twain's writing was providing a handsome living, and he devoted the next seventeen years to writing the major novels that would be his legacy.

Primarily known as a humorist, Twain used his acerbic wit to comment on religion and death. Nominally a Presbyterian, he was nonetheless caustically critical of organized religion. "Faith," he once remarked, "is believing what you know ain't so." And he said, "If Christ were here now there is one thing he would not be—a Christian." Although Twain attended church services and asserted that he believed in God, he discounted many of the tenets of Christianity, such as the infallibility of the Bible and retribution for sins in an afterlife. "Death," Twain once remarked, "is the only immortal who treats us all alike, whose pity and whose peace and whose refuge are for all—the soiled and the pure, the rich and the poor, the loved and the unloved."

For a decade or so, during the 1890s, Twain and Olivia traveled widely as he lectured throughout the world. By this time, a series of bad investments had plunged him into bankruptcy, and he relied upon lecture tours to restore his finances. In 1896, the Twains' daughter Susy died of meningitis at the age of twenty-four while visiting their Hartford home. Twain never returned there, and he and Olivia settled in New York.

After Olivia's death, Twain's last years saw a gradual lessening of his mental capacity, and he became a cantankerous and cynical curmudgeon, speaking against the government so vehemently that some accused him of treason. In 1908, he moved to his final home, Stormfield, in Redding, Connecticut, which is where he died of heart disease on April 21, 1910, at the age of seventy-four.

The *New York Times* had a detailed account of his final hours, which read in part:

> Samuel Langhorne Clemens, "Mark Twain," died at 22 minutes after 6 tonight....
>
> Although the end had been foreseen by the doctors and would not have been a shock at any time, the apparently strong rally of this morning had given basis for the hope that it would be postponed for several days. Mr. Clemens awoke at about 4 o'clock this morning after a few hours of the first natural sleep he has had for several days, and the nurses could see by the brightness of his eyes that his vitality had been considerably restored.
>
> His strength seemed to increase enough to allow him to enjoy the sunrise, the first signs of which he could see out of the windows in the three sides of the room where he lay. The increasing sunlight seemed to bring ease to him, and by the time the family was about he was strong enough to sit up in bed and overjoyed them by recognizing all of them and speaking a few words to each.
>
> For two hours he lay in bed enjoying the feeling of this return of strength. Then he made a movement [and]

asked in a faint voice for the copy of Carlyle's "French Revolution," which he has always had near him for the last year, and which he has read and re-read and brooded over.

With his glasses on he read a little and then slowly put the book down with a sigh. Soon he appeared to become drowsy and settled on his pillow. Gradually he sank and settled into a lethargy.... At 3 o'clock he went into complete unconsciousness. At twenty-two minutes past 6, with the sunlight just turning red as it stole into the window in perfect silence he breathed his last.

It is certain to be recalled that Mark Twain was for more than fifty years an inveterate smoker, and the first conjecture of the layman would be that he had weakened his heart by overindulgence in tobacco. Dr. Halsey said to-night that he was unable to say that the angina pectoris from which Mark Twain died was in any way [related to] nicotine poisoning. Some constitutions, he said, seem immune from the effects of tobacco, and his was one of them. Yet it is true that since his illness began the doctors had cut down Mark Twain's daily allowance of twenty cigars and countless pipes to four cigars a day....

Twain's funeral was two days later at the Brick Presbyterian Church on 5th Avenue at 37th Street in New York. The Associated Press reported:

The body reached New York shortly before noon in a private car, in which rode Mrs. Ossip Gabrilowitsch, Samuel Clemens' only surviving daughter, and her husband; Dan Beard, the artist, Twain's lifelong friend; James Langdon of Elmira; Katie Leary, for thirty years the housekeeper at Stormfield, and other house servants. At the head of the coffin stood Claude Benzollete, for many years Twain's valet, who refused to move from the side of his dead master.

Only a handful of people met the body at Grand Central Station. No loving hands lifted it from the car to the hearse. That task was delegated to the undertaker and his assistants.

Slowly the cortege drove to the old brick church, where the body remained until the funeral services began at 3 o'clock. The church filled quickly. Holders of tickets were admitted first. Millionaires and paupers rubbed elbows in the vast crowd that stood outside. The body, clad in the immaculate white serge suit which marked Twain in his old age, lay coffined in front of the altar. The only floral piece was a wreath garlanded by the hand of Dan Beard.

At 3 o'clock the immediate family seated themselves in front of the coffin. Rev. Dr. Henry Van Dyke of Princeton and Rev. Joseph H. Twitchell of Hartford, Twain's old chums, robed in their vestments, took their places in the chancel. For a quarter of an hour the two ministers sat silent, their heads bowed in prayer.

No sound was heard through the dark old edifice save a muffled sob. Dr. Twitchell, Twain's oldest and dearest friend, was convulsed with tears. His massive frame shook as he brushed the white locks from his forehead and gazed down into the face of his dead friend.

Then Dr. Van Dyke rose and read the beautiful funeral service of the Presbyterian faith. At its conclusion he spoke briefly of Samuel L. Clemens, his friend, not Mark Twain, the author.

[Then] Dr. Twitchell walked to the altar, from which he might gaze down at Mark Twain's face. His voice was inaudible, and the tears poured down his cheeks as he asked God's blessing upon his friend, and the world's friend. He clasped the altar rail and seemed to be speaking to his old chum as he brokenly sobbed out a prayer.

Twain was buried in his wife's family plot at Woodlawn Cemetery in Elmira, New York, his grave marked by a twelve-foot (two fathoms, or "mark twain,") monument.

THOMAS HARDY

Thomas Hardy, the preeminent English novelist and poet, who lived to be eighty-seven, almost became the baby thrown out with the proverbial bath water. At his birth on June 2, 1840, in the tiny Dorset hamlet of Higher Bockhampton, the attending doctor believed him to have been stillborn and was prepared to dispose of the "corpse." A vigilant midwife, however, detected signs of life and rescued the infant from an exceedingly premature departure. Having survived this close call, Thomas grew up in a middle-class household headed by his fiddle-playing, stonemason father. His mother home-schooled him until he was eight, when he was sent to Mr. Last's Academy for Young Gentlemen in Dorchester, where he learned Latin and read widely on his own.

There was no money for a university education, so Thomas was apprenticed to an architect in Dorchester, then headed for London to study at King's College, after which he launched his career. While successfully working as an architect and winning some notable prizes for his designs, he began to write novels, though with less success. One of his early novels, serialized in a magazine, gave rise to the term "cliffhanger," as a character was literally left hanging off a cliff at the end of one episode.

Hardy moved back to Dorset for a time, and in 1870, while working on a commission in Cornwall, he met Emma Lavinia Gifford, whom he married in 1874. That was also the year that he had a major success with his novel *Far from the Madding Crowd*, which enabled him to give up architecture and become a full-time writer. The Hardys moved often among various locales in Dorset, also maintaining a London home.

Hardy's later novels, which included *The Mayor of Casterbridge*, *The Woodlanders*, *Tess of the D'Urbervilles*, and *Jude the Obscure*, were fairly gritty slices of realism for their time. *Jude the Obscure* met with such criticism for its perceived attack on the institution of marriage that the Anglican Bishop of Wakefield burned it—"Probably in despair," said Hardy, "at not being able to burn me." He wrote no more novels after 1895, and instead turned his attention to several books of existentially bleak poetry.

In 1912, the death of his wife, from whom he had been estranged, contributed to Hardy's dreary outlook on life—which brightened a bit in 1914, when at the age of seventy-four, he married his thirty-nine-year-old secretary, Florence Dugdale.

Having previously declined a knighthood because he felt it was an unsuitable way to honor a literary man, Hardy in 1910 accepted the more prestigious Order of Merit, which is limited to twenty-four members. Incidentally, Hardy was repeatedly passed over for a Nobel Prize in literature (as were such contemporaries of his as Leo Tolstoy, Mark Twain, Emile Zola, and Joseph Conrad, during years when the Prize was granted to such now largely forgotten authors as Sully Prudhomme, Rudolf Eucken, Paul Heyse, Selma Lagerlöf, and Carl Spitteler).

Hardy was raised in a nominally Anglican family, but as an adult he was skeptical of Christian orthodoxy and wavered among a variety of beliefs—agnosticism, Deism, and spiritualism. Fascinated by ghosts, he also retained a fondness for Christian rituals. His pessimistic worldview is often expressed in his poetry, most of which was written in the latter part of his life.

In "The Impercipient," published in 1898, he laments his lack of faith:

That from this bright believing band
   An outcast I should be,
That faiths by which my comrades stand
   Seem fantasies to me,
And mirage-mists their Shining Land,
   Is a drear destiny.

Four years later, in "In Tenebris," he writes:

Black is night's cope;
But death will not appal
One who, past doubtings all,
   Waits in unhope.

In December of 1927, Hardy fell ill with pleurisy, which taxed his heart, and just after nine o'clock in the evening on January 11, 1928, at the age of eighty-seven, he died at Max Gate, the home he had built near Dorchester. The cause of death was listed as "cardiac syncope" (inadequate blood flow to the brain), compounded by "old age."

Hardy had wished to be buried next to his first wife in Stinsford, a Dorset village near his birthplace, but his executor, Sir Sydney Carlyle Cockerell, felt that the great author should be interred in Westminster Abbey. Prime Minister Stanley Baldwin agreed, and a tug-of-war ensued over Hardy's remains. A compromise was reached by removing his heart, to be buried in Stinsford, and cremating the rest of him, with the ashes to repose in Westminster Abbey.

A widely circulated story claimed that after his family physician, Dr. E. Mann, had excised the heart, it was stored in a biscuit tin in a garden shed to await burial. The family cat, named Cobweb, somehow managed to open the can and, finding what it took to be a massive treat for a carnivore, ate the heart. Next morning, the undertaker realized what had happened, dispatched the cat, and buried it with the partially digested contents of its stomach in the grave in St. Michael's churchyard next to Mrs. Hardy. This story is denied—heartily—by most Hardy experts.

The pallbearers at the Abbey funeral were a distinguished literary lot that included Rudyard Kipling, George Bernard Shaw, John Galsworthy, A. E. Housman, J. M. Barrie, and Edmund Gosse, plus Prime Minister Baldwin.

ROBERT LOUIS STEVENSON

Robert Louis Stevenson, author of such much-read works as *Treasure Island*, *Kidnapped*, *The Strange Case of Doctor Jekyll and Mister Hyde*, and *A Child's Garden of Verses*, is the twenty-sixth most-translated author in history—according to a UNESCO list on which he ranks well below Barbara Cartland, Danielle Steele, and Nora Roberts.

Born in Edinburgh on November 13, 1850, Stevenson came from a family of lighthouse engineers. After studying at Edinburgh Academy, he enrolled in the University of Edinburgh with the intention of following in his family's engineering footsteps. He switched to law, but after finishing his degree, decided instead to be a writer. As such, he felt it only appropriate to adopt the ways of a dissolute bohemian, sporting long hair, wearing velveteen jackets, and frequenting Edinburgh's taverns and brothels, as writers were (and may still be) wont to do.

Stevenson's visits to France yielded some travel articles and also introduced him to an American woman, Fanny Osbourne, eleven years his senior, separated from her husband and with two children. When Fanny returned to California in order to obtain a divorce, the love-struck Stevenson followed her, sailing second-class on a steamer and then traveling by train from New York to Nevada. He became ill during the journey and spent months recuperating before he and Fanny married in San Francisco. The new family returned to Britain to make their home in Scotland.

Stevenson continued to write short fiction, virtually inventing the literary genre of the short story. During one wintry Scottish afternoon, his stepson entertained himself by drawing a map of a "treasure island," which inspired Stevenson to write one of his most famous works. *Treasure Island* established Stevenson as a popular and financially successful writer.

The family returned to America, intending to live in Colorado for its healthful air, but wound up instead at Saranac Lake, a spa in New York's Adirondack Mountains. In 1888, fulfilling a long-held dream, Stevenson decided to sail around the world with his family. He chartered a yacht in San Francisco and went first to the Society Islands, then to the Sandwich Islands (now Hawaii), where he befriended King Kalakaua and finished his novel *The Master of Ballantrae.* Finally, the family settled in Samoa, where they constructed a house and Stevenson became a revered figure in Samoan society.

Stevenson was reared by a Presbyterian family and a staunch Calvinist nanny, but as a young man, he declared that he was an atheist. His views on religion and an afterlife have been the subject of much speculation. He wrote to his friend Edmund Gosse: "If I could believe in the immortality business, the world would indeed be too good to be true; but . . . the sods cover us, and the worm that never dies, the conscience, sleeps well at last." He went on to say that a man "can tell himself this fairy tale of an eternal tea-party; and enjoy the notion . . . that his friends will yet meet him. But the truth is, we must fight on until we die . . . when all these desperate tricks will lie spellbound at last."

Despite this rejection of Christian belief, Stevenson held regular family prayers in Samoa and even taught briefly in a Presbyterian Sunday school. Perhaps his religious views are best summed up in a vague theism, as he expressed when he wrote to a friend, "I am religious in my own way, but I am hardly brave enough to interpose a theory of my own between life and death. Here both our creeds and our philosophies seem to me to fail."

Sickly all his life, Stevenson suffered from childhood with chronic tuberculosis, several bouts of meningitis, and sciatica. His health was probably not enhanced by his chain-smoking, heavy use of alcohol, and occasional reliance upon cocaine.

On the evening of December 3, 1894, on the verandah of his home in Vallima, Samoa, Stevenson was chatting with his wife while straining to open a bottle of wine. Suddenly he put the wine down, and said to her, "What's that? Does my face look strange?" Then he collapsed and died within a few hours of a brain hemorrhage, at the age of forty-four.

His body was carried the next day by six Samoans to the peak of Mount Vaea, where he was buried in a Presbyterian service overlooking the Pacific Ocean. As Stevenson had wished, his tomb was inscribed with his poem, "Requiem":

Under the wide and starry sky,
Dig the grave and let me lie.

Glad did I live and gladly die,
And I laid me down with a will.

This be the verse you grave for me:
Here he lies where he longed to be;
Home is the sailor, home from the sea,
And the hunter home from the hill.

Although the text of the original poem was "home from sea," it was misquoted on his tomb as "home from *the* sea," as it usually appears today.

OSCAR WILDE

"I put all of my genius into my life; I put only my talent into my works." So said Oscar Fin-gal O'Flahertie Wills Wilde, who was born in Dublin, October 16, 1854, with a name as flamboy-ant as his later lifestyle. Second of three children, Wilde was tutored at home in the classics by his parents, an eye surgeon and his poet wife. After three years at the University of Dublin, he matriculated at Oxford, where he was tutored by such big aca-demic guns as Walter Pater and John Ruskin, winning a degree in classics with "double first-class  honours." His stellar achievement elicited this comment in a let-ter to a friend, "The dons are 'astonied' beyond words—the Bad Boy doing so well at the end." At Oxford, he espoused the theory of aestheticism, which idealized beauty over social or political content in art. He wore his hair unfashionably long, decorated his room with peacock feathers and flowers, and dressed like a dandy in knee breeches; a flowing tie; velvet coat; wide, turned-down collar; and a drooping lily.

Settling in London, Wilde published a book of poems, worked as a journalist, became editor of *The Woman's World* magazine, and in 1881 married Constance Lloyd, daughter of a promi-nent Queen's Counsel, with whom he had two sons. In 1882, he embarked upon a year-long lecture tour of more than a hundred cities in the United States, sponsored by Richard D'Oyly Carte to promote his American production of Gilbert and Sullivan's *Patience*, a parody of the aesthetic movement with which Wilde was closely identified. Wilde's only novel, *The Picture of Dorian Gray*, about a young man whose aging is transferred to a portrait, was inspired by aestheticism.

By 1886, Wilde's marriage had begun to fray, and at the same time he was fatefully seduced into a homosexual affair by Robert Ross, a seventeen-year-old admirer. Through Ross, Wilde met Lord Alfred Douglas, the son of the Marquess of Queensberry—the same British peer who invented the rules of modern boxing. Wilde and Douglas, who was known as "Bosie," began an affair that lasted for years, involving Wilde in the sordid world of homosexual prostitution, and resulting ultimately in his imprisonment.

Wilde was also becoming widely known as the West End's leading boulevard dramatist. Between 1891 and 1895, there were productions of *Salome*, *Lady Windermere's Fan*, *A Woman of No Importance*, *An Ideal Husband*, and Wilde's comic masterpiece, *The Importance of Being Earnest.*

The feisty Marquess of Queensberry vehemently opposed the relationship between his son and Wilde. On one occasion, the Marquess—full of vitriol, but low on spelling skills—left his calling card at Wilde's club addressed to "Oscar Wilde, posing somdomite [sic]." Homosexual acts, officially referred to as sodomy, were illegal in Britain, and Wilde filed a libel suit against Queensberry. This proved to be an unfortunate tactic, and at the trial, evidence was produced to show the truth of Queensberry's assertions, resulting in Wilde's prosecution for "gross indecency" and imprisonment for two years.

When he was released in May of 1897, Wilde went to France, began calling himself Sebastian Melmoth, and though impoverished, managed to indulge in promiscuous sex and heavy consumption of absinthe. When told by doctors that the absinthe would kill him, he replied, "I am dying as I lived, beyond my means." At this low point of his life, Wilde might well have recalled what he said of death in *The Canterville Ghost*, his first published story:

> Death must be so beautiful. To lie in the soft brown earth, with the grasses waving above one's head, and listen to silence. To have no yesterday, and no to-morrow. To forget time, to forget life, to be at peace.

Scraping a living from the small stipend sent to him by his estranged wife, the aptly named Constance, Wilde was reduced to making his home in a single room in Paris's modest Hôtel d'Alsace in the rue des Beaux-Arts. When Constance died in 1898, following a fall, Wilde relied upon friends. A typical day started at eleven o'clock with breakfast, followed by lunch at two o'clock, drinks at the Café de la Régence at five o'clock, and supper after midnight at the Café de Paris. The owner of the Alsace, Jean Dupoirier, supplied Wilde with five bottles of Courvoisier cognac each week. Dupoirier said that a liter would hardly last him through the night.

Despite his dissipation, Wilde did manage to write a poetic account of prison life, *The Ballad of Reading Gaol*, and to prepare *An Ideal Husband* and *The Importance of Being Earnest* for publication, before falling ill in October of 1900 with an ear infection, caused by a perforated eardrum he had suffered in prison. To relieve the condition, Dr. Maurice A'Court Tucker, the British Embassy's physician, advised a mastoidectomy, which was done in his hotel room on October 10.

Wilde telegraphed his old lover, Robert Ross, "Terribly weak. Please come." While recuperating, Wilde said of his surroundings, "My *wallpaper* and I are fighting a duel to the death. One or other of us has to go." By November, the infection had spread to his brain and developed into cerebral meningitis. Morphine would no longer stop his pain, so Wilde tried opium, chloral hydrate, and generous slugs of champagne. Ross finally arrived on November 29. He found Wilde "thin, his flesh livid, his breathing heavy," and with a two-week growth of beard.

Wilde, who had been baptized in the Protestant Church of Ireland, but had flirted with Roman Catholicism all his life—he said it "is the only religion to die in"—wanted to see a Catholic priest. Ross, who was a Catholic, found Father Cuthbert Dunne, an Irish priest of the Passionist order, who came to Wilde's room and presided over his deathbed conversion. Dunne administered conditional baptism and extreme unction to Wilde, but because he was semi-comatose, he did not attempt to give him communion. Even so, Dunne was satisfied that the dying man was lucid enough to assent to the basics of the Catholic faith.

The next day, November 30, Ross and another friend reported they heard grinding sounds from Wilde's throat, and a nurse dabbed blood coming from his mouth. His pulse weakened, and Oscar Wilde died at 1:50 p.m., at the age of forty-six. His corpse was dressed in a white nightshirt and covered in a white sheet and palm branches. The accumulated bill for his four-month stay at the hotel was £200, which was never paid.

The cause of Wilde's meningitis has been much debated. Some thought it was a result of syphilis, but others blamed a botched mastoidectomy. Wilde's own physician simply attributed it to complications of the old eardrum injury.

Bosie arrived on December 2 for the funeral the next day. A requiem mass was celebrated by Dunne in the church of Saint-Germain-des-Prés, with fifty-six people in attendance, and Wilde was given a pauper's burial in the remote Cimetière de Bagneux outside Paris. In 1909, his old friend Ross came up with funds to move his remains to Père Lachaise Cemetery.

In 1913, Ross commissioned the noted sculptor Jacob Epstein to design a monument. The modernist work was in the

form of a nine-foot nude "demon-angel" whose genitalia were
so prominent that the cemetery manager insisted they be covered in plaster. A year later, Ross substituted a bronze butterfly
for the plaster. The butterfly was stolen, and for decades thereafter the exposed pendulous testicles were regarded as tokens of
good luck for visitors to Wilde's tomb, and became shiny from
frequent rubbing. In 1961, two Englishwomen walking in the
cemetery were so offended by the statuary that they hacked off
the testicles and took them to the cemetery office, where they
were used as paperweights. Today, the desexed monument is
protected from further vandalism by a glass barrier. It bears an
inscription from *The Ballad of Reading Gaol*:

> And alien tears will fill for him
> Pity's long-broken urn,
> For his mourners will be outcast men,
> And outcasts always mourn.

The Modern Era

GEORGE BERNARD SHAW

Author of sixty-three plays, critic of music and literature, Socialist reformer, co-founder of the London School of Economics, and the only person ever to win both the Nobel Prize for literature and an Oscar, George Bernard Shaw began his long, productive life on July 26, 1856, in Dublin, the youngest of three children of a corn merchant and a concert singer.

He attended a Methodist grammar school, Central Model School, and, finally, the Dublin English Scientific and Commercial Day School. He said of his schooling that he "had learned little and was largely self-educated." He worked in Dublin as a clerk for a real estate company, and when he was twenty, he went to London to join his mother, who had abandoned the Shaw household three years earlier to live with a conductor and music teacher named Vandeleur Lee. Young Shaw wrote several novels, which were rejected by publishers, then began to earn a modest living working for the Edison Telephone Company while also writing music reviews.

He lost his virginity on his twenty-ninth birthday to a lusty Irish widow who was a family friend, evidently a very close one. Thereafter, Shaw was infatuated with numerous women, including the actresses Ellen Terry and Mrs. Patrick (Stella) Campbell, but by most accounts his only other sexual experience was

with an actress named Florence Farr. Shaw married Charlotte
Payne-Townshend, a well-to-do fellow Socialist in the Fabian
Society, but, owing to her fear of pregnancy at age forty-one,
their marriage was never consummated during its forty-five
years.

Beginning with a production of *Widowers' Houses*, Shaw
began to write popular comedies with social and political mes-
sages. Among the most notable are *Mrs. Warren's Profession*,
Arms and the Man, *Candida*, *The Devil's Disciple*, *Caesar and
Cleopatra* (all in the 1890s), *Man and Superman*, *Major Barbara*, *The Doctor's Dilemma*, *Misalliance*, *Androcles and the
Lion*, *Pygmalion*, *Back to Methuselah*, *Saint Joan*, and *The Apple
Cart* (all between 1900 and 1929). Recognized as the leading
English-speaking playwright, he won the Nobel Prize in 1925
and the Oscar in 1938 (for the screenplay of *Pygmalion*). Shaw
declined all other honors, including the offer of a knighthood.

A teetotaler, a nonsmoker, and, in his later years, a vegetarian, he led an ascetic life. He continued to write plays, essays,
and political pamphlets, and voluminous correspondence with
his platonic lovers and others—an astonishing 250,000 letters
are attributed to him, or an average of about ten a day for his
adult life.

Shaw's interests were centered on the present life, and very
little serious attention is given in his works to notions of personal immortality. In his youth, he called himself an atheist—"I
am an atheist, and I thank God for it," he allegedly said. But in
later life, he espoused a kind of mystical evolutionary theology,
sparked by a "Life Force," and based partly on the Creative
Evolution promulgated by Henri Bergson and partly on Friedrich Nietzsche's concept of a "Superman." Shaw argued in a
speech called "The New Theology":

I do not want to be uncomplimentary, but can you conceive
God deliberately creating you if he could have created

anything better? What you have got to understand is that somehow or other there is at the back of the universe a will, a life-force. You cannot think of him as a person, you have to think of him as a great purpose, a great will, and, furthermore, you have to think of him as engaged in a continual struggle to produce something higher and higher, to create organs to carry out his purpose; as wanting hands, and saying, 'I must create something with hands'; arriving at that very slowly, after innumerable experiments and innumerable mistakes, because this power must be proceeding as we proceed, because if there were any other way it would put us in that way: we know that in all the progress we make we proceed by way of trial and error and experiment.

The possibilities of Heaven and Hell did emerge in his work—but it was tongue-in-cheek, as in the exchange between Don Juan and Dona Ana in the *Don Juan in Hell* section of *Man and Superman:*

ANA: I am going to heaven for happiness. I have had quite enough reality on earth.
DON JUAN: Then you must stay here; for hell is the home of the unreal and of the seekers for happiness. It is the only refuge from heaven, which is, as I tell you, the home of the masters of reality, and from earth, which is the home of the slaves of reality. . . . But here you escape this tyranny of the flesh; for here you are not an animal at all: you are a ghost, an appearance, an illusion, a convention, deathless, ageless: in a word, bodiless. There are no social questions here, no political questions, no religious questions, best of all, perhaps, no sanitary questions. Here you call your appearance beauty, your emotions love, your sentiments heroism, your aspirations virtue, just as you did on earth;

but here there are no hard facts to contradict you, no ironic contrast of your needs with your pretensions, no human comedy, nothing but a perpetual romance, a universal melodrama….

ANA: But if Hell be so beautiful as this, how glorious must heaven be!…

DON JUAN: In Heaven, as I picture it, dear lady, you live and work instead of playing and pretending. You face things as they are; you escape nothing but glamor; and your steadfastness and your peril are your glory…. Thither I shall go presently, because there I hope to escape at last from lies and from the tedious, vulgar pursuit of happiness, to spend my eons in contemplation….

ANA: Is there nothing in Heaven but contemplation, Juan?

DON JUAN: In the Heaven I seek, no other joy….

Shaw's long life came to an end in 1950 at the age of ninety-four at his home, known as Shaw's Corner, in Ayot St. Lawrence in Hertfordshire. On September 10, he had fallen from a ladder while pruning a tree. He was taken to a nearby hospital and underwent surgery for a fractured thigh. The trauma reinflamed a chronic infection in his bladder and kidneys, and more surgery was done to alleviate that condition. He returned home, but the infection worsened, and by late October, he was in a much-weakened condition.

In his final days, Shaw was visited by the Reverend R. G. Davies, the local Anglican vicar, who said prayers over the non-believer. "It is wrong to say that he was an atheist," Davies later said. "I would call him rather an Irishman. He believed in God."

At three o'clock in the morning on November 1, Shaw fell into a coma and never regained consciousness. With only his two nurses at his bedside, he expired at 4:59 a.m. on November 2. Later that morning, his housekeeper, Alice Laden, dressed in black, appeared at the gate and told waiting reporters, "Mr. Shaw is dead."

Shaw had left instructions that there be no religious service and that his tombstone not "take the form of a cross or any other instrument of torture or symbol of blood sacrifice." Nonetheless, the vicar conducted a five-minute service at Shaw's Corner, attended by several local parishioners.

For his cremation at the local Welwyn chapel, Shaw had instructed that no clergymen be present and that two of his favorite musical compositions should be played: "We Are the Music-Makers," a poem by Arthur O'Shaughnessy set to music by Elgar, and "Libera Mea" from Verdi's "Requiem." It was his wish that his ashes be mixed with those of his wife, Charlotte, who had died seven years earlier, and then scattered in their garden.

Shaw's will left a sizeable sum to promote a phonetic alphabet he had invented. In a ruling that probably would have infuriated him, a court ruled this project was "impossible" and ordered the money distributed instead to the British Museum, the Royal Academy of Dramatic Art, and the National Gallery of Ireland.

ARTHUR CONAN DOYLE

Sherlock Holmes may have been a highly rational detective whose methods depended on close empirical observation and rigid logic, but his creator, Arthur Conan Doyle, was a spiritualist who believed in fairies. Doyle, who added his middle name to his surname so that he would be known more elegantly as Conan Doyle, entered the world on May 22, 1859, in Edinburgh. His father was a down-at-heels alcoholic, and the family was supported by wealthy Roman Catholic uncles, who saw to it that Arthur received a rigorous Jesuit education before studying medicine at the University of Edinburgh.

As a dashing medical student, Arthur fancied himself a ladies' man and bragged about keeping five women on the string at the same time. Whimsically, he made a sketch of himself receiving his medical diploma with the caption "Licenced to Kill." After graduation, he sailed to West Africa as a ship's surgeon and then returned to England to set up an unsuccessful medical practice, first in Plymouth, then in Portsmouth. In the long gaps between patients, he wrote stories, and he sold *A Study in Scarlet*, the first story to feature sleuth Holmes and his sidekick Dr. Watson, to *Beeton's Christmas Annual* for £25. Conan Doyle married Louise Hawkins, the sister of a patient, and they had two children.

In 1890, Conan Doyle set up practice in London as an ophthalmologist. He claimed, seemingly without regret, that not a single patient came to see him, and he was able to devote himself full-time to writing. It was just as well, for detective stories were more lucrative than medicine, and he needed money to support his stable of horses, his Swiss skiing trips, and his newfangled motor car. By this time, the Sherlock Holmes stories had attracted millions of fans on both sides of the Atlantic, including King Edward VII, who knighted Conan Doyle for his service as a physician in the Boer War.

Conan Doyle decided to kill off Holmes, in order to have more time for serious historical novels, and Holmes, along with his archenemy Professor Moriarty, met a watery doom in "The Final Problem." Readers, including Conan Doyle's mother, were outraged. "You won't! You can't! You mustn't!" she wrote to him. The chorus of protest was so loud and vehement that Holmes was resurrected in *The Hound of the Baskervilles*.

Conan Doyle's first wife died of tuberculosis, and the widower married Jean Leckie, with whom he had been in love for ten years and had even carried on an affair during his wife's illness. They had three children.

Besides the loss of his first wife, Conan Doyle experienced the death of one of his sons, a brother, and two brothers-in-law—and he began to try to communicate with their departed souls. Becoming an ardent spiritualist, he claimed to have spoken to Joseph Conrad, Cecil Rhodes, and other talkative, though deceased, Britons. On a trip to America, he struck up a friendship with the illusionist Harry Houdini, whom he credited with supernatural powers, despite Houdini's dogged insistence that his feats were mere (albeit brilliant) trickery.

When he was seventy, Conan Doyle began to experience frequent chest pain, which was diagnosed as acute angina pectoris. Seriously ailing, he made a visit to psychics in Holland and Scandinavia, but was so ill that he had to be carried ashore on his return home. As death approached, he observed, "I have had many adventures. The greatest and most glorious of all awaits me now."

He embarked upon that great and glorious adventure on July 7, 1930, when he was found gasping and clutching his chest in the hallway of Windlesham Manor, his country home in Crowborough, East Sussex. As his son Adrian told an *Associated Press* reporter: "My mother's and father's devotion to each other at all times was one of the most wonderful things I have ever known. His last words were to her, and they show just how much he thought of her. He simply smiled up at her and said, 'You are wonderful.' He was in too much pain to say a lot. His breathing was very bad, and what he said was during a brief flash of consciousness."

Conan Doyle, surrounded by his wife, two sons, and a daughter, died at the age of seventy-one.

At his memorial service the following week at Royal Albert Hall, attended by six thousand mourners, an empty chair was placed next to that of his wife. A medium named Estelle Roberts tried to summon Conan Doyle's spirit, and after half an hour, pointed to the empty chair and announced, "He is here!" No one except her, however, was able to see him. She whispered a message from him to the widow, but what he said was never revealed—except that the medium did report that Sir Arthur had congratulated her on her superb performance.

Conan Doyle was first buried in the rose garden at Windlesham, but was later reinterred in Minstead Churchyard, New Forest, Hampshire. The epitaph on his gravestone reads:

Steel True
Blade Straight
Arthur Conan Doyle
Knight
Patriot, Physician & Man of Letters.

ANTON CHEKHOV

Anton Chekhov was both a writer and a physician, but like an earlier poet-doctor, John Keats, he found his medical skills could not spare him an early death from a dreaded disease. On the bright side, only moments before he died, Chekhov was sipping champagne.

Born in Taganrog, in southern Russia, on January 29, 1860, the son of a grocer who was a religious fanatic, Anton attended local schools. When he was sixteen, he was left in his hometown to fend for himself while the family relocated in Moscow after his father's bankruptcy. After finishing school, he rejoined his family and enrolled in Moscow University Medical School, where he graduated when he was twenty-four.

During this time, he began to publish short stories, which received considerable acclaim. He maintained a dual career for eight years, practicing medicine and continuing his writing, winning the Pushkin Prize for literary excellence. "Medicine is my lawful wife," he said, "and literature is my mistress." After his play *The Wood Demon* flopped, he quit writing for several years and embarked upon medical research among prisoners in a Siberian penal colony. He then decided to see the world, traveling to Asia, India, and the Middle East.

He returned to Russia, bought a country estate near Moscow, and devoted himself full-time to writing. He turned out dozens of short stories and began to write plays again, notably his four supreme achievements: *The Seagull, Uncle Vanya, The Three Sisters,* and *The Cherry Orchard.* At first they were not successful, but a revival of *The Seagull* by Konstantin Stanislavsky was a huge hit.

The actress who played Nina in that production was Olga Knipper, with whom Chekhov began an affair, culminating in their marriage. Unfortunately, Chekhov's health began to deteriorate rapidly at that time. Since leaving medical school, he had suffered from tuberculosis, an illness that ran in his family, and his tempestuous marriage to Olga weakened him further. He spent most of his time in Yalta by the sea while Olga was performing in Moscow.

As a boy, Chekhov was dominated by his father's religious fervor, and he dutifully attended Russian Orthodox services. As he grew older, his religious views became more humanist, but he never lost an underlying affinity for the doctrines and rituals of Orthodoxy. While not specifically advocating Christian concepts in his works, Chekhov let his characters embrace them, with his seeming approval. In *Uncle Vanya,* for example, Sonia talks of an afterlife with this vision of Heaven as a welcome rest from this life's vicissitudes:

And when our final hour comes, we shall meet it humbly, and there beyond the grave, we shall say that we have known suffering and tears, that our life was bitter. And God will pity us. Ah, then, dear, dear Uncle, we shall enter on a bright and beautiful life. We shall rejoice and look back upon our grief here. A tender smile—and—we shall rest. I have faith, Uncle, fervent, passionate faith. We shall rest. We shall rest. We shall hear the angels. We shall see heaven shining like a jewel. We shall see evil and all our pain disappear in the great mercy that shall enfold the world. Our life will be as peaceful and gentle and sweet as a caress. I have faith; I have faith. My poor, poor Uncle Vanya, you are crying! [*Weeping*] You have never known what it is to be happy, but wait, Uncle Vanya, wait! We shall rest. We shall rest.

In the summer of 1901 at Yalta, Chekhov was coughing blood, but steeled himself to return to Moscow for rehearsals of *The Three Sisters*. The following year, he finished his final play, *The Cherry Orchard*, and against doctors' orders returned to Moscow for rehearsals with Stanislavsky's company. It was not a happy experience: As with most of the Chekhov-Stanislavsky collaborations, the two were at cross purposes; Stanislavsky saw the plays as stark tragedies, and Chekhov thought they were amusing comedies. "He turned my characters into crybabies," the playwright complained.

When *The Cherry Orchard* opened in January of 1904, the tuberculosis had become terminal, and Chekhov's friends and family knew the end was near. By this time, as one friend observed, he could hardly walk and "noises were coming from his chest." Opening night was a farewell tribute to Russia's greatest playwright.

Chekhov held on until June. Then, accompanied by Olga, he went to the German spa of Badenweiler, seeking some relief.

On the night of July 14, he stayed up late to work on a story. After going to bed, he woke up feeling ill, sat up straight, and said, *"Ich sterbe"* (German for "I am dying")—which was surprising, since he knew only a little German. Olga summoned a physician, who calmed him, gave him an injection of camphor (used to treat minor heart symptoms), and offered him a glass of champagne—an incongruously festive custom of German doctors when attending a fellow doctor on his deathbed. Chekhov drained the glass, smiled at Olga, and said, "It's a long time since I drank champagne." He then lay down on his left side and died. He was forty-four years old.

Chekhov's body was transported to Moscow in a refrigerated railway car marked "FOR OYSTERS," a perceived indignity that outraged Chekhov's friend Maxim Gorky. Chekhov was buried in Novdevichy Cemetery, next to his father, after a four-mile funeral procession of four thousand mourners. During the procession, some of the Chekhov crowd became confused by the cortege of another funeral and marched off by mistake to the martial strains of an army band to services for General Fyodor Keller.

RUDYARD KIPLING

Although he hated receiving honors and turned down many, including the Poet Laureateship, a knighthood, and the Order of Merit, Rudyard Kipling did accept the Nobel Prize for literature in 1907, becoming the first English-speaking writer to win it. An Anglo-Indian, he was born December 30, 1865, in Bombay, where his father headed an art school. Named Rudyard after an English lake where his parents had courted, he had an idyllic early childhood, which ended abruptly at age five when his lackadaisical parents sent him and his younger sister to England for an education, in the care of total strangers whose names they got from an advertisement.

When he was sixteen, Ruddy returned to India and began to write for English-language newspapers, but after a dispute with one of his editors, he was fired and departed India for a visit to the United States. He saw such American locales as Seattle, Salt Lake City, Yellowstone National Park, Omaha, Chicago, Boston, and Elmira, New York, where he met and favorably impressed Mark Twain. Twain said of Kipling, who was only twenty-three at the time, but looked much older: "He is a most remarkable man—and I am the other one. . . . he knows all that can be known, and I know the rest."

Kipling wound up back in England and embarked upon his literary career. In short order, he published a novel, *The Light That Failed*, suffered a nervous breakdown, recuperated on a whirlwind tour of India and South Africa, returned to London, and became friendly with Wolcott Balestier, an American writer and agent, whose younger sister Carrie became Kipling's wife. They settled in America, which is how Kipling came to write *Captains Courageous* and *The Jungle Book*, in Brattleboro, Vermont, of all places. A son and a daughter were also born there, and Kipling completed a new version of *Barrack-Room Ballads*, which contained the famous "Gunga Din" ("You're a better man than I am, Gunga Din") and "Mandalay" ("On the road to Mandalay, / Where the flyin'-fishes play").

A long-running feud over property and money with his wife's younger brother, who threatened either to blow Kipling's brains out or to give him the worst hiding he had ever had (not surprisingly, their accounts differed), persuaded Kipling to move his family back to England. By this time, his writing had made him famous and wealthy—he was reputedly the highest paid writer in the world—and the family settled into the first of two stately homes in Sussex.

Kipling's other most famous works of fiction (all of them later notable movies or TV series) were *Kim, The Man Who Would Be King,* and *Just So Stories.* Oft-quoted poems are "The Ballad of East and West," ("Oh, East is East, and West is West, and never the twain shall meet"), "Danny Deever," ("An' they're hangin' Danny Deever in the mornin'"), "Recessional" ("Lord God of Hosts, be with us yet, / Lest we forget, lest we forget"), "The Female of the Species" (". . . is more deadly than the male"), "The Betrothed" ("A woman is only a woman, but a good cigar is a smoke"), and "If" ("If you can keep your head when all about you / Are losing theirs and blaming it on you").

Although his personal religious views were unclear—probably a Deist; he once called himself a "God-fearing Christian atheist"—he could write in the vernacular of sentimental orthodoxy about a future life, as he did in an 1892 poem some may regard as more than a wee bit treacly:

> When Earth's last picture is painted and the tubes are
>   twisted and dried,
> When the oldest colours have faded, and the youngest critic
>   has died,
> We shall rest, and, faith, we shall need it—lie down for an
>   aeon or two,
> Till the Master of All Good Workmen shall put us to work
>   anew.
>
> And those that were good shall be happy; they shall sit in a
>   golden chair;
> They shall splash at a ten-league canvas with brushes of
>   comets' hair.
> They shall find real saints to draw from—Magdalene, Peter,
>   and Paul;
> They shall work for an age at a sitting and never be tired at
>   all!

And only The Master shall praise us, and only The Master
    shall blame;
And no one shall work for money, and no one shall work for
    fame,
But each for the joy of the working, and each, in his separate
    star,
Shall draw the Thing as he sees It for the God of Things as
    They are!

Kipling got to try out his golden chair in 1936, when an ulcer
from which he had suffered for many years proved his final
undoing. A magazine's earlier erroneous report of his death
prompted Kipling to write to the offending publication: "I've
just read that I am dead. Don't forget to delete me from your list
of subscribers." This time, however, his demise was real. He and
his wife were stopping over in London en route to a vacation in
the south of France, when he became ill and was transported to
Middlesex Hospital. That old ulcer had perforated and hemor-
rhaged in his small intestine, and he underwent seemingly successful surgery—but after twenty-four hours, peritonitis set in.
Kipling survived four more days, receiving frequent oxygen and
blood transfusions, but at 12:10 a.m. on Saturday, January 18,
he died at the age of seventy.

Kipling was cremated at Golders Green Crematorium, and
his cremains were buried beneath a simple stone in Poets' Corner of Westminster Abbey, next to Charles Dickens. T. S. Eliot's
memorial stone later found a space on Kipling's other side.

ROBERT FROST

Robert Frost's religious sentiments seemed to swing like a pendulum. In a whimsical poem entitled "Not All There," he laments
about God's absence when he tries to speak to him. But Frost
sometimes referred to himself as an "Old Testament Christian,"

and when it came to an afterlife, apparently he wasn't sure. He left this piece of useful advice: "You ought to live so's if there isn't anything, it will be an awful shame."

Named Robert Lee for the Confederate general, Frost was born in San Francisco on March 26, 1874. He was the son of a hard-drinking newspaper editor and religious skeptic and his wife, who started as Presbyterian, but through the influence of reading Emerson, became a Unitarian and then a Swedenborgian. Young Robert was baptized in the Swedenborgian Church and remained influenced by its Christian mysticism throughout his life. When Frost was eleven, his father died, leaving the family with just eight dollars to its name, and Robert, his mother, and nine-year-old sister moved to Lawrence, Massachusetts, where his father's parents lived.

Robert attended public school and then went on to Dartmouth and Harvard, failing to graduate from either. He worked at various jobs: teaching, delivering newspapers, cobbling shoes, changing arclight carbon filaments, and editing the Lawrence *Sentinel*. In 1894, he had his first poem published in a New York newspaper. The following year, he married a high school classmate, Elinor Miriam White, with whom he had six children. He tried his hand at farming for several years on land inherited from his grandfather, but when the farm failed, he moved with his family to England. There he met a number of literary figures, including Ezra Pound, who took a liking to his work and helped him get two volumes of poetry published.

After World War I erupted, Frost returned to the United States, his reputation as a major poet secure. Thereafter he lived in Massachusetts and Vermont, teaching at Amherst College and Middlebury College and continuing to turn out poetry, which won a total of four Pulitzer Prizes. Among his most familiar poems, many of which use pastoral New England imagery to make philosophical comments, are "Mending Wall," "The Death of the Hired Man," "Birches," "Fire and Ice," "Departmental," "Stopping by Woods on a Snowy Evening," "The Road Not Taken," and "The Gift Outright," which he recited at President John F. Kennedy's inauguration.

Frost's family life was plagued by illness and premature deaths. His mother, his sister, his wife, some of his children, and Frost himself suffered bouts of depression, and Frost had to commit his sister to a mental institution. His daughter Irma was similarly institutionalized. Frost's mother died of cancer when he was twenty-six, his son Eliot died four years later of cholera, his daughter Elinor died three days after her birth, and his daughter Marjorie died in childbirth. Frost's wife developed breast cancer in 1937 and died of a heart ailment the following year. Two years later, their son Carol committed suicide.

Frost himself lived until 1963, when he died of an embolism at the age of eighty-eight. He had entered Peter Bent Brigham Hospital in Boston for prostate cancer surgery on December 10. He then suffered a heart attack, and blood clots settled in his lungs. An operation in early January to tie the veins in both his legs attempted to ease the blockage, but shortly after midnight on January 29, Frost complained of shortness of breath and severe chest pains. He died at 1:50 a.m., "probably of a pulmonary embolism," according to his death certificate.

A family service was conducted by a Unitarian minister in Appleton Chapel at Harvard University, and Frost was buried in a family plot in Old Bennington, Vermont. Beneath his name on the gravestone is a quotation from his poem "The Lesson for Today": "I had a lover's quarrel with the world." Later, in Johnson Chapel at Amherst College, there was a public memorial service, at which President Kennedy delivered a eulogy.

JACK LONDON

When Jack London heard the call of the wild, he answered it. The man who would become the highest paid author in America was born in San Francisco on January 12, 1876, in modest circumstances to an unmarried mother named Flora Wellman. His father was probably William Chaney, an astrologist, and as an infant, Jack was handed over by his neurotic mother to a former slave named Jennie Prentiss, who raised him like one of her own children. Flora later married John London, a Civil War veteran, and Jack took his name.

The family settled in Oakland, where Jack finished grade school and then worked at various jobs, one of which was pirating oysters on San Francisco Bay in a sloop he purchased with money borrowed from his nanny. He decided to switch sides and worked for a while with the harbor patrol, catching poachers. An alcoholic by the time he was fifteen, he sailed the Pacific on a Scandinavian seal-catching boat, hoboed around the country, marched in Coxey's army of the unemployed, got arrested in Niagara Falls and served jail time for vagrancy, then returned to Oakland to attend high school, work in a power plant, and engage in the political activism that made him famous as the "Boy Socialist of Oakland."

London won a national short story contest, and then began to submit other stories and poems to magazines with little success, until he spent the winter of 1897 looking for gold in the Klondike. He experienced frostbite, scurvy, malaria, and dysentery, netted only $4.50 worth of gold dust, but came up with material that would set him up as a successful writer, beginning with stories such as "To Build A Fire," and culminating with *The Call of the Wild*. Other books followed, including *White Fang*, *The Sea-Wolf* (which was the basis of Hollywood's first full-length feature film), *The Iron Heel*, *Martin Eden*, *The People and the Abyss* (a critique of capitalism), *John Barleycorn* (a memoir of his alcoholism), and *The Cruise of the Snark* (an account of an abortive attempt to sail the Pacific in a ketch with his wife).

By now an international celebrity, he was earning the equivalent of $250,000 a month from his writing and endorsements of clothing and grape juice—but he squandered his fortune on a yacht; a money-draining ranch in Sonoma County, where he pioneered sustainable agriculture; and a mansion that cost two million dollars in today's money, but burned down just before it was finished.

London married twice, first to Bess Maddern, with whom he had two daughters before divorcing her to marry Charmian Kittredge, who remained his wife, his muse, and his editor for the rest of his life.

Major influences on London's thought and writing were Rudyard Kipling, Robert Louis Stevenson, Charles Darwin, Aldous Huxley, Karl Marx, and Friedrich Nietszche, from whom he acquired a fierce anti-religious bent. He identified himself as an atheist and was sometimes quoted as saying, "I believe that when I am dead, I am dead. I believe that with my death I am just as much obliterated as the last mosquito you and I squashed."

Never in good health since the ailments he contracted in the Klondike, London suffered in his later years from gout, pyorrhea, and severe and painful chronic kidney disease, which might have been caused by heavy drinking and a weird diet filled with raw fish and nearly raw duck. In addition to a reliance on alcohol for relief, he also took strong opiates. He died on his ranch near Glen Ellen, California, on November 22, 1916, and his death certificate attributed the cause to "uraemia following renal colic," complicated by "chronic interstitial nephritis." He was forty years old.

His good friend George Sterling claimed that London committed suicide, but solid evidence is lacking. It is certainly possible that London, mortally ill and in chronic pain, may have taken an overdose of morphine either accidentally or purposely. London's ashes are buried on his ranch, now known as Jack London State Historic Park, under a red boulder on a knoll that overlooks his ranch house.

In his handwritten will, London left his whole estate and all rights to his works to his wife, Charmian, except for monthly allowances of $45 to his mother, $35 to his sister, $25 to each of his two daughters, and $15 to his "old mammy," Jennie Prentiss—and a one-time payment of $5 to his former wife, Bessie.

SHERWOOD ANDERSON

Death by toothpick was the sad fate of American writer Sherwood Anderson, best known for his story sequence *Winesburg, Ohio.* A true son of Ohio, Anderson was the third of seven children, born in Camden on September 13, 1876, to a harness-maker who moved around frequently to avoid debt collectors. Anderson quit school at age fourteen (though he later attended classes at Wittenberg College in Springfield). He worked for a while as an advertising salesman for a Chicago magazine publisher.

During this period, he began to write character sketches that were published in some of the magazines.

Anderson then moved to Cleveland to run his own mail-order business. One of the products he sold was a defective incubator, and hundreds of complaints from angry customers drove him to a nervous breakdown. He regrouped and started another business in Elyria, Ohio, selling a preservative paint called Roof-Fix, but again suffered a mental breakdown. He walked thirty miles to Cleveland, where after three days he was found, delirious, in a drug store.

That experience was evidently an epiphany of sorts: Anderson left his wife and three children, moved to Chicago, took up a bohemian lifestyle, met young Ernest Hemingway and Carl Sandburg, and devoted himself fulltime to the literary life. He spent some time in New Orleans, where he hobnobbed with William Faulkner. During a stay in Paris Anderson became close friends with Gertrude Stein and Ezra Pound, and on his return to New York socialized with F. Scott Fitzgerald. Though he fared reasonably well as a writer of novels, essays, poetry, and especially short stories, his novel *Dark Laughter*, inspired by his New Orleans days, was the only bestseller of his career.

Although raised in a home with a devoutly Presbyterian mother, Anderson evidenced scant interest in formal religion. He was far more interested as a writer in how people lived their lives than in what happened to them after they were dead. In one short story from *Winesburg, Ohio*, which Anderson called "Death," he romanticizes the figure of the Grim Reaper:

The sick woman spent the last few months of her life hungering for death. Along the road of death she went, seeking, hungering. She personified the figure of death and made him now a strong black-haired youth running over hills, now a stern quiet man marked and scarred by the business of living. In the darkness of her room she put out her hand, thrusting it from under the covers of her bed, and she thought that death like a living thing put out his hand to her. "Be patient, lover," she whispered. "Keep yourself young and beautiful and be patient."

By 1941, Anderson's works had faded from popularity, and he and his fourth wife went on a South American cruise with playwright Thornton Wilder aboard the liner *Santa Lucia*. Anderson was fond of martinis, a drink that is often served with an olive speared on a toothpick. Somehow or other Anderson managed to swallow a toothpick while imbibing, and the next day he fell ill. After suffering abdominal pains for several days, he was diagnosed with peritonitis by the ship's doctor, and the captain made port in Colón, Panama, where Anderson was taken to a hospital. He died there on March 8, at the age of sixty-four, of the massive infection caused when the toothpick perforated his intestine.

Anderson's body was returned to the United States, where he was buried at Round Hill Cemetery in Marion, Virginia. His epitaph reads, "Life, Not Death, is the Great Adventure." His obituary in the Elyria, Ohio, paper gave little notice of his literary career; it was headed "Former Elyria Manufacturer Dies."

CARL SANDBURG

Carl Sandburg, American poet, journalist, biographer, film critic, and three-time Pulitzer Prize–winner, was concerned less about the afterlife than the present lives of common people, especially in the Midwest.

One of the common people himself, Sandburg was born January 6, 1878, in Galesburg, Illinois, to a Swedish

immigrant railroad worker who changed his name to August Sandburg from August Johnson, because there were too many other August Johnsons at the railyard. Young Carl had to start work at age thirteen, and he found employment as a porter in a barber shop, a milk delivery man, a bricklayer, a farm laborer, and a hotel servant.

After a stint in the Army during the Spanish-American War, he attended Lombard College in Galesburg and then went to work for the *Chicago Daily News* as a film critic. He became an organizer for the Social Democratic Party in Milwaukee, where he met fellow organizer Lillian Steichen, known as Paula, sister of the photographer Edward Steichen. They married in 1908 and raised a family of three daughters, whom he whimsically nicknamed his "homeyglomeys."

Sandburg began to write poetry, inspired both by Walt Whitman and by his own rough-and-tumble Midwestern life. Most of it was free verse, nonmetrical and nonrhyming, a form that his contemporary Robert Frost disdained as "playing tennis without a net." Sandburg's first volume was *Chicago Poems*; followed by *Cornhuskers*, which won a Pulitzer Prize; then *Smoke and Steel*; and *Slabs of the Sunburnt West*. Despite poetic fame, a notoriously ill-compensated distinction, he didn't have financial success until the publication of the first in his three-volume biography of Abraham Lincoln. Among his later works are "Good Morning, America," *The People, Yes*, and *Abraham Lincoln: The War Years*, which won him another Pulitzer Prize. His *Complete Poems* won him a third Pulitzer in 1951.

Sandburg was raised a Lutheran, but according to his biographer Harry Golden, after his confirmation at age thirteen, he was never a member of any church. Golden once asked him directly what his religion was, and Sandburg replied: "I am a Christian, a Quaker, a Moslem, a Buddhist, a Shintoist, a Confucian, and maybe a Catholic pantheist or a Joan of Arc who hears voices. I am all of these and more. Definitely I have more religions than I have time or zeal to practice in true faith."

"Death Snips Proud Men," published in 1920, is a memorable Sandburg commentary on the end of life:

Death is stronger than all the governments because the governments are men and men die and then death laughs: Now you see 'em, now you don't.

Death is stronger than all proud men and so death snips proud men on the nose, throws a pair of dice and says: Read 'em and weep.

Death sends a radiogram every day: When I want you I'll drop in—and then one day he comes with a master-key and lets himself in and says: We'll go now.

Death is a nurse mother with big arms: 'Twon't hurt you at all; it's your time now; you just need a long sleep, child; what have you had anyhow better than sleep?

In one of his last poems, "Timesweep," Sandburg accepts the inevitability of his own mortality, which he calls "the final announcement from the Black Void," with quiet resignation.

The last twenty-two years of Sandburg's life were spent with Paula on their 245-acre farm, called Connemara, in Flat Rock, North Carolina. He enjoyed a nip of whisky or cognac, and he smoked cigars—although he was known to limit his intake by cutting them into thirds. He continued to work; writing poetry, traveling to speaking engagements, even spending time in Hollywood to work on the screenplay of *The Greatest Story Ever Told*. But his age eventually caught up with him. Sandburg began to have frequent attacks of bronchitis and pneumonia, and suffered increasing memory loss. When he was eighty-seven, he was hospitalized with diverticulitis.

In June of 1967, Sandburg had two heart attacks, and by mid-July, he was bedridden. As he lay dying, he asked to hear a recording by classical guitarist Andrés Segovia, who years earlier had written a piece in Sandburg's honor. Sandburg died of heart failure about nine o'clock in the morning on July 22, at the age of eighty-nine. His last word was his wife's name, "Paula."

Nearly six thousand people gathered at the Lincoln Memorial in Washington for a memorial service on September 17, and Sandburg's ashes were buried on October 1 under "Remembrance Rock" at his Galesburg birthplace.

VIRGINIA WOOLF

What was Virginia Woolf afraid of? On the day of her death, the author of *Mrs. Dalloway* and *To the Lighthouse* left a note for her husband that read in part: "I feel certain that I am going mad again. I feel we can't go through another of those terrible times. And I shan't recover this time. I begin to hear voices, and I can't concentrate. So I am doing what seems the best thing to do."

A victim of mental disorders for much of her life, Woolf was born in London on January 25, 1882, to Sir Leslie Stephen, editor of the *Dictionary of National Biography*, and his wife, Julia. Virginia received all of her schooling at home. She had several breakdowns and bouts of depression, some requiring hospitalization. The first was after the death of her mother when Virginia was thirteen, and another occurred when her father died nine years later. Between 1910 and 1913, she had three stays in nursing homes.

In 1912, Virginia married Leonard Woolf, a novelist and political theorist, and they eventually settled in a house on

Tavistock Square in the Bloomsbury section of London. This was one of the meeting places of the literary circle known as the Bloomsbury Group, which included the Woolfs, E. M. Forster, John Maynard Keynes, Rupert Brooke, Desmond McCarthy, Roger Fry, Lytton Strachey, and others.

The Woolfs acquired a small hand printing press as a hobby for Virginia, and from this activity grew the Hogarth Press, which the couple managed for more than twenty years and which published most of her works, including *Orlando*, *A Room of One's Own*, *The Waves*, *Flush*, *Roger Fry: A Biography*, and *Between the Acts*, which she finished shortly before her death and which was published posthumously.

During the blitz of World War II, the Woolfs' London flat was destroyed, and they went to live in Sussex. Both of them had suffered depression and contemplated suicide, and they had stockpiled morphine and petrol for just such a purpose. These proved unnecessary. At 11:30 a.m. on March 28, 1941, Virginia Woolf put on her hat and coat, filled her pockets with rocks, took her walking stick, and went to the Ouse River near her home. She removed her hat, laid down her cane, and jumped into the river. Her body, weighted by the stones, was recovered April 18. She was fifty-nine years old.

Her husband buried her ashes under am elm tree in the garden of their home, Monk's House, in Rodmell, Sussex.

JAMES JOYCE

When asked to provide a guide to his riddle-strewn novel *Ulysses*, James Joyce demurred: "If I gave it all up immediately, I'd lose my immortality." His bid for eternal life was to keep experts guessing forever about what his words meant. But, having cast off the Catholic teaching of his youth, a personal afterlife was probably not something Joyce would have expected.

Born in Rathgar, Ireland, on February 2, 1882, Joyce was the eldest of a large family described vaguely as "sixteen or seventeen children" by his father, an impecunious, heavy-drinking Irish tenor. One of only ten who survived past infancy, James was a precocious child who immersed himself in Aristotle, Dante, Thomas Aquinas, and Henrik Ibsen, while receiving a Jesuit education and then earning a degree at University College, Dublin.

He went to Paris and started writing, returning to Ireland for his mother's funeral in 1903 and remaining there only long enough to meet and woo a chambermaid named Nora Barnacle, with whom he had two children and whom he finally married in 1931. James and Nora lived in various European cities, including Paris, Rome, Trieste, and Zurich. Able to speak seventeen languages, Joyce taught English to support the family as he continued writing.

Joyce published a volume of short stories, *Dubliners*, followed by *A Portrait of the Artist as a Young Man*. In 1922, he published his controversial landmark novel *Ulysses*, whose obscurity did not prevent eager readers from gleefully trying to decipher its alleged obscenity. Not until 1934 in the United States and 1936 in Great Britain was the book allowed to circulate legally. The even more enigmatic *Finnegans Wake* came in 1939.

Despite his rejection of Christianity, Joyce often attended both Catholic and Orthodox services, especially during Holy Week. One friend called him "a believer at heart," and T. S. Eliot, among others, regarded Joyce's novels as fundamentally Christian in outlook.

Joyce, who had undergone numerous operations for eye ailments, had surgery again—this time for a perforated ulcer—in

January of 1941 in Zurich, where the Joyces had settled at the outset of World War II. The day after surgery, he suffered a relapse and was given transfusions, but fell into a coma. He awoke at two o'clock in the morning on Monday, January 13, asked a nurse to call his wife and son, Giorgio, and then lapsed back into the coma. Fifteen minutes later he died, at the age of fifty-eight, before Nora and Giorgio reached the hospital. Joyce's last words were, "Does nobody understand?" What he meant was not clear.

The funeral was Wednesday afternoon, January 15, in the Friedhof Chapel at Fluntern Cemetery in Zurich. A Catholic priest offered to officiate, but Nora declined, saying, "I couldn't do that to him." Instead, there were eulogies by Lord Derwent, the British minister to Bern, poet Max Gellinger, and Professor Heinrich Straumann. The tenor Max Meili sang an aria from Monteverdi's *Orfeo*. Two Irish diplomats were in Switzerland at the time, but neither attended the funeral, and a rather petulant Irish government refused Nora's request to repatriate Joyce's remains, which are still interred at Fluntern.

FRANZ KAFKA

If there are days when you feel squashed like a bug, remember that Franz Kafka felt that way first. "The meaning of life," he said, "is that it stops." Human beings in his most famous works are the helpless pawns of an unfeeling cosmos. Kafka is remembered for the novels *The Trial, The Castle,* and *Amerika,* and for such stories as "The Hunger Artist" and, most of all, "The Metamorphosis"—which is memorable for its image of a man who wakes up and finds he has turned into a giant insect. "Kafkaesque" is a term that describes surreal, menacing situations, and this stark existentialism was a major influence on Jean-Paul Sartre and Albert Camus.

Kafka, eldest of six children in a middle-class, German-speaking, Jewish family, was born on July 3, 1883, in Prague, the capital of Bohemia in what was then the Austro-Hungarian Empire. He received his early education at a German boys' school and at the local synagogue until his bar mitzvah. At Prague's Charles University, he earned a law degree and then toiled several years at an insurance company at what he called his "bread work," to earn money to live on while writing in his spare time.

Never married, Kafka had a series of lovers, but to satisfy his voracious sexual appetite, he consorted frequently with prostitutes and indulged his avid interest in pornography. Not an observant Jew, Kafka nonetheless had a lifelong interest in the Talmud and other Jewish traditions.

The notion of death, for Kafka, like most of life, was bleak, cold, and impersonal. In "The Metamorphosis," Gregor Samsa, the protagonist who becomes a giant insect, is found dead, "dried up and flat," by a housekeeper who pokes him with a broom to determine if there's any life left. The housekeeper promises to get rid of the "thing," and Gregor's father, mother, and sister resume their lives with little more thought for "it."

Always sickly, Kafka suffered from anorexia nervosa, migraine headaches, insomnia, constipation, and boils—all aggravated by acute hypochondria—for which he turned to various naturopathic remedies and a vegetarian diet. It was tuberculosis of the larynx that did him in. Diagnosed when he was thirty-four, it steadily worsened, and he sought treatment at a sanatorium near Vienna in April of 1924, where he died on June 3 at the age of forty. The actual cause of death was attributed to starvation, owing to the tubercular swelling in his throat that made it impossible for him to eat.

His body was returned to Prague and buried on June 11 in the New Jewish Cemetery. He achieved no recognition as a writer during his lifetime, since most of his works were published only after his death.

EZRA POUND

Genius, visionary, reformer, traitor, lunatic—these all describe Ezra Pound. Probably the most important influence on twentieth-century British-American literature, Pound befriended and offered assistance to a long list of writers that included T. S. Eliot, James Joyce, William Butler Yeats, Robert Frost, Ernest Hemingway, D. H. Lawrence, Sherwood Anderson, William Carlos Williams, Marianne Moore, and H. D. (Hilda Doolittle). Pound's own major work was the epic *Cantos*, a sprawling and often opaque poem, which deals, so to speak, with the history of the world. Pound was accused of treason against the United States for his pro-Axis broadcasts during World War II, judged insane, and confined in a mental hospital.

This poet-provocateur was born on October 30, 1885, in Hailey, Idaho, the son of a federal official. He grew up near Philadelphia, attended Cheltenham Military Academy, the University of Pennsylvania, and Hamilton College, earning a B.A. in philosophy before taking a teaching job at Wabash College in Indiana. He was fired after an incident involving a young woman whom he allowed to sleep in his room at the college. With a nest egg of just eighty dollars, he sailed for Europe in 1908.

After a brief stay in Venice, where he paid for the publication of his first book of verse, he settled in London, where he became an increasingly well-known part of the literary scene. He pioneered the school of Imagism, a poetic movement that stressed precision of language and a loose meter. His major works, besides the unfinished *Cantos*, include *A Lume Spento* (*With Tapers Spent*), *Personae*, *Provenca*, *Homage to Sextus Propertius*, *Hugh Selwyn Mauberley*, and numerous pieces of literary and social criticism.

In 1914, Pound married Dorothy Shakespear, a British painter, and the couple lived in London and then Paris, where Pound met an American violinist named Olga Rudge, with whom he began a fifty-year affair. Tiring of Paris and ill with what his friend Hemingway called "a small nervous break-down," Pound took Dorothy in 1924 to Rapallo, Italy, followed shortly by Olga. An equal opportunity procreator, Pound sired a son by his wife and a daughter by his mistress.

Pound and his good friend T. S. Eliot argued over the role of religion in civilization, Eliot maintaining that the evils of the world could be attributed to the decay of medieval Christianity, and Pound vigorously attacking organized religion of all kinds. Not precisely an atheist, Pound expressed a belief in a superior force that he called an "intimate essence" or "eternal state of mind," but he was never specific in these beliefs, and was much influenced by Confucian humanism derived from his early interest in Chinese and Japanese poetry.

Falling under the influence of Fascist politicians, Pound became an outspoken anti-Semitic and ardent supporter of Italian dictator Benito Mussolini. In 1939, Pound returned briefly to the United States to try to persuade the American government to stay out of the European war. Back in Italy, he made a series of propaganda broadcasts supporting Mussolini and condemning the United States.

Following the war, Pound was imprisoned in Pisa by Italian partisans for six months, then was handed over to Allied authorities and returned to the United States to be tried for treason. Found insane, he was sent to St. Elizabeth Hospital in Washington, D.C., where he remained for twelve years. The Library of Congress awarded him the Bollingen Prize for a section of the *Cantos* known as *The Pisan Cantos*, completed while he was held at Pisa after the war. The furor the award caused resulted in Congressional action to end the Library's involvement in future prizes.

Freed from St. Elizabeth's in 1958 through the efforts of Archibald MacLeish, Robert Frost, and other writers, Pound returned to Italy, where he lived out his life in Venice with Olga, working on the *Cantos*, while his wife, Dorothy, lived for a time at Merano, about a hundred miles away, before retreating to London. When asked by a friend in Venice on what date he had been released from the asylum, Pound replied, "I never was released. When I left the hospital I was still in America, and all America is an insane asylum."

During his last years, Pound and Olga lived in her small three-story house on Venice's Calle Querini, one street away from the Giudecca Canal on the Rio della Fornace. Their daily routine consisted of early-morning shopping by Olga as Pound snoozed, followed by a leisurely breakfast, a late morning walk along the Giudecca Canal, lunch *al fresco* at the Pensione Cici, then another walk along the Grand Canal.

Dorothy arranged for Olga to be paid $100 a month for her services—which an indignant Olga regarded as an insult. Olga had graduated from mistress and now served as nurse, housekeeper, secretary, and watchdog to screen the many visitors who came to pay homage. She complained especially about inquiries from so-called "biographers," whom she called "hogs after truffles."

Details from Olga's diary in Anne Conover's *Olga Rudge and Ezra Pound* chronicle Pound's last five days. On October 29, 1972, the day before his eighty-seventh birthday, Pound was plagued by an intestinal obstruction. He drank some hot water and a cup of coffee, then took a purgative called Guttalax, followed by vegetable and apple purees. On his birthday, there were no results from the Guttalax, and Pound, dressed in apricot pajamas, took only a demitasse of coffee and some broth with pasta at teatime. That evening, as well-wishers sipped champagne and visited Pound's room two at a time, a cake with eighty-seven candles was brought in, and he blew them all out. Still suffering from unrelieved constipation on the night of October 31, Pound walked to a gondola ambulance summoned by Olga and was taken to Sts. Giovanni and Paolo Hospital. He died there in his sleep on November 1 of an intestinal obstruction with Olga at his side.

A friend described Pound's funeral at the church of San Giorgio Maggiore as "grim," with no flowers and only a single candle. A Roman Catholic mass was followed by an Anglican benediction.

Pound was buried in San Michele Cemetery in the Protestant section beneath a simple marble tombstone engraved with his name by Venetian sculptor Joan Fitzgerald, a close friend. Twenty-four years later, Olga was buried next to him.

T. S. ELIOT

Uneasy for most of a life spent wearing the crown of the twentieth century's leading poet, Thomas Stearns Eliot was also a whiz-bang at literary and social criticism, playwriting, book publishing, and prize-winning—a Nobel and three Broadway Tony Awards, two of them after he had been dead for eighteen years. American by birth, British by temperament and choice, Eliot was born in St. Louis, Missouri, on

September 26, 1888, youngest of six children in a middle-class family that sent him to Harvard University, where he earned bachelor's and master's degrees in literature.

Just before the outbreak of World War I, he decided to pull up stakes and move to London, where he went to work as a clerk at Lloyds Bank and met the eccentric and influential poet Ezra Pound, who helped him find publishers for his verse—notably the iconic poem that every college freshman knows, "The Love Song of J. Alfred Prufrock," which established Eliot's reputation.

In 1915, Eliot married Vivienne Haigh-Wood, a would-be writer whom he met at a tea dance, and after a wedding night on which they found they were sexually incompatible, they spent a miserable eighteen years together before separating. Their friend Virginia Woolf referred to Vivienne as "a bag of ferrets" around Eliot's neck. To escape the anguish, Eliot relied on alcohol—to the extent that novelist Anthony Powell noted in his diary: "Eliot always drunk these days." In 1938, after having an affair with Eliot's friend and mentor Bertrand Russell, Vivienne was committed to a mental institution, where she stayed until her death in 1947. Though they remained married, Eliot never visited her.

Eliot worked at Lloyds Bank for eight years and continued to turn out acclaimed modernist poems that included *The Waste Land*, *Ash Wednesday*, *The Hollow Men*, and *Four Quartets*. When a woman asked him where he got his inspiration, Eliot replied, "Gin and drugs, dear lady, gin and drugs." His manner and appearance were more like a banker than a poet—"very yellow and glum," according to diplomat and author Harold Nicolson. After a nervous breakdown, Eliot joined the publishing house of Faber & Faber, of which he eventually became a major editor and co-owner.

Eliot became a British subject and also converted from Unitarianism to Anglo-Catholicism, joining the parish of St. Stephen's in Gloucester Road, where he served as a warden. Years after his conversion, Eliot characterized his religious beliefs as "a Catholic cast of mind, a Calvinist heritage, and a Puritanical temperament."

He won the Nobel Prize for Literature in 1948, the same year King George VI named him to the exclusive Order of Merit, limited to twenty-four living members. He captured his first Tony Award in 1950 for the Broadway production of *The Cocktail Party*. His other major plays include *Murder in the Cathedral* and *The Family Reunion*. Posthumous Tony Awards were in 1983 for the musical *Cats*, based on his children's poems in *Old Possum's Book of Practical Cats*, which earned him double honors for best book and best lyrics.

After Vivienne's death, Eliot was wooed by two women: Emily Hale, an old flame from his Harvard days, and Mary Trevelyan, his constant companion in London. But the efforts of both were in vain, and Eliot married his longtime secretary, Valerie Fletcher, in 1957, when he was sixty-eight and she was thirty. The ceremony at St. Barnabas Church in north London at 6:15 a.m. was attended only by the bride's parents and one friend of Valerie's.

No children issued from either of Eliot's marriages. He was reputed to have a distaste for sex of any kind, at least until his second marriage, which was a very happy one. Basking in its glow, he called himself "the luckiest man in the world," and told an interviewer, "I am thinking of taking up dancing lessons again."

A heavy smoker most of his life, Eliot suffered from chronic lung problems, including bronchitis and emphysema, and a pathologically rapid heartbeat known as tachycardia. According to newspaper accounts, he was hospitalized on oxygen for five weeks in January of 1963, then returned to his ground-floor flat in Kensington Court Gardens for two more years, being "coddled," as he called it, by Valerie. In October of 1964, he lapsed into a coma and was hospitalized again, but Valerie nursed him through this illness and he returned home once more. By Christmas, however, his heart was failing, and on January 4, 1965, at the age of seventy-six, he awoke from a final coma, uttered Valerie's name, and died.

Eliot was cremated at Golders Green Crematorium and his ashes interred at the Church of St. Michael and All Angels in East Coker, the Somerset village from which his ancestors had come, and the title of one of the poems in *Four Quartets*. A commemorative plaque quotes that poem: "In my beginning is my end. In my end is my beginning." There is also a memorial stone in Poets' Corner of Westminster Abbey.

EUGENE O'NEILL

"I knew it, I knew it—born in a hotel room and, goddammit, died in a hotel room." These were the last words of playwright Eugene O'Neill, whispered before he died in Suite 401 of the Sheraton Hotel on Bay State Road in Boston on November 27, 1953. He was born on October 16, 1888, in a room in the Barrett House hotel on Longacre Square (now Times Square) in New York City.

His father, James O'Neill, was an Irish immigrant actor, famous for barnstorming in the title role in *The Count of Monte Cristo*. Eugene's itinerant parents sent him to a Catholic boarding school in the Bronx, and he spent his summers in New London, Connecticut, at Monte Cristo Cottage, his parents' summer home. He was expelled after a year at Princeton University, allegedly for throwing a beer bottle through the window of Professor Woodrow Wilson, the future U.S. president.

O'Neill spent several years as a merchant seaman before falling ill with tuberculosis. While recuperating, he decided to devote himself to playwriting. He enrolled in a drama course at Harvard, then took a "trunkful" of his plays to the Provincetown Players on Cape Cod. Several of his early plays, volubly tragic for the most part, were produced there and at the Provincetown Playhouse in Greenwich Village. One of them, *Beyond the Horizon*, went on to Broadway and won the Pulitzer Prize in 1920. He had a major Broadway hit with *The Emperor Jones* the same year, followed by *Anna Christie* (Pulitzer Prize), *Desire Under the Elms*, *Strange Interlude* (Pulitzer Prize), *Mourning Becomes Electra*, and *Ah, Wilderness!*, O'Neill's only comedy. He won the Nobel Prize for Literature in 1938.

O'Neill married three times, first in 1909 to Kathleen Jenkins, with whom he had one son; in 1918 to novelist Agnes Boulton, with whom he had a son and a daughter; and finally, in 1929, to actress Carlotta Monterey. O'Neill was estranged from all three of his children. Both sons committed suicide, and his daughter, Oona, married the actor Charlie Chaplin, over O'Neill's strong objection.

As well as his early tuberculosis, depression and alcoholism haunted O'Neill for much of his life. After the Broadway success of his most highly regarded tragedy, *The Iceman Cometh*, O'Neill in his early fifties began to develop a palsy that made it difficult for him to write. Nonetheless, he was able to complete *A Moon for the Misbegotten* and *Long Day's Journey into Night*, although the latter was not produced until years after his death, as were the other plays he left only partly finished, *A Touch of the Poet* and *More Stately Mansions*.

Educated in Catholic schools, O'Neill distanced himself from any religious observance, although many of his plays have theological themes, and O'Neill acknowledged that his work explores the relationship between man and God. The critic Robert Brustein has characterized O'Neill's attitude as anguish at an inability to confirm or deny the existence of God. The playwright instructed Carlotta, "When I'm dying, don't let a priest or Protestant minister or Salvation Army captain near me. Let me die in dignity. Keep it as simple and brief as possible. No fuss, no man of God there. If there is a God, I'll see him and we'll talk things over."

With worsening palsy, thought to be Parkinson's disease, O'Neill went with Carlotta in 1953 to Boston, where he sought treatment. He rarely left the Sheraton suite, seeing only Carlotta; his physician, Dr. Harry Kozol; and a nurse. He died in his room on November 27, at the age of sixty-five. An autopsy disclosed that he did not suffer from Parkinson's disease, but from a degenerative neurological disorder known as cerebellar cortical abiotrophy, which causes brain cells to die.

O'Neill was privately buried in Forest Hills Cemetery, Jamaica Plain, Suffolk County, Massachusetts.

The hotel where O'Neill died is now a Boston University residence hall. The fourth floor frequently experiences unexplained knocks on doors, dimming lights, and random elevator stops. These phenomena are said to be caused by the playwright's ghost.

ROBERT BENCHLEY

"Except for the occasional heart attack, I feel as young as I ever did," humorist Robert Benchley humorously quipped. It wasn't a heart attack, however, but a cerebral hemorrhage, combined with cirrhosis of the liver after years of heavy drinking, that did him in. Benchley, the master of literary whimsy and a droll performer in many Hollywood films, was—by his own account—never quite a writer and never quite an actor.

Born in Worcester, Massachusetts, on September 15, 1889, he claimed in an autobiographical parody that he wrote *A Tale of Two Cities* and *Uncle Tom's Cabin*; married Princess Anastacia of Portugal, with whom he had Prince Rupprecht and several little girls; and was buried in Westminster Abbey. In fact, he went to Harvard, worked on the college literary and humor magazines, married Gertrude Darling (whom he had known since he was eight years old), fathered two sons, wrote more than six hundred witty essays and countless reviews, appeared in goofy roles in at least fifty major movies and short films, and left a string of *bons mots* that inspired such humorists as James Thurber and Dave Barry.

Benchley's early career was checkered, as he bounced from one job to another, spending time as columnist, critic, and editor with the *New York Tribune*, *Vanity Fair*, and the *New Yorker* before devoting himself primarily to film and radio. He was a founding member of the Algonquin Round Table, a group of wags including Dorothy Parker, Robert Sherwood, George S. Kaufman, and Alexander Woollcott, who regularly lunched (and, even more regularly, drank) as they traded quotable quips at the Algonquin Hotel on West 44th Street in New York.

A militant teetotaler until he was thirty-four, Benchley more than made up for his abstemiousness during the last twenty years of his life. "I know I'm drinking myself to a slow death," he said, "but then I'm in no hurry." He also observed, "The only cure for a real hangover is death."

In 1945, Benchley was in about a dozen films in Hollywood, including the Bob Hope-Bing Crosby *Road to Utopia* and *Weekend at the Waldorf* with Ginger Rogers, Lana Turner, Walter Pidgeon, and Van Johnson. In October of that year, he returned to his home in Scarsdale, New York, and was working on some radio shows when he suffered a stroke. Hospitalized at Columbia Presbyterian Medical Center in New York City, he died there a week later, on November 21, 1945, at the age of fifty-six, and his death was attributed to a cerebral hemorrhage.

Benchley was cremated and the remains buried privately in a family plot on Nantucket Island. His family decided not to use an epitaph he had written for his gravestone: "This is all over my head."

AGATHA CHRISTIE

Agatha Christie is the bestsell-ing novelist of all time, according to the Guinness Book of World Records, and the most translated author in world history, according to UNESCO—and that adds up to a lot of bodies in the library. Known primarily for her sixty-six mur-der mystery novels and numerous  short stories, as well as six romances under the pen name Mary Westmacott, Christie was born Agatha Mary Clarissa Miller to a wealthy family in Torquay, Devonshire, on September 15, 1890.

She married Colonel Archibald Christie in 1914 and worked in the local hospital as a nurse and pharmacy assistant while he was at war. It was there that she learned about the poisons that would figure prominently in many of her murder mysteries.

Her first novel, *The Mysterious Affair at Styles*, published in 1920, featured a detective named Hercule Poirot and estab-lished her as a major mystery writer. Most of her other works featured Poirot, Miss (Jane) Marple, or Tommy and Tuppence Beresford as detectives. All told, they have sold more than two billion copies in more than a hundred languages.

In 1926, Christie herself was the subject of a mystery when she vanished for eleven days. Her husband had asked her for a divorce, saying he was in love with a mutual friend named

Nancy Neele. This evidently unhinged Agatha, and she left home in her Morris Cowley car, which she abandoned in a chalk pit in Surrey. She then took a train to the seaside town of Harrowgate in Yorkshire, where she registered at a hydropathic spa under the name Theresa Neele. Her husband instigated a nationwide search for her. Police were baffled, and even such fellow mystery writers as Sir Arthur Conan Doyle and Dorothy L. Sayers tried to find her. When guests at the spa recognized her, her husband was summoned to bring her home. It was presumed that she was suffering from some form of temporary memory loss, but there was also speculation that she had intended suicide and planned to frame her husband's mistress for her murder.

The Christies finally divorced a year and half later. He married his mistress, and Agatha married the noted archeologist Sir Max Mallowan, who was fifteen years younger. She divided her time between traveling with him to far-flung archeological digs and writing no more than one bestselling mystery per year—limiting her output reputedly in order to avoid excessive income tax. Among her many feats is authorship of the longest-running play in history, *The Mousetrap*, which has had more than 25,000 consecutive performances in London since 1952. In 1971, Christie was made a Dame of the British Empire by Queen Elizabeth II.

In her works, Christie reveals nothing about her religious beliefs or views of death. She was a nominal member of the Church of England, and some critics have viewed her mysteries as Christian allegories of good versus evil. She makes it clear that the Belgian detective Poirot is a devout Catholic, and she had enough interest in religious liturgy to sign a petition to Pope Paul VI asking for continued permission for the Latin mass to be said in Great Britain.

Dame Agatha died at the age of eighty-five on January 12, 1976, at her country home, Winterbrook, near Wallingford in Oxfordshire. Death came "peacefully and gently," according to her husband, and was attributed to unspecified "natural causes," very likely pneumonia resulting from a stubborn cold.

She is buried in the churchyard of St. Mary's, Cholsey, in Oxfordshire. Her estate was valued at only £106,000, since she had shrewdly transferred most of her vast wealth before her death in order to minimize taxes.

DOROTHY L. SAYERS

Dorothy L. Sayers hoped that her translation of Dante's *Divine Comedy* would be her most lasting work, but as fate would have it, she is best remembered for her mysteries featuring the insouciant amateur sleuth Lord Peter Wimsey, whom her readers found less daunting than Dante. Also a playwright, poet, essayist, literary critic, and Christian apologist, Sayers was an only child, born on June 13, 1893, in the headmaster's house of Christ Church Cathedral in Oxford.

Her father, the chaplain there, tutored precocious little Dorothy in Latin when she was six. Dorothy grew up in the village of Bluntisham-cum-Earith in Huntingdonshire, where her father became rector. She won a scholarship to Somerville College, Oxford, and took first-class honours in modern languages and medieval literature—although regulations prevented women from receiving degrees until 1920, when Dorothy belatedly became one of the first women to be awarded an Oxford M.A.

She went to work for a London advertising agency, where her clients included Colman's Mustard and Guinness stout, for whom she created this jingle to accompany the image of a toucan and two glasses of Guinness:

If he can say as you can
"Guinness is good for you,"
How grand to be a Toucan,
Just think what Toucan do.

When she was thirty, Sayers took up motorcycle riding and became infatuated with a fellow biker and car salesman named Bill White, with whom she had a son. She farmed the boy out to a cousin to raise, passing him off as her nephew. She began to write mystery novels, beginning with *Whose Body?* in 1923, followed by a dozen more, including *Clouds of Witness*, *Strong Poison*, *Five Red Herrings*, *Murder Must Advertise*, *The Nine Tailors*, and *Gaudy Night*.

In 1926, Sayers married Captain Oswald Atherton Fleming, a Scottish journalist, and moved to a flat in Bloomsbury, where she lived the rest of her life. Fleming suffered from war injuries and tippled too much—but he was an accomplished cook, and Sayers was an avid appreciator of his cuisine.

A devout high-church Anglican, Sayers wrote influential theological works, lectured extensively, and served as a church-warden in her parish, St. Thomas-cum-St. Anne's in Soho. She devoted the last years of her life to her *magnum opus*, a translation of Dante's *Divine Comedy*, of which *Hell* appeared in 1949, *Purgatory* in 1955, and *Paradise*, completed by her colleague Barbara Reynolds, posthumously in 1962.

A heavy woman who relished her food and drink, and a smoker who often used a clay pipe as a cigarette holder, Sayers fell victim to heart disease in her sixties. On December 17, 1957, she was found by her gardener in the front hall of her London home, dead of a massive coronary thrombosis at the age of sixty-four.

At her funeral service, the eulogy was delivered by her friend and fellow Christian writer C. S. Lewis. Her ashes were interred beneath the tower of her parish church. Sayers left her entire estate to the son she had never acknowledged.

DOROTHY PARKER

Once the queen of quips at the Algonquin Round Table and the wise-
cracking toast of New York's literati,
Dorothy Parker died alone and financially strapped in a rented room, with
only her poodle for company. Born
on August 22, 1893, in Long Branch,
New Jersey, where her parents had
a summer cottage, Parker grew up
on New York's Upper West Side. Her

father was a garment manufacturer named Rothschild (unre-
lated to the banking family), and her mother died shortly after
she was born. Dorothy's staunchly Catholic stepmother sent her
to school at the Convent of the Blessed Sacrament.

After graduating from Miss Dana's Finishing School, Dorothy worked at *Vogue* and *Vanity Fair* magazines and published
her first book of poems, *Enough Rope*, which became a bestseller. She moved on to the *New Yorker* magazine, and with her
pals Robert Benchley, Robert E. Sherwood, Alexander Woollcott, George S. Kaufman, and others formed the witty circle
at the Algonquin Hotel known as the Round Table. A cynical
Parker later called the legendary Algonquin wags "just a bunch
of loudmouths showing off." Author of several books of poetry
and numerous short stories, Parker is said to have coined such
terms as "ball of fire," "with bells on," "birdbrain," "face-lift,"
"doesn't have a prayer," "scaredy-cat," "the sky's the limit," and
"wisecrack."

In 1916, she married a Wall Street Banker named Eddie
Parker, whom she divorced in 1928. Despite her celebrity status, Parker led a troubled life in the 1920s. She drank heavily,
had a string of affairs, underwent an abortion, and attempted
suicide three times.

In the 1930s, she went to Hollywood, married a writer-actor named Alan Campbell, and made pots of money writing screenplays, including the 1937 *A Star Is Born* and Alfred Hitchcock's 1942 *Saboteur.* Parker became identified with liberal political causes, including civil rights and anti-fascist groups.

Her marriage to Campbell, who drank even more than she did and also enjoyed the frequent favors of other women, was stormy, and they divorced, remarried, separated again, then reconciled once more in 1961, remaining together until Campbell died of a drug overdose in 1963. The day he died, a solicitous neighbor came to offer condolences and asked if she could bring the grieving widow anything. "A new husband," said Parker. The stunned neighbor stammered a shocked response to such irreverence. "All right, then," said Parker, "how about a ham and cheese on rye, and tell them to hold the mayo."

Although half-Jewish, half-Scottish, and educated by Catholic nuns, Parker never practiced the religion of Abraham, of Calvin, or of Rome—or any other. She did ponder death on occasion, but always with sardonic humor. She proposed several epitaphs for herself, including "Excuse my dust," "This is on me," and "Wherever she went, including here, it was against her better judgment."

After Campbell's death in California, Parker moved back to New York with her poodle Troy (short for *Troisième*) into a two-room suite on the eighth floor of the Volney Hotel on East 74th Street. When she turned seventy, she said, "If I had any decency, I'd be dead. All my friends are." On June 7, 1967, a hotel housekeeper found Parker in her bed, dead of a heart attack at the age of seventy-three, with Troy in attendance.

As her executor, Parker had named playwright Lillian Hellman, who arranged a funeral at Frank E. Campbell Funeral Chapel. About 150 people attended, including actor Zero Mostel, who spoke, saying, "Dorothy didn't want a funeral service, and if she had her way I suspect she wouldn't be here at all." Parker's good friend Gloria Vanderbilt Cooper was unable to attend, since she was recuperating from having given birth to her son, Anderson. She had, however, furnished the designer dress in which Parker was laid out.

Hellman arranged for Parker's cremation, but neglected to tell the crematory what to do with the ashes, which remained on a shelf for six years, when they were sent to Parker's lawyer, Paul O'Dwyer, in whose filing cabinet they sat for another fifteen years. Finally they were given to the National Association for the Advancement of Colored People, which became the beneficiary of Parker's will after the death of her primary beneficiary, Martin Luther King, Jr. The remains were buried in 1988 at the NAACP national headquarters in Baltimore. Parker's estate consisted of a mere $20,000—but also included future royalties on her work, which still go to the NAACP.

JAMES THURBER

"If I have any beliefs about immortality," James Thurber once said, "it is that certain dogs I have known will go to heaven, and very, very few persons." He didn't say if he thought he was one of the few. Along with Robert Benchley, one of the two leading American humorists of the first half of the twentieth century, Thurber was the son of a frequently unemployed political clerk and an eccentric mother named Mame, whom Thurber called a "born comedienne." Born on December 8, 1894, in Columbus, Ohio, he lost vision in one eye when his brother accidentally shot him with an arrow while playing at "William Tell." Because the eye was not removed, as modern medical practice would indicate, he later lost most of the sight in the other one as well. Thurber attended Ohio State University, but his vision prevented his participation in compulsory ROTC, so he failed to get a degree.

He worked for the American Embassy in Paris, then became a newspaper reporter, first in Columbus and then in New York, while beginning to freelance with pieces of wry humor and whimsical cartoons. Through his friend E. B. White, he met Harold Ross, editor of the *New Yorker*, who hired him as a staff writer. Thurber and White collaborated on *Is Sex Necessary?*, a spoof of sex manuals, which established Thurber's reputation as a major humorist and cartoonist.

He married Althea Adams in 1922, they had one daughter, and they divorced in 1935, when Thurber married his second wife, Helen Wismer, who also became his editor, manager, and caretaker until his death.

Among Thurber's notable works are such books as *The 13 Clocks*, *My World and Welcome to It*, *The Seal in the Bedroom and Other Predicaments*, *The Thurber Carnival*, *The Wonderful O*, *My Life and Hard Times*, *The Middle-Aged Man on the Flying Trapeze*, *Fables for Our Time*, and *The Years With Ross*. Some of them are collections of stories that include the classics "The Unicorn in the Garden," "The Day the Dam Broke," "The Night the Bed Fell," "University Days," "The Catbird Seat," and "The Secret Life of Walter Mitty." With Elliott Nugent, Thurber also wrote a successful Broadway play, *The Male Animal*, and his stories provided material for a revue, *A Thurber Carnival*, in which he sometimes played himself uncredited during the Broadway run.

Very much a man of the world, Thurber was not much given to speculation about an afterlife. His biographer Harrison Kinney observed, "Thurber had never allowed his probing, restless mind to settle on any single theological insurance policy concerning the possibilities of the hereafter. He remained an agnostic."

Although never an actual member of the Algonquin Round Table, Thurber frequently strayed into its gatherings to lift a glass and trade stories with Benchley, Dorothy Parker, George S. Kaufman, and others. A hearty drinker who was especially fond of martinis, Thurber was ejected from more than one New York bar. "One martini is all right," he said, "two are too many, and three are not enough." Also a ladies' man, he prided himself on what he thought of as his sexual prowess into his later years.

Such a rough-and-tumble high life did not result in longevity, and on October 4, 1961, Thurber was stricken with a blood clot of the brain and underwent emergency surgery. As often happens, he developed an infection while in the hospital, lingered several weeks, and died of pneumonia on November 2, at the age of sixty-six. According to his wife, his last intelligible words were, "God bless . . . God damn."

In a graveside service at Greenlawn Cemetery in Columbus, Thurber's ashes were buried in a family plot. His friend and *A Thurber Carnival* director Burgess Meredith attended, along with Thurber's wife, daughter, two brothers, his literary agent, and some forty relatives, friends, and colleagues from Columbus and New York. The Reverend Karl Scheufler, pastor of Columbus's First Methodist Church, read some short prayers.

OSCAR HAMMERSTEIN II

Oscar Hammerstein II is often thought of simply as the second half of "Rodgers and Hammerstein," but he had a major career as author and lyricist before he teamed with Richard Rodgers. Hammerstein (it's "stine" not "steen," as he often pointed out, usually in vain) contributed more than any other single person to the development of American musical theatre. A quintessential New York theatre man, he was born July 12, 1895, in New York City. His grandfather, the first Oscar Hammerstein, was an opera producer who had a Broadway theatre named for him.

Young Oscar's father, William, was the manager of a Manhattan vaudeville theatre, and his Uncle Arthur was a Broadway producer. Although his father was Jewish, Oscar's Scottish Presbyterian mother had him baptized in the Episcopal Church.

Oscar got a law degree at Columbia, but abandoned that career for theatre soon after graduation. His first collaborators were composers Herbert Stothart and Vincent Youmans and librettist Otto Harbach, with whom he wrote the book and lyrics for his first Broadway musical, *Wildflower*, in 1923, followed by *Rose Marie* with composers Stothart and Rudolf Friml. With Jerome Kern, the Harbach-Hammerstein team wrote *Sunny*, and with Sigmund Romberg and Frank Mandel the classic operetta *The Desert Song*.

In 1927, Hammerstein without Harbach teamed with Kern again to create a show that was a watershed in the development of musical theatre. *Show Boat*, based on a novel by Edna Ferber, was a revolutionary musical with an epic plot dealing with such issues as racial and social bigotry, miscegenation, poverty, alcoholism, compulsive gambling, and prostitution. It was also innovative in melding the musical numbers, including such classics as "Ol' Man River," "Make Believe," "Why Do I Love You?," "Can't Help Lovin' Dat Man," and "Bill," organically into the plot. The next important Broadway musical that would advance the art form was *Oklahoma!*—also Hammerstein's creation, in 1943, with his new partner, Richard Rodgers.

In between *Show Boat* and *Oklahoma!*, Hammerstein had a varied career with Kern and others, turning out both hits and flops on Broadway, and writing lyrics for songs that are now standards, such as "Lover, Come Back to Me," "All the Things You Are," "I've Told Every Little Star," "The Song Is You," and

"The Last Time I Saw Paris." His lyrics were typically optimistic, full of hope for better things to come in a basically wholesome world.

By the 1940s, however, Hammerstein's career was fading, so he eagerly accepted an invitation to team with composer Richard Rodgers, who had lost all patience with his alcoholic and often absentee lyricist, Lorenz Hart. Rodgers and Hammerstein produced *Oklahoma!*, which realized Hammerstein's goal of integrating all the elements of a musical—book, music, lyrics, dance, and setting—into a unified whole. After that came more R&H smash hits—*Carousel, South Pacific, The King and I*, and Hammerstein's last show, *The Sound of Music*.

In 1959, several weeks before *The Sound of Music* was to open on Broadway, Hammerstein was diagnosed with stomach cancer. Friends were shocked at his illness, since Hammerstein was the epitome of good health and salubrious habits; a nonsmoker, he drank little and exercised regularly on the tennis court.

Following his surgery, Hammerstein rejected more aggressive treatment and returned to his Bucks County home, Highland Farm, in Doylestown, Pennsylvania, to await the end. He lived several months, and his protégé Stephen Sondheim recalls a lunch at which Hammerstein gave him a photograph of himself, which he had signed, "To Stevie, my pupil and teacher." Hammerstein and his wife, Dorothy, slept side by side in their bedroom, with his morphine doses steadily increasing, until the night he died peacefully, August 23, 1960, at the age of sixty-five.

Hammerstein was cremated and the ashes buried in Ferncliff Cemetery in Hartsdale, New York, after a brief ceremony attended by family and close friends, including his collaborator Rodgers. The Reverend Donald Harrington of New York City's Community Church said prayers and read some lines from Hammerstein's "Climb Every Mountain," and actor-playwright

Howard Lindsay, coauthor of *The Sound of Music*, delivered a eulogy.

On September 1, theatre lights on Broadway were extinguished for one minute in Hammerstein's memory—the first time the lights had gone dark since World War II. London's West End theatres also dimmed their lights in tribute.

F. SCOTT FITZGERALD

Echoing a line spoken by one of the few mourners at the funeral of Jay Gatsby in F. Scott Fitzgerald's *The Great Gatsby*, Dorothy Parker viewed Fitzgerald's body at a Los Angeles funeral home and murmured, "The poor son-of-a-bitch." At the time of his death in 1940, Fitzgerald was generally regarded as a failure, even by himself. His flame had burned brightly as a novelist and writer of short stories in the 1920s "Jazz Age" that inspired his work, but it had flickered and died in the last ten years of his life.

Born on September 24, 1896, in St. Paul, Minnesota, he was named Francis Scott Key, in honor of his distant cousin who wrote "The Star-Spangled Banner." His father, a failed furniture maker and soap salesman, and mother, daughter of an Irish immigrant grocer, sent him to the St. Paul Academy and then to Newman School, an exclusive Catholic prep school in New Jersey. He attended Princeton, wrote scripts for the Triangle Club and stories for the literary magazine, but wound up on academic probation and failed to graduate.

Fitzgerald joined the Army in 1917 and was stationed in Alabama, where he met Zelda Sayre, daughter of a state supreme court justice. The two became engaged, but she broke it off the following year, when the newly discharged Fitzgerald took a job in New York as an advertising copy writer on a tiny salary. Fitzgerald began to write money-making short stories, primarily for *The Saturday Evening Post*, and when his much rewritten first novel, *This Side of Paradise*, was published and he suddenly became famous, Zelda changed her mind. They were married in 1920 in an informal ceremony at New York's St. Patrick's Cathedral, and then embarked on a riotous, hard-drinking life as devil-may-care celebrities.

A second novel, *The Beautiful and the Damned*, was issued the following year, and the Fitzgeralds celebrated with a trip to Paris. They returned to St. Paul for the birth of their only child, a daughter. Drinking more heavily and unable to make progress on his next novel, Fitzgerald took his family back to Paris, and he was able to finish *The Great Gatsby* while hobnobbing with Gerald and Sara Murphy, Cole and Linda Porter, and Ernest Hemingway—and Zelda was flirting with a French aviator she met on a beach.

The Fitzgeralds returned to the United States, and he continued to turn out lucrative short stories, tried his hand (without success) at Hollywood screenplays, and finished his fourth novel, *Tender Is the Night*. Fitzgerald was earning an average of $25,000 annually during the 1920s, equivalent to $300,000-400,000 today, but the high-living couple spent more than he earned. Meanwhile, Zelda was experiencing the beginnings of schizophrenia, which would put her in and out of mental institutions for the rest of her life.

In 1937, suffering chronic ill effects from alcoholism and with his reputation on the wane, Fitzgerald returned to Hollywood and tried once again to write screenplays. During his three years there, he contributed material to several films, but received screen credit for only one: *Three Comrades*, starring Robert Taylor, Margaret Sullavan, Franchot Tone, and Robert

Young. Fitzgerald fell in love with Sheilah Graham, a movie columnist, and after he had a heart attack in Schwab's Drug Store, he moved into Graham's first-floor apartment so he wouldn't have to walk up two flights to his own.

On the evening of December 20, 1940, Fitzgerald and Graham went to the Pantages Theatre to see Rosalind Russell and Melvyn Douglas in a new film, *This Thing Called Love.* Fitzgerald had another heart episode and dizzily staggered out of the theatre, people around him assuming he was drunk. He didn't seek medical help because he was planning to see his own physician the following day. The next afternoon, at Graham's apartment, while munching a Hershey bar, listening to a recording of Beethoven's "Eroica" symphony, and reading the *Princeton Alumni News*, Fitzgerald suddenly jumped up, gasped, clutched the mantelpiece, and fell dead of a final heart attack at the age of forty-four. Sheilah tried vainly to revive him by pouring brandy through his clenched teeth.

Fitzgerald's will stipulated that he be given "the cheapest funeral and burial." His body was shipped to Bethesda, Maryland, where about thirty people, including his daughter, Scottie, and his editor Maxwell Perkins, attended a simple funeral home ceremony, at which Fitzgerald was laid out wearing a necktie in Princeton's orange and black colors. He had hoped to be buried with his parents at St. Mary's Catholic Cemetery in Rockville, but the Archbishop of Baltimore regarded Fitzgerald, who had not practiced Catholicism since his teens, as an apostate and refused permission. Instead he was interred at the nondenominational Rockville Cemetery, where Zelda was also buried after her death in a fire at a North Carolina hospital in 1948. In 1975, with a new archbishop in place, Scottie at last obtained permission to allow burial at St. Mary's, and both Fitzgerald bodies were exhumed and reinterred. Scottie joined them there in 1986.

WILLIAM FAULKNER

Novelist William Faulkner, who regularly earned Ds in English at the University of Mississippi, won the Nobel Prize for Literature anyway. There must be a moral there somewhere. Faulkner, who was born September 25, 1897, in New Albany, Mississippi, had a sketchy education. His mother and grandmother were great readers, and he grew up with the novels of Charles Dickens and the tales of the Brothers Grimm,  before attending but not finishing high school, and then attending—but not graduating from—Ole Miss.

He served in both the Canadian and British air forces in World War I, worked for a while in a New York bookstore, spent time in Paris, and wrote for a New Orleans newspaper before settling down in Oxford, Mississippi, where he lived most of his life. During his time in New Orleans, he was befriended by the established novelist Sherwood Anderson, who helped him get his first novel, *Soldier's Pay*, published in 1925. Faulkner's other principal works were *The Sound and the Fury*; *Sanctuary*; *Requiem for a Nun*; *As I Lay Dying*; *Light in August*; *Absalom, Absalom!*; *Intruder in the Dust*; *A Fable*; and his final novel, *The Reivers*, published in 1962, the year of his death. He won Pulitzer Prizes for *A Fable* and *The Reivers*, which ironically are both considered among his "minor" works. The Nobel Prize came in 1949.

Faulkner married Estelle Oldham in 1929. She was his childhood sweetheart, but her family had insisted she marry a young lawyer whose future seemed brighter than Faulkner's.

That marriage failed, and Estelle and Faulkner were reunited and settled down at Rowan Oak, a house on twenty-nine acres that Faulkner bought in Oxford. He tried to support his wife, their daughter, and his two stepchildren with his short stories and novels, but MGM beckoned with much more lucrative opportunities as a screenwriter. Faulkner spent much of the 1930s and 1940s in Hollywood, creating and doctoring scripts for such movies as *Gunga Din, Drums Along the Mohawk, To Have and Have Not, God Is My Co-Pilot, Mildred Pierce,* and *The Big Sleep.*

Although known as a hard drinker, Faulkner rarely imbibed heavily while he was working, preferring to celebrate completion of a project with a bourbon binge. "There is no such thing as bad whiskey," he was quoted. "Some whiskeys just happen to be better than others. But a man shouldn't fool with booze until he's fifty; then he's a damn fool if he doesn't."

Faulkner also had numerous sexual liaisons, including one three-year affair with a woman he met at the Nobel Prize ceremony, the widow of a journalist who had introduced Faulkner's works to Sweden.

Faulkner's religious views were vague. Raised as a Methodist, he was married in a Presbyterian church, and joined but rarely attended St. Peter's Episcopal Church in Oxford. There are spiritual overtones in all his work, and in his Nobel Prize acceptance speech, Faulkner asserted the immortality of the human soul. Whether this meant he expected a personal afterlife is not clear.

On June 17, 1962, Faulkner took his horse Stonewall out for a ride in a forested area near Rowan Oak. As Faulkner's friend and biographer Joseph Leo Blotner relates, Stonewall, who was known to be intractable, was spooked and threw Faulkner to the ground. Badly hurt, Faulkner limped back to Rowan Oak, where he found the horse. Despite agonizing back pain, he mounted him again and made several jumps. When Faulkner's doctor told him he could have killed himself, he replied, "You don't think I'd let that damned horse conquer me, do you? I had to conquer him."

The pain from his injury wouldn't go away, and Faulkner was forced to get around on crutches as he began to drink even more heavily than his usual generous allotment. On the night of July 5, he felt worse and was taken to Wright's Sanatorium, a private clinic in nearby Byhalia, where Faulkner had sometimes stayed to recover from binges. At one-thirty the next morning, he awoke, groaned, and collapsed with a myocardial infarction. Doctors tried to revive him for forty-five minutes, but Faulkner was dead at the age of sixty-four.

The simple funeral service at Rowan Oak was conducted by the Reverend Duncan Gray, rector of St. Peter's Church, and attended by only a handful of mourners, including the immediate family, writers William Styron and Shelby Foote, and publisher Bennett Cerf. The body was then taken in a sixteen-car motorcade around the Oxford town square and buried at St. Peter's Cemetery. Faulkner wished his epitaph to read simply: "He made the books and he died."

FEDERICO GARCÍA LORCA

Federico García Lorca's brilliant literary flame was snuffed out by a rain of bullets when he was thirty-eight. The details of his assassination and the whereabouts of his body remain mysteries to this day. Regarded as the most important playwright and poet of modern Spain, García Lorca was born June 5, 1898, in Fuente Vaqueros, a small town near Granada. His father was a farm owner and his mother a concert pianist. Federico attended local schools and then studied law briefly at Sacred Heart University.

He moved to Madrid and plunged into the literary and theatrical world. He produced performances of his plays, organized readings of his poetry, published his first book, and became part of an artist group including filmmaker Luis Buñuel and painter Salvador Dalí. Lorca and Dalí were especially close and may have been lovers. In 1929, Lorca visited New York, haunting the jazz clubs, literary circles, and art galleries in Harlem.

Returning to Spain the following year, he produced his most famous folk tragedies, *Blood Wedding*, *Yerma*, and *The House of Bernarda Alba*. Lorca was developing into a multitalented artist: playwright, poet, actor, director, designer, pianist, guitarist, painter, and essayist, and is now the most widely translated Spanish author of all time. While immersing himself in artistic creation, Lorca also involved himself in Liberal political causes as Fascist opposition to Spain's republican government developed.

In addition to his attachment to Dalí, Lorca also had a passionate relationship with an art critic named Juan Ramírez de Lucas, who was not yet twenty at the time. Lorca's homosexual orientation and his rebellion against dogmas of any kind put him at odds with the Church, and he bitterly rejected all organized religion—although he identified deeply with Jesus Christ, even writing a play about him.

Death was an obsession for Lorca, and he had often sensed omens of his own demise. "Life is laughter," he once said, "amidst a rosary of death." When a close friend, who was a matador, was killed in the bullring, Lorca felt it was a "trial run" for his own death. In 1936, when military uprisings erupted in Spain, Lorca wanted to leave Madrid and return to his family home in Granada, but his friend Buñuel warned him, "Stay here. Dreadful things will happen to you." Lorca went anyway to his family home, Callejones de García, and three days later, the Spanish Civil War broke out.

With Granada in the hands of the Fascist forces of General Francisco Franco, Lorca was in serious peril from right-wing, pro-Franco death squads, who targeted him not only for his left-wing views, but also for his homosexual lifestyle. As Lorca's biographer Ian Gibson relates, on August 17, 1936, Lorca was arrested by pro-Franco forces and thrown into jail. On August 19, he was taken to Fuente Grande, on the road between Viznar and Alfacar, supposedly to visit his brother-in-law, the Socialist former mayor of Granada, whom the soldiers had in fact killed earlier. Thirty-eight-year-old Lorca was clubbed senseless with rifle butts and then, together with two bullfighters who were anarchists and a leftist schoolteacher with only one leg, he was riddled with bullets. His body has never been found. Franco, who won the civil war and ruled Spain as an iron-handed dictator for thirty-six years, died in 1975 and is still dead.

ERNEST HEMINGWAY

"The real reason for not committing suicide," wrote Ernest Hemingway when he was twenty-seven, "is because you always know how swell life gets again after the hell is over." By the time the Nobel Prize-winning novelist was sixty-one, life was no longer getting swell again, and he failed to follow his own advice.

Hemingway was born to a physician and his musician wife in Cicero, Illinois, on July 21, 1899. His childhood was peculiar for a man later famous for rugged machismo: until he was six, his mother frequently dressed him as a girl and called him "Ernestine." Hemingway did get early experience as an outdoorsman when he hunted, fished, and camped with his father. In high school Hemingway excelled at boxing, track and field, football—and English.

Shunning college, he found work as a reporter for the *Kansas City Star*, whose stylebook provided a guide for Hemingway's later fiction style: "Use short sentences. Use short first paragraphs. Use vigorous English. Be positive, not negative."

At the outbreak of World War I, Hemingway volunteered for ambulance service at the Italian front. Seriously wounded, he returned to the United States and married the first of four wives, Hadley Richardson, a reclusive woman of delicate health who was eight years older than Hemingway. The couple moved to Paris, where Hemingway wrote dispatches for the *Toronto Star* and began to associate with the "lost generation" of expatriate writers—Gertrude Stein, James Joyce, Ford Madox Ford, and Ezra Pound.

In 1926 Hemingway published his first novel, *The Sun Also Rises*, and the following year he divorced Hadley and married Pauline Pfeiffer, an Arkansas heiress who worked in Paris for *Vogue*. Pfeiffer was a Roman Catholic, and Hemingway nominally converted, but there is no evidence that he ever practiced his new-found religion. He probably believed, as he once wrote, that "all thinking men are atheists."

The Hemingways returned to the United States, dividing their time between Wyoming and Key West, Florida, as Hemingway honed his skills as a world-renowned novelist, daring sportsman—and champion drinker, fortified by the rum elixirs of a local bar called Sloppy Joe's. *A Farewell to Arms* came out in 1929, and in 1933 Hemingway went to Africa, where a safari provided ideas for his short stories "The Snows of Kilimanjaro" and "The Short Happy Life of Francis Macomber."

In 1937, Hemingway went to Spain to report on the civil war. He was joined there by Martha Gellhorn, a journalist he had met in Key West. She inspired him to write his most famous novel, *For Whom the Bell Tolls*, published in 1940, the same year that he divorced Pauline and made Martha Mrs. Hemingway No. 3.

During World War II, Hemingway was in London and Europe and began to spend time with Mary Welsh, a *Time* magazine correspondent. Always eager to be at the front lines, Hemingway was at the Normandy landings, the liberation of Paris, and the Battle of the Bulge. He was awarded a Bronze Star for bravery. Mary became the fourth and final Mrs. Hemingway in 1946.

Hemingway, whose career was at an ebb in the late 1940s, had a home in Cuba, where he wrote *The Old Man and the Sea*, which returned him to literary prominence—leading to the Nobel Prize in 1954.

On an African trip, two successive plane crashes left him with two cracked vertebral discs, kidney and liver damage, a dislocated shoulder, and a fractured skull. He was in poor health the rest of his life and self-medicated with increasingly large doses of liquor. On a visit to Paris, Hemingway discovered some unpublished manuscripts from the 1920s in a trunk he had stored at the Ritz Hotel, and this provided material for his memoir *A Moveable Feast*. Ailing with arteriosclerosis, liver disease, diabetes, and hypertension, he left Cuba with Mary and settled in Ketchum, Idaho.

Suicide was frequently on Hemingway's mind and shows up in his writing. He sometimes speculated about ending his life by jumping overboard from an ocean liner. He once threatened—perhaps not seriously—to open fire with a tommygun in the offices of *The New Republic* and then kill himself. In *To Have and Have Not*, published in 1937 in the Great Depression, when suicide was a way out for those who had lost everything, Hemingway provided a whole catalogue of the means by which those unfortunates took their leave: jumping from office windows, breathing carbon monoxide from automobile exhausts, shooting themselves in the head. In the last year of his life, Hemingway wrote, "A long life deprives a man of his optimism. [It is better] to die happy . . . to go out in a blaze of light, than to have your body worn out and old and illusions shattered."

A manic-depressive, Hemingway developed paranoia and believed, actually with some justification, that the FBI was spying on him. In February of 1961, he received shock treatments at the Mayo Clinic. After he returned to Idaho, Mary found him one morning in April sitting at the kitchen window with a loaded shotgun. She shipped him off to Mayo for more electroshock, and he returned to Ketchum on June 30.

Mary had locked his guns in the basement, but crafty old Hemingway knew where the keys were, and early Sunday morning, July 2, dressed in robe and pajamas, he took a twelve-gauge shotgun to the front foyer, loaded both barrels, put the gun to his forehead, and fired. Dr. Scott Earle was summoned at 7:40 a.m., and his death certificate stated that Hemingway had accidentally shot himself cleaning his gun, but Mary later acknowledged that his death at the age of sixty-one was suicide.

Medical records released after Hemingway's death disclosed that he suffered from hemochromatosis, an inability to metabolize iron. Among its symptoms are liver disease and diabetes, as well as some mental deterioration. It is a genetic disorder and, left untreated as it was, may have been a contributing factor in the suicides not only of Hemingway, but also his father, his brother, his sister, and a granddaughter.

Hemingway's funeral at the Ketchum Cemetery was private, with only Mary, Hemingway's three sons, and a few other family members and close friends. Hemingway's body was dressed casually in a sport coat and slacks. The Reverend Robert J. Waldemann, pastor of Our Lady of the Snows Catholic Church in Ketchum, offered prayers at the gravesite as an altar boy, overcome by heat or emotion, fainted and fell on the coffin.

HART CRANE

Poet Harold Hart Crane might well have been a fabulously wealthy heir to a candy fortune had it not been for one fateful business transaction. His father, Clarence Crane, invented Life Savers mints, but sold the patent for the popular circular sweet to a couple of advertising men for the grand sum of $2,900. Although the elder Crane continued to do well enough financially with chocolate bars, he and his wife, a Christian Scientist, were constantly bickering, and Har-

old, born July 21, 1899, in Garrettsville, Ohio—the same day as Ernest Hemingway—grew up in a troubled household. He dropped out of high school and moved to Cleveland, where he worked as an ad copywriter, then to New York, then back to Ohio to work in his father's chocolate factory.

Dropping his first name and going by Hart, Crane published a volume of enigmatic lyrical verses called *White Buildings*, which attracted favorable attention from Eugene O'Neill, Randall Jarrell, and Allen Tate. Back in New York, where he felt at home, Crane moved in with his lover, a young Danish merchant sailor, whose father had a home in Brooklyn Heights. From there, Crane could see the Brooklyn Bridge, which was the inspiration for his epic *The Bridge*, "a mystical synthesis of America," which he was sure would rival T. S. Eliot's *The Waste Land* in poetic significance.

Crane moved to Paris in 1929 to continue his work on the poem, but spent much of his time getting drunk and carousing with sailors. After a brawl in a Paris bar, he was fined and jailed in *La Santé*, the reassuringly named "Prison of Good Health." A friend bailed him out and gave him money to return to the United States, where he finished *The Bridge*. It was savaged by critics, and Crane felt that his life was pointless.

Influenced in his youth by his mother's Christian Science, Crane employed many Christian symbols in his poetry, although in such an opaquely symbolic way that his beliefs are difficult to discern. The critic Harold Bloom characterizes Crane's personal religion as an "inchoate mixture of a Christian Science background, an immersion in Ouspensky [the Russian scholar of esoteric religion], and an all but Catholic yearning."

With a Guggenheim fellowship, Crane went to Mexico in 1931, intending to write an epic about the Aztecs, but it was not completed, and his major accomplishment was a love poem called "The Broken Tower." He was accompanied to Mexico by his only known heterosexual romantic interest, Peggy Cowley, recently divorced from writer Malcolm Cowley.

But Crane just couldn't leave the sailors alone, and on the steamer *Orizaba*, en route from Mexico back to New York, he made sexual advances to a young crew member who didn't take kindly to Crane's attention and beat him severely, leaving him bruised and bloody with a black eye.

Crane, whose body and mind were already damaged by years of heavy drinking, administered first aid to himself with copious amounts of alcohol, internally applied. In a whisky-soaked daze just before noon on April 27, 1932, he approached the ship's rail, removed and neatly folded the light topcoat he wore over pajamas, waved to several onlookers, cried, "Goodbye, everybody!" and threw himself overboard into the Atlantic Ocean, some 250 miles north of Havana and ten miles east of Florida. Someone shouted, "Man overboard!" Lifeboats were dispatched for about two hours, but his body was never recovered, and it was speculated that a shark might have devoured him. Crane was thirty-two years old.

NOËL COWARD

Celebrated as "the Master" for his frivolous wit, stylish stage presence, and prodigious output of sophisticated plays, musicals, and songs, Noël Coward was also an unlikely wartime spy. Born in the London suburb of Teddington on December 16, 1899, Coward made his professional stage debut at age eleven, playing Prince Mussel in "The Goldfish."

Coward's path to success was primarily through his plays, beginning in 1924 with his first big hit, *The Vortex*, and continuing with some fifty more, mostly comedies of upper-class manners, including *Hay Fever*, *Private Lives*, *Design for Living*, *Tonight at 8:30*, *Present Laughter*, *Blithe Spirit*, and *Nude with Violin*. He also composed hundreds of songs for revues and his own cabaret performances; wrote poetry and short stories; created a dozen musical theatre pieces, notably *Bitter Sweet* and *Sail Away!*; and acted and directed on stage and in films. Among his most enduring songs are "Mad Dogs and Englishmen," "I Went to a Marvellous Party," "Mad About the Boy," "I'll See You Again," "Someday I'll Find You," "I'll Follow My Secret Heart," "The Stately Homes of England," "The Party's Over," "Poor Little Rich Girl," "London Pride," and his satirical war song, "Don't Let's Be Beastly to the Germans."

Coward always insisted on using the diaeresis, the two dots over the "e" in "Noël," claiming that without it, his name would be pronounced something like "Nool."

In World War II, Coward volunteered to work with the British secret service, collecting information and influencing public opinion during his overseas travel. He also headed the British propaganda office in Paris.

Coward was always reticent about sex, partly because homosexual activity was in violation of British law until six years before his death. He had affairs with several men, including actors Louis Hayward and Alan Webb, producer-director John C. Wilson, and composer Ned Rorem. (Rorem told an interviewer that sleeping with Coward was unexciting, since they were both unadventurous in bed.) Coward's longest lasting relationship was with the actor Graham Payn, from the 1940s until Coward's death. Although his sexual orientation was an open secret, Coward never acknowledged it, noting drolly, "There are still one or two old ladies in Worthing who don't know." Coward was denied a knighthood by Prime Minister Winston Churchill, partly owing to his homosexuality and partly because of his violation of some post-war currency regulations. The sexual issue arose again in 1969—along with Coward's avoidance of British taxes by maintaining homes in Switzerland and Jamaica—when Prime Minister Harold Wilson also objected to a knighthood. The royal family, who were close friends of Coward's, overruled that decision, and he was finally knighted by Queen Elizabeth II in 1969.

An avowed agnostic, Coward wrote a poem called "Do I Believe in God?" in which his answer was that he couldn't say yes, and he couldn't say no. In various diary notations, he expressed his disbelief in an afterlife and his wish that death would bring "ultimate oblivion." When he was sixty-six and feared he might have cancer, Coward stoically wrote in his diary, "I don't relish prolonged illness . . . and attenuated death. But I suppose I shall have to cope with it as well as I can."

Beset by debilitating arthritis, pleurisy, and advancing arteriosclerosis during the last three years of his life, Coward suffered memory loss and lack of mobility that made acting and writing impossible. In a 1971 letter, he complained that his doctor had ordered him to walk every day to maintain circulation in his legs, and he confessed that he hoped he wouldn't live too long, asking that Fate "let me go to sleep when it's my proper bedtime." On a wall at Firefly Estate, his home in Jamaica, is Coward's last poem, which comments wistfully on his approaching end. It echoes Keats' "When I have fears that I may cease to be," but unlike Keats, Coward finds consolation in his memories and in the peaceful sea.

Coward made his last public appearance on January 14, 1973, at a New York performance of *Oh, Coward!*, a revue of his songs—on the arm of his close friend, Marlene Dietrich. Bent nearly double, he painfully made his way with her up three flights to reach their seats. The next day he, Payn, and his secretary, Cole Lesley, returned to Firefly, where he spent his evenings sipping brandy and ginger ale and watching the birds around his swimming pool.

On Sunday evening, March 25, he told Payn and Lesley, "Good night, my darlings, I'll see you tomorrow," and retired to his second-floor bedroom. Early the next morning, the housekeeper, Imogene Graves, heard him moaning in his room and called the butler, Miguel Fraser. The two tried unsuccessfully to gain entry through the locked bedroom door, and Fraser then brought a ladder to the outside window and climbed in. He found Coward facedown on the bathroom floor, moved him to the bed, and called a doctor. Gentlemanly to the end, Coward insisted that the household not be disturbed until morning. He died of a coronary thrombosis just before dawn at the age of seventy-three.

Coward had frequently said he wished to be buried wherever he died, so Payn and Lesley arranged for interment at Firefly

Hill. The British High Commissioner and an attaché from the Governor-General's office attended the simple service conducted by the Bishop of Kingston and the local vicar, as Coward was laid to rest in a plain oak coffin placed in a concrete tomb in the garden near his house.

Westminster Abbey refused to allow a London memorial service, since Coward "was not a church-goer," so the church of St. Martin's-in-the-Fields in Trafalgar Square was the venue for an event on May 29 that included a poem written and read by Poet Laureate John Betjeman, Laurence Olivier's reading of Psalm 100, John Gielgud's reading of Shakespeare's "Sonnet XXX," and violinist Yehudi Menuhin's playing of a Bach sonata. Mourners in attendance included Lord Mountbatten, the Duke of Kent, the Earl of Snowdon, David Niven, Ralph Richardson, Charlie Chaplin, Ava Gardner, Liza Minnelli, and Peter Sellers. Coward's patriotic song "London Pride" concluded the service.

Years later, Westminster Abbey deigned to allow a stone honoring Coward to be placed in Poets' Corner. It was unveiled by Queen Elizabeth, the Queen Mother, one of Coward's closest friends.

EVELYN WAUGH

Imagine the confusion in the household of novelist Evelyn Waugh during the time that he was married to a woman whose name was also Evelyn. Friends even had to resort to calling them "He-Evelyn" and "She-Evelyn." Even though Evelyn (usually pronounced EE-vuh-lin) is a fairly common name in Britain for both men and women, to Waugh's great annoyance, the *Times Literary*

Supplement's review of his first novel referred to him as "Miss Waugh."

Arthur Evelyn St. John Waugh, called Evelyn to distinguish him from his father, also named Arthur, was born on October 28, 1903, in West Hampstead in north London. Son of a publishing executive, he was the younger brother of Alec Waugh, who also became a novelist of note. Evelyn attended Lancing College, where he was said to be a belligerent boy who bullied younger students, among them Cecil Beaton, later a famous photographer and designer. At Hertford College in Oxford, Evelyn had a zesty social life and an undistinguished academic career, earning a third-class degree in history, sometimes known as a "gentleman's third." He taught school for a while, wrote a well-received biography of Dante Gabriel Rossetti, and worked as a freelance journalist and reviewer.

Waugh married Evelyn Gardner in 1928, the same year that *Decline and Fall*, the first of several savagely satirical novels skewering British society, made Waugh a celebrity. It was followed in the 1930s and 1940s by *Vile Bodies, Black Mischief, A Handful of Dust, Scoop, Put Out More Flags, Brideshead Revisited*, and *The Loved One*, in which he turned his mordant wit on the funeral industry in California.

Waugh became a Roman Catholic in 1930 and remained a staunch traditionalist throughout his life, opposing changes made by the Second Vatican Council and championing the Latin mass. In 1934, he and Evelyn were divorced (a hard-won papal annulment followed), and three years later he married Laura Herbert, with whom he had six children, including the writer Auberon Waugh.

During World War II, Waugh served as a captain in the Royal Marines, but saw very little combat. After the war, he suffered a mental breakdown, which he self-medicated for the rest of his life with ample quantities of liquor, cigars, and various opiates—which he reputedly gave up every year for Lent.

More novels, travel books, and biographies flowed from his pen during the 1950s and early 1960s, as Waugh gained a reputation as an irascible, bigoted, embittered curmudgeon. He hated having visitors at his country home, disdained talking on the telephone, and refused to drive a car. His son Auberon said that if an afterlife existed, the last person he would wish to meet there was his father. The author Nancy Mitford once asked Waugh how he could behave so abominably to other people and yet still consider himself a practicing Catholic. "You have no idea," Waugh replied, "how much nastier I would be if I was not a Catholic. Without supernatural aid I would hardly be a human being."

On Easter Sunday, April 10, 1966, having attended mass— Latin, of course—at the nearby village of Wiveliscombe, Waugh was in the toilet at Combe Florey, his home in Somerset, when he collapsed of a heart attack. He was found with a gash on his head from having hit it on the door handle, and the family's cook tried mouth-to-mouth resuscitation in a vain attempt to revive him. When a doctor arrived, all he could do was pro- nounce Waugh dead, at the age of sixty-two.

Waugh's daughter Margaret wrote to a friend: "You know how he longed to die and dying as he did on Easter Sunday, when all the liturgy is about death and resurrection, after a Latin mass and holy communion, would be exactly what he wanted. I am sure he had prayed for death at Mass."

The novelist Graham Greene, a fellow Catholic, commented on Waugh's passing in a radio broadcast: "It was Easter Sun- day, symbolizing his religion, and he died . . . on the lavatory . . . symbolizing his humor." It was Greene who also maintained, perhaps with more than a touch of facetiousness, that Waugh had killed himself by drowning in the toilet bowl.

Waugh was buried on a snowy day in a plot consecrated by a Catholic priest just outside the Anglican churchyard in Combe Florey. Only family and close friends attended. A Latin requiem mass on April 21 was celebrated before a packed congregation at London's Westminster Cathedral.

GRAHAM GREENE

"I suppose I'd call myself a Catholic atheist," the novelist Graham Greene once said. "I don't like conventional religious piety. I've always found it difficult to believe in God." A convert in 1926 so that he could marry devout Catholic Vivienne Dayrell-Browning, Greene took the confirmation name of St. Thomas— the Doubter. His work is infused with theological questions, but always with morally ambiguous answers. In an interview in his eighties, he amended his self-description to "Catholic agnostic."

Denied a Nobel Prize (it was rumored that the left-wing judges considered him too Catholic, and the right-wing judges thought him too much a Communist), he nonetheless received Britain's highest honors from Queen Elizabeth II—the exclusive Order of Merit and elevation as a Companion of Honour.

Greene was born October 2, 1904, at St. John's House, a faculty house at Berkhamsted School in Hertfordshire, England, where his father taught and later was headmaster. The fourth of six children, he had an older brother, Raymond, who became a noted physician, and a younger brother, Hugh, who rose to the post of director-general of the BBC. Greene attended Berkhamsted School and then Balliol College, Oxford. Bipolar from an early age, he attempted suicide several times—by Russian roulette, overdosing on aspirins, and swallowing eyedrops, hay fever lotion, and deadly nightshade. His Oxford contemporary

Evelyn Waugh said of him, "He looked down on the rest of us as childish and ostentatious. He certainly shared in none of our revelry."

After taking a second-class degree in history, Greene worked briefly as a tutor, then became a journalist, first with the *Nottingham Journal* and then with the *Times* in London. The success in 1929 of his first novel, *The Man Within*, enabled him to quit his day job and devote himself to fiction, travel books, and film reviewing.

One of his reviews—of *Wee Willie Winkie* starring Shirley Temple—provoked a libel suit by Twentieth Century Fox on behalf of its wee star. The studio alleged that Greene had implied that Temple deliberately played to "a public of licentious old men, ready to enjoy the fine flavour of such an unripe, charming little creature." In his review, Greene commented on the eight-year-old Shirley's "neat and well-developed rump," "agile studio eyes," and "dimpled depravity." Infuriated by the lawsuit, Greene complained, "The little bitch is going to cost me £250—if I'm lucky." In fact, the suit was settled for £500, and Shirley Temple later said she forgave him for what he wrote.

Greene divided his fiction into two categories: thrillers of a sort, which he called "entertainments," and serious novels. The entertainments included *Stamboul Train, A Gun for Sale, The Confidential Agent, The Ministry of Fear, The Third Man,* and *Our Man in Havana,* and notable among the novels are *Brighton Rock, The Power and the Glory, The Heart of the Matter, The End of the Affair, The Quiet American, A Burnt-Out Case, The Comedians, Travels with My Aunt, The Honorary Consul,* and *The Human Factor.* Many of them were made into successful movies. Greene also wrote travel books about his sojourns in Africa, the Caribbean, and Asia, and several plays that were hits on the West End and on Broadway.

In 1953, the Holy Office of the Catholic Church put *The Power and the Glory* on its index of forbidden books, owing to its anti-clerical theme. Greene later had a private audience with Pope Paul VI, who told him he had read and enjoyed the book, and Greene should pay no attention to the critics.

During World War II, Greene was recruited into MI6, Britain's spy agency, by his sister Elizabeth, and was posted to Sierra Leone. During his years in espionage, he befriended Kim Philby and spoke out for him when Philby was later charged with treason as a double agent.

Greene and Vivienne had two children and separated in 1947. They never divorced, although Greene had dozens of affairs, including long-lasting ones with two mistresses, Catherine Walston (with whom he reportedly once had sex in the backseat of a car while her husband was driving) and Yvonne Cloetta, and flings with Australian artist Jocelyn Rickards and Swedish sexpot Anita Bjork. An opium smoker and an alcoholic, Greene had a seemingly insatiable sexual appetite, which he often satisfied with visits to brothels.

In 1966, having lost a great deal of money in a swindle, Greene moved to Antibes in order to be near Yvonne Cloetta. In the 1970s, diagnosed with leukemia, he moved to Vevey, on Lake Geneva, in Switzerland, to be near his daughter. He often visited with his neighbor in Vevey, Charlie Chaplin.

In March of 1991, Greene fell gravely ill with the leukemia he had managed for years. He was rushed to La Providence Hospital in Vevey. While he had ceased going to mass and confession almost forty years earlier, Greene had recently begun to receive communion again from the Reverend Leopoldo Durán, a Spanish priest who was the model for the protagonist of Greene's novel *Monsignor Quixote* and with whom Greene liked to lift a glass or two. Durán was summoned from Madrid to the hospital, and at Greene's funeral he gave this account of the dying man's final moments:

I told him most directly, "Graham, God is waiting for you just now—pray for us where you will be for ever in God's blessing. I now give the last absolution." This I did. He passed away in the most peaceful manner. Without a gesture, he fell asleep. My faith tells me that he is now with God or on the way there.

Greene had refused to see his estranged wife, but was persuaded to allow his son, Francis, to visit. Just before lapsing into a coma, Greene cried, "Why must it take so long to come?" Death did come, just before noon on Wednesday, April 3. Greene was eighty-six years old.

The funeral was held in the Church of St. Jean in Corseaux, attended by both Greene's wife, Vivienne (now styled Vivien), and his latest mistress, Yvonne. His son, Francis, his daughter, Caroline Bourget, a grandson, and other family members were also there, as was the honorary British consul for Nice and Antibes. Burial was in the Cimetière des Monts-de-Corsier.

A sung Latin requiem mass was offered for Greene the first week of June at London's Westminster Cathedral. The homilist was the Reverend Roderick Strange, former chaplain of Oxford University. Two fellow Catholics, novelist Muriel Spark and actor Alec Guinness, also spoke. Greene's niece, Louise Dennys, recalled some words her uncle had written a few days before he died: "Sometimes I pray not *for* dead friends but *to* dead friends, asking their help. I picture Paradise as a place of activity."

SAMUEL BECKETT

Samuel Beckett liked to say that he was born on Good Friday, April 13, 1906, the day on which Christ's crucifixion is commemorated, and to use that coincidence to draw parallels between the suffering of Christ and of the desperate characters who inhabited the bleak world of his plays and novels. One minor inconvenience, however, is that Beckett's birth certificate insists that the date was Sunday, May 13. There is no dispute about the place— Foxrock, a well-to-do suburb of Dublin. A sickly child who constantly cried, Beckett later claimed to have vivid memories of his prenatal life in the womb—"an existence where no voice, no possible movement could free me from the agony and darkness I was subjected to."

Be that as it may, he grew up in the Protestant Church of Ireland, attended the Royal Portora School in County Fermanagh, where Oscar Wilde had also been a student, and then Trinity College, Dublin, where he studied English, French, and Italian, and excelled at cricket, earning a listing in the *Wisden Cricketers' Almanack*.

After graduating from the university, he went to Paris to teach in the École Normale Supérieure, began publishing stories and essays, and rubbed elbows with expatriate Irish literati, including James Joyce, for whom he worked as an assistant on *Finnegans Wake*. Beckett returned to Trinity College for a year, but then settled more or less permanently in Paris, where he began to write in French because it made it easier for him to write "without style." He published his first novel, *Murphy*, in 1938 and adopted a bohemian Parisian lifestyle, having an affair with socialite art collector Peggy Guggenheim. On one occasion, Beckett was nearly killed when he was stabbed for refusing the solicitation of a pimp. Joyce arranged a VIP hospital room for him, and he was looked after by a friend named Suzanne Decheveaux-Dumesnil, who became his lifelong companion and eventually his wife.

During World War II, Beckett joined the French Resistance in occupied Paris as a courier. A French traitor revealed his identity to the Gestapo, and Beckett and Suzanne fled to the south of France, where he continued to aid the Resistance by storing munitions in his back garden. He was awarded the Croix de Guerre and the Médaille de la Résistance for bravery, but later downplayed his exploits as "boy scout stuff."

In the 1950s, he completed his trilogy of novels, *Molloy*, *Malone Dies*, and *The Unnameable*, and turned his attention to dramas, in order to move out of Joyce's shadow. He also began an affair with Barbara Bray, a BBC editor, whose affections he juggled with those of Suzanne for the rest of his life.

Beckett's most famous work, *Waiting for Godot*, premiered in 1953 before an audience of the playwright's friends and a few high-brow theatre-goers at Paris's 230-seat Théâtre de Babylone. As became his custom with all his plays, Beckett skipped the opening. The play puzzled critics and was followed by a London production, which was generally dismissed, except by Harold Hobson of the *Sunday Times*, who said it would "securely lodge in a corner of your mind as long as you live." New York critics were equally unimpressed, and it was several years before *Godot* was recognized as one of the great works of twentieth-century theatre.

Other plays—notably *Endgame*, *Krapp's Last Tape*, and *Happy Days*—followed, and Beckett won the Nobel Prize for Literature in 1969, an event that Suzanne regarded as a "catastrophe," because it would make him a public figure and destroy the privacy he cherished.

Beckett's stark outlook on life is evident in the story told by a friend who was walking with him one fine spring morning in Paris. "Ahh," said the friend, "doesn't a day like this make you feel glad to be alive?" Beckett answered, "I wouldn't go as far as that."

Beckett used Christian symbolism throughout his work, acknowledging that it was natural for him to do so, since

Christianity was a "mythology" with which he was perfectly familiar. One critic, Colin Duckworth, maintained that Beckett could not "make up his mind about God and His intentions toward His creatures. Hence, his attitude toward things divine varies from the scatological to the reverent." "What do I know about man's destiny?" Beckett said. "I could tell you more about radishes."

Devoted to thin, dark Gitanes cigarettes, bolstered by espresso and Irish whiskey, in which he indulged during late-night conversations in cafés, Beckett was diagnosed with emphysema when he turned eighty and began to use a portable oxygen machine.

When he injured himself in a fall at his apartment, Beckett moved at the suggestion of his physician into Le Tiers Temps, a modest, public nursing home in the Montparnasse district of Paris. He had a sparsely furnished room, painted dark blue, with a bed, a wardrobe, an overhead light fixture with three bare bulbs, a small refrigerator, a borrowed television set on which he watched sports events, and a shelf on which he kept a few books, including Dante's *Divine Comedy* and a biography of Oscar Wilde. He had no phone and took calls at the desk in the lobby. There was a tiny courtyard near his room where he liked to feed pigeons. Many of his friends thought it was not a suitable place for a wealthy Nobel Prize–winner, but Beckett loved the simple monastic quality of his lodgings and was perfectly content, as long as his accommodating doctor kept him supplied with newspapers, cigarettes, and Irish whiskey.

Beckett's health, however, continued to deteriorate, and he was plagued with psoriasis and what he called "disorders of the feet" and "trouble with the joints." In July of 1989, his wife, Suzanne, died at the age of eighty-nine, and Beckett was well enough to attend her funeral. On December 6 of that year, a nurse found Beckett unconscious in his room and he was rushed to a hospital. As he was carried to an ambulance, he regained consciousness and called out to the bystanders, "I'll be back!" Alas, he was not destined to leave the hospital alive, and on December 19, he lapsed into a coma and died of respiratory failure on December 22 at the age of eighty-three.

He was buried in secrecy at eight-thirty in the morning of December 26 at the Montparnasse Cemetery. There were no speeches, no religious service, and no clergy. He and Suzanne share a simple gravestone that follows Beckett's instruction: that it could be any color, "as long as it's gray."

W. H. AUDEN

"We must love one another or die" is one of the most famous lines of contemporary poetry. It appeared in W. H. Auden's "September 1, 1939," which was published in *The New Republic*. Curiously, Auden came to loathe the poem, and he omitted the stanza containing that quote in his collected works. He permitted it to be reprinted in one anthology, with a note that said he considered it "to be trash which he is ashamed to have written." It is difficult to understand why, since the line summarizes a theme that appears throughout Auden's poems—the redemptive power of human love.

Wystan Hugh Auden was born on February 21, 1907, in York, England. His father, a physician, took a post in Birmingham, the industrial Midlands city, which is where Auden grew up, wanting to be a mining engineer, before being sent off to boarding schools. At St. Edmund's School in Surrey, he met Christopher Isherwood, the writer who would become his lifelong friend and, briefly, his lover. At Christ Church College, Oxford, Auden read English literature and began to publish poetry and criticism with a left-wing bent. He moved among a circle of future famous poets—C. Day Lewis, Louis MacNeice, and Stephen Spender, who became known, probably to their annoyance, as "the Auden Group."

Auden left Oxford with a third-class degree, spent some time in Berlin, returned to England to work as a schoolmaster and later a freelance film reviewer, and began to publish his poems, under the thrall of Isherwood and with the backing of T. S. Eliot. In 1939, Auden moved to New York and met the poet Chester Kallman, who became his lover for a period of about two years, and thereafter was his lifelong live-in companion and collaborator, although no longer a romantic partner.

When war broke out in Europe, Auden volunteered to join the British army—but at his age of thirty-two, the army said "no thanks," and he was advised to stay in America, where he taught at the University of Michigan and at Swarthmore College. After the war, Auden taught at the New School for Social Research, Bennington College, and Smith College. He became a U.S. citizen in 1946.

Auden grew up in an Anglo-Catholic household, but abandoned religion at the age of thirteen—only to take it up again at the age of thirty-three, when he joined the Episcopal Church. Thereafter, an existential Christianity became central to his work, under the influence of theologians Kierkegaard and Niebuhr.

A heavy smoker—as his deeply wrinkled face would suggest— and an equally devoted martini drinker, Auden undoubtedly hastened his own premature death. His brother John described his habits during his years in New York: "Although strictly disciplined in regard to work every morning, and with only a beer or a plain martini [vermouth] at lunch, the evenings brought

stiff vodkas and martinis from the freezer." Auden's seriousness
about his martinis can be seen in fellow poet Richard Wilbur's
description of a conversation they once had: "Auden had ordered
a martini and I had ordered a martini, and we talked about martinis, and we discussed the fact that if you are devoted to martinis, it's very hard to get a good one away from home. I think that
was the essence of our deep conversation, but it was heartfelt."

In 1972, his health failing, Auden moved from New York to
Oxford for the winter months. He continued to spend summers
in Austria, as he had done since buying a farmhouse in Kirchstetten in 1958. On the evening of September 28, 1973, Auden
spoke and read poetry at the Austrian Society of Literature in
Vienna. He stayed overnight in the modest Altenburger Hotel
near the Staatsoper. Next morning he was found dead, victim of
a heart attack. He was sixty-six.

In keeping with Austrian custom, Auden's body was laid out
at his house for several days before the funeral, which was held
at the white-walled, onion-domed Kirchstetten Catholic parish
church of St. Vitus, where Auden had regularly danced attendance. Stephen Spender and Chester Kallman led the procession, which included a brass band. The church was packed with
mourners for a service conducted jointly by two priests, one
Anglican and one Roman Catholic.

Auden is buried in the St. Vitus churchyard, and a plaque in
his memory is in Poets' Corner at Westminster Abbey.

TENNESSEE WILLIAMS

Did a bottle cap cause the death of one of America's leading
playwrights? That was the opinion of some people when Tennessee Williams departed this life. Others concluded it was drink
and drugs, while his brother hinted darkly that it was murder.

Thomas Lanier Williams, as he was first known, was born
March 26, 1911, in Columbus, Mississippi, to a hard-drinking

traveling shoe salesman and the puritanical daughter of an Episcopal clergyman. When he was eight, the family moved to St. Louis, where Tom attended high school. He showed an early aptitude for creative writing, and even as a teenager, began to win recognition for his stories and plays. After high school, he enrolled in journalism courses at the University of Missouri in Columbia. When a childhood girlfriend also enrolled there, his father broke up what he thought was a budding romance and pulled young Tom out of school.

He went to work for his father's shoe company, a job he called "a living death," while writing plays in his spare time. He quit work when he had a mental breakdown and spent some time in Memphis, where he joined an amateur theatre group. Finally he settled at the University of Iowa, where he graduated with a B.A. in English, followed by study in dramatic arts at The New School in New York.

Seeking a change in his lifestyle, Williams moved to New Orleans, where he began to call himself Tennessee, partly because it was his father's birthplace. He also explained that it was a college nickname based on his Southern accent and that he liked its "distinctive" sound. He won a playwriting contest, which attracted the literary agent Audrey Wood. She got him a job writing screenplays in Hollywood, where he tinkered unsuccessfully on scripts for Lana Turner and Margaret O'Brien.

He also finished a play called *The Glass Menagerie* in which the daughter, Laura, is based on his schizophrenic sister, Rose. Its Broadway production in 1945 brought Williams overnight fame as a playwright. This play was followed by a string of successes through the 1940s and 1950s: *A Streetcar Named Desire*,

Summer and Smoke, The Rose Tattoo, Camino Real, Cat on a Hot Tin Roof, Orpheus Descending, Sweet Bird of Youth, and *The Night of the Iguana.*

In 1948, Williams began a fourteen-year relationship with an actor named Frank Merlo, and the pair lived happily in New York and Key West. When Merlo died of lung cancer in 1963, Williams fell into a long period of severe depression. "I went to pieces," he later said. "I retreated into a shell."

Williams was hospitalized repeatedly and began to rely on amphetamines, barbiturates, and frequent injections of drugs prescribed by physician Max Jacobson, known as "Doctor Feelgood," whose patients also included Elvis Presley, Marilyn Monroe, Marlene Dietrich, Truman Capote, Nelson Rockefeller, and President John F. Kennedy. Increasingly reliant on a regimen of coffee, cigarettes, drugs, and alcohol, Williams split bitterly with his longtime agent and mentor, Audrey Wood. But he continued to write, churning out a dreary procession of flop plays. He would rise at five o'clock in the morning and, during the course of a day's work at the typewriter, would consume dozens of pills, several quarts of strong coffee, and two or three bottles of wine.

During the period of his depression, Williams's brother, Dakin, a Catholic convert, urged Tennessee to join the Church. Whether the conversion was genuine is a matter of speculation. In a 1981 interview in the *Paris Review,* on his seventieth birthday, Williams claimed to be "a Catholic by nature," based on his family's high-Anglican background, but he called his "conversion" a "joke . . . while I was taking Dr. Jacobson's miracle shots." Williams went on to say that he believed that after death, humans were absorbed back into "the eternal flux." He added that he was reconciled to the inevitability of his own death, but he hoped it would not be before his work was finished.

Whether or not he thought his work was finished, it came to an end willy-nilly in 1983. Williams and his secretary, John Uecker, were staying in a two-bedroom suite in the Hotel Elysée

on East 54th Street in New York. About eleven o'clock in the
evening on Thursday, February 24, Uecker heard a noise from
Williams's room, but did not investigate. The next morning at
10:25, Ueckert went to Williams's room and found him dead
on the floor near his bed. Beneath the night table was an open
bottle of Visine eye drops, its screw-on cap lodged in Williams's
throat, and two open wine bottles with their corks beside them.
Williams was seventy-one.

As John L. Sime recounts in *American Funeral Director*
magazine (reprinted at the Sime Funeral Home's web site), it
was originally thought that Williams died when he choked on
the Visine cap, which he was holding in his mouth as he put the
drops in his eyes. Williams's brother, Dakin, claimed that he was
murdered, and he offered a $50,000 reward to find the killer.
He maintained that a "strange, eerie man" forced his way onto
the hotel elevator, got off on Williams's floor, entered his suite,
smothered him with a pillow, and then inserted the bottle cap in
his throat as a ruse.

The official autopsy mentioned some marks on the body that
lent credence to Dakin's claim: "There is pronounced anterior
lividity involving the head, the chest and the upper extremities.
There are intense hemorrhages about the face, about the chest
and left arm. There is some subconjunctival congestion and
hemorrhages as well. The tip of the tongue has a slight pinkish
discoloration."

The police report, however, indicates that Williams died of
an overdose of drugs and alcohol. The *New York Times* reported
that he had also been under treatment for heart disease.

For a nonchurchgoer, Williams was accorded an impres-
sive array of religious obsequies. Sime's article notes that a service on March 1 at the Frank E. Campbell Funeral Home on
Madison Avenue was conducted by the Reverend Sidney Lanier,
an Episcopal priest and Williams's cousin. The body was also
blessed by both a Catholic and a Russian Orthodox priest, the

latter at the request of Maria St. Just, a confidante of Williams. A requiem mass was celebrated on March 3 at St. Malachy's Catholic Church on West 49th Street, known as the "Actors' Parish."

Williams's body was then moved to the Lupton Funeral Home in St. Louis, where it lay in state for two days. On Saturday, March 5, at ten o'clock in the morning, with more than 1,200 people present, a funeral mass was celebrated at the Roman Catholic Cathedral Basilica of St. Louis by the Reverend Jerome F. Wilkerson. In his homily, Wilkerson said, "The tragedy of Tennessee seems to be that the revelatory sword of suffering that pierced his heart seemed to be so much more therapeutic to others than to himself. He would seem to have remained all of his life among the walking wounded...He did a lot of dying and apparently had little difficulty in 'hating his life in this world.'" Episcopalian Lanier also participated in the service, reading a passage from the Book of Ecclesiastes.

Williams had said that he wanted to be buried at sea, in a clean, white sack, at the same spot off Florida where his idol Hart Crane had thrown himself overboard. But Dakin thought otherwise, and the body was interred in the Calvary Cemetery in St. Louis next to their mother. A monument of pink Tennessee granite was installed bearing a quotation from Williams's *Camino Real*: "The violets in the mountains have broken the rocks."

On March 8, at eight o'clock in the evening, the marquees of twenty Broadway theatres dimmed for one minute in memory of Williams, and on March 26, a memorial service was held in the Shubert Theatre. Some 1,500 people packed the auditorium, where Jessica Tandy did a monologue by Blanche from *A Streetcar Named Desire*, Geraldine Fitzgerald sang Williams's favorite song, "Danny Boy," and the recorded voice of Williams read the opening speech of *The Glass Menagerie*. Williams's friend, the actress Maureen Stapleton, commented, "I think Tenn would be glad to know that he had a full house."

DYLAN THOMAS

"I've had eighteen straight whiskeys. I think that's the record." That's the boast that poet Dylan Thomas made shortly before he was carted off to St. Vincent's Hospital in New York's Greenwich Village, where he died four days later. Whether he actually consumed that many shots, he unquestionably drank a prodigious quantity of alcohol during his lifetime, a great deal of it in the twenty-one days before his death while visiting America for poetry readings and rehearsals of his play *Under Milk Wood*.

Thomas got his start on October 27, 1914, on a typically consonant-heavy Welsh street, Cwmdonkin Drive in Swansea. His father was an English teacher at the local grammar school who, along with his wife, spoke fluent Welsh. Dylan, however, never learned the language, and although he is revered as the Welsh national poet, wrote exclusively in English. Dylan quit school when he was sixteen and went to work as a reporter for the *South Wales Daily Post*, a job that lasted little more than a year. After that stint, Thomas was never employed fulltime again, devoting himself to his poetry—a notoriously ill-paying occupation, even compared with other literary pursuits, and Thomas was perpetually short of money for the rest of his life.

In his late teen years, Thomas wrote more than half of his total output of poetry, which comprises only about a hundred poems; his first collection, *18 Poems*, appeared in 1934 and won favorable notice. Thomas divided his time between Wales and London.

In 1937, he married twenty-four-year-old Caitlin Macnamara, a dancer who, at the time, was the mistress of the sixty-year-old painter Augustus John. Dylan had to borrow £3 for the wedding license, and the penurious couple resided alternately with both sets of parents. From the moment they said "I do," the marriage was tempestuous, punctuated by money woes, drinking bouts, and adultery by both partners. In the height of World War II, the Thomases moved to London, where Dylan served as an anti-aircraft gunner. After four years of the constant danger of the blitz, they moved back to Wales and settled at Lougharne.

Thomas's well-known poems include "And Death Shall Have No Dominion," "Fern Hill," "In My Craft or Sullen Art," "A Refusal to Mourn the Death, by Fire, of a Child in London," and perhaps his most famous work, "Do Not Go Gentle Into That Good Night," in which he urges the reader to resist death with fierce effort. Thomas also wrote the popular memoir *A Child's Christmas in Wales* and the much-produced play for voices, *Under Milk Wood*.

Many readers regard Thomas's poems as difficult to interpret. He himself once described his poetic deficiencies as "Immature violence, rhythmic monotony, frequent muddle-headedness, and a very much overweighted imagery that leads often to incoherence."

Although young Dylan had early exposure to religious education at the Walter Road Congregational Church in Swansea and his poetry is filled with Christian allusions, most commentators regard these trappings as devices used for their poetic imagery and not from any genuine religious feeling.

In 1950, Thomas made the first of four visits to the United States, where he was a popular lecturer and reader of his romantic, image-filled poetry. His death, on the last such trip, was a chronicle of dissipation, multiple illnesses, and medical mismanagement.

On October 19, 1953, he arrived in New York for the final fateful tour and checked into the Chelsea Hotel on West 23rd Street, a favorite haunt of artists and writers. According to his biographer Paul Ferris, Thomas unfortunately showed up several days late for his reservation, and he had to settle for a small, dingy back room, where he said there were "cockroaches with teeth." With him was one of his several mistresses, Liz Reitell, the assistant of American poet and critic John Malcolm Brinnin, who had arranged Thomas's visit.

Ferris has reconstructed a chronology of events leading up to Thomas's death. Between rehearsals for a production of *Under Milk Wood* and various lectures and symposia, Thomas spent most of his idle hours at the White Horse Tavern and various other watering holes, or in his room at the Chelsea with a bottle. Suffering from chronic asthma, gastritis, and gout, he dosed himself with beer and Old Granddad bourbon. On Friday, October 23, feeling unwell, Thomas visited Dr. Milton Feltenstein, a physician Reitell had recommended to him, and was given steroid injections. The next few days he attended performances of *Under Milk Wood* and other public appearances, including a party for his thirty-ninth birthday on the evening of the 27th— and downed more rounds of whiskey and beer.

On the evening of Tuesday, November 3, Thomas went out in the evening for drinks, and when he returned to the Chelsea, he burst into tears and told Reitell he wanted to die "and go to the garden of Eden." At two o'clock in the morning, he got out of bed, said he needed a drink, and left the hotel. When he returned an hour and a half later, he made the infamous remark about eighteen whiskeys, and then went to sleep.

He awoke mid-morning on November 4, said he was suffocating, and went to the White Horse for two glasses of beer. When he returned to the hotel, still unwell, Dr. Feltenstein was summoned and gave him a steroid injection. Thomas slept through the afternoon, and when he awoke he had severe gastritis, with vomiting and hallucinations. Feltenstein came back and concluded Thomas had alcoholic delirium tremens and administered morphine. At midnight, Thomas's breathing became more labored and he turned blue. An ambulance was summoned to take him to St. Vincent's Hospital, where he was given artificial respiration and oxygen.

The medical examiner reported: "Patient brought into hospital in coma at 1:58 a.m. Remained in coma during hospital stay. History of heavy alcoholic intake. Impression on admission was acute alcoholic encephalopathy [damage to the brain], for which patient was treated without response."

Caitlin was notified of his illness and flew to New York. At the hospital, she was allowed only forty minutes with him, but returned later in a drunken rage, threatening to do violence to Thomas's friends, as well as the hospital nuns and nurses. Dr. Feltenstein had her placed in a straitjacket and taken to a detox center on Long Island.

Meanwhile, a tracheotomy was performed on Thomas to facilitate his breathing, and he was placed in an oxygen tent. He remained in a coma until November 9, when he died, at the age of thirty-nine. Evidence now indicates that Thomas never had as many as eighteen whiskeys, and that alcohol was not the direct cause of his death, which instead was a result of undiagnosed and untreated bronchitis and pneumonia, complicated by emphysema, untreated diabetes, a fatty liver, and swelling of the brain caused by lack of oxygen. A lifetime of smoking, drinking, and unhealthful eating habits undoubtedly contributed to his weakened condition.

Thomas's body was returned to Wales, where he was buried on November 24 from the parish church of St. Martin's in Laugharne, followed by a reception at Brown's Hotel. A plaque in his memory was unveiled in Poets' Corner at Westminster Abbey some thirty years later.

THOMAS MERTON

Thomas Merton was a Trappist monk under a vow of silence, but he simply wouldn't keep quiet. Anti-war activist, civil rights crusader, poet, and mystic, he was accused by fellow Catholics of being a heretic, a Communist, and a Buddhist, and his writings were frequently censored by his monastic superiors. After an attempt to stifle a pacifist work of his, Merton's caustic comment, reported in the Jesuit magazine *America*, was: "The Peace Book is not to be published. Too controversial,

doesn't give a nice image of monk. Monk concerned with peace. Bad image." He accepted the restrictive discipline reluctantly: "I have just been instructed to shut my trap and behave, which I do since these are orders that must be obeyed and I have said what I had to say."

Author of countless articles and more than seventy books, including his bestselling autobiography, *The Seven Storey Mountain*, this unlikely cloistered monk was born January 31, 1915, in Prades, France, the son of two artists, an American mother and a New Zealander father. His mother died when he was six, and Thomas lived in Bermuda, France, and England with his father, who died when Thomas was seventeen. Thomas attended Cambridge, where he led a rambunctious life of drinking and womanizing, and finally enrolled at Columbia University, where he converted to Catholicism.

In 1941, having been snubbed by the Franciscan order for his earlier debauchery, he entered the Abbey of Gethsemani, a Kentucky monastery of the ascetic monks of the Cistercian Order of the Strict Observance, known as Trappists from their origin in France at the Abbey of La Trappe. Merton was ordained to the priesthood in 1948 and spent the next twenty years writing,

lecturing, advocating various progressive causes, and dodging
frequent attempts by higher-ups to muzzle him.

In the 1960s, he became interested in Asian religions, and
had frequent dialogue with spiritual figures such as the Dalai
Lama, the Vietnamese monk Thich Nhat Hanh, and Japanese
writer D. T. Suzuki. "If Catholics had a little more Zen," he said,
"they would be less ridiculous than they are."

Merton had constant health problems, both physical and
psychological. He often suffered from exhaustion, and his
actions were sometimes impetuous to the point of recklessness.
Questions were raised about the nature of his relationship with
a young nurse who treated him during a hospital stay for a back
injury; some thought their friendship might have escalated into
a secret love affair.

On December 10, 1968, Merton was in Bangkok, where he
spoke at an interfaith meeting of some seventy Asian Cister-
cians and Benedictines, as well as non-Christians. That afternoon at his hotel, he stepped out of the shower, still wet, and
attempted to move an electric fan, which electrocuted him. He
was fifty-three.

There were, however, lingering doubts about the cause of
his death. The initial report in the media was that he had had
a heart attack, and others have suggested a more sinister sce-
nario—that he was assassinated by fanatics who objected to his
unorthodox views. Merton's friend Dom Jacques Leclercq concluded, "In all probability the death of Thomas Merton was due
in part to heart failure, in part to an electric shock. Neither of
them alone would normally be fatal."

Ironically, Merton's body was flown back to the United States
in a military plane returning from Viet Nam, transporting bodies of those killed in the war that Merton so vigorously opposed.
After a ceremony in which monks, according to ancient custom, stood and recited Psalms next to his coffin, followed by
a requiem mass attended by his fellow monks and numerous

notable visitors, Merton was buried as a misty rain fell outside the Abbey of Gethsemani. In another touch of irony, instead of the usual Trappist practice of easing the body into its grave on hand-held ropes, Merton's steel casket was noisily lowered by an elaborate metal contraption powered by electricity.

ARTHUR MILLER

Many people know him primarily as Mr. Marilyn Monroe—but playwright Arthur Miller had a life before and after his five-year marriage to the Hollywood goddess. Born October 17, 1915, in the fashionable Upper East Side of New York City to a family of Polish Jewish immigrants, Arthur was the second of three children. His father was a well-to-do clothing manufacturer who employed  a chauffeur and had a seaside summer home in Queens, but he suffered huge losses in the stock market crash of 1929, and the impoverished family moved to modest quarters in Brooklyn.

After high school, Miller worked in odd jobs until he had the money to attend the University of Michigan, where he wrote his first play, called *No Villain.* He went to New York to join the Federal Theatre Project, and there he married Mary Slattery, with whom he had two children.

Miller's first Broadway play, *The Man Who Had All the Luck,* ran for only four performances, but he bounced back three years later with *All My Sons,* a wartime drama that had a respectable 328 performances, won two Tony Awards, and established both Miller's reputation and his association with director Elia Kazan. In 1949, Miller's *Death of A Salesman* won the theatre's triple crown: Tony Award, Pulitzer Prize, and New York Critics' Circle Award. *The Crucible*, a play that indirectly commented on the anti-Communist phobia of McCarthyism by comparing it to the Salem witch trials, cemented his stature—and aroused suspicions among rabid Red-hunters.

In 1956, Miller divorced Mary, married Marilyn Monroe, and was summoned to testify before the House Un-American Activities Committee—not about his marital adventures, titillating though they may have been, but for his espousal of liberal causes and for the anti-authoritarian sentiments of *The Crucible*. The committee chair offered to exempt him from questioning in exchange for a signed photo of Monroe—but Miller declined the offer. Unlike his pal Kazan, with whom he bitterly split, Miller refused to name names, and he was held guilty of contempt of Congress and sentenced to a fine, thirty days in prison, and revocation of his passport—a conviction that was overturned.

In 1961 Miller wrote the screenplay for *The Misfits*, starring Monroe and Clark Gable. Its title was prophetic, for he divorced Monroe shortly thereafter and married photographer Inge Morath. They had two children, a daughter, Rebecca, who later married actor Daniel Day-Lewis, and a son with Down syndrome, whom Miller had little to do with until Day-Lewis engineered a reconciliation. Morath died in 2002, and Miller, then eighty-seven, promptly invited a thirty-four-year-old painter named Agnes Barley to move in with him. Miller said he regarded her as his "soul mate," but their relationship was said to be nonsexual.

Miller was born into a moderately observant Orthodox Jewish household, but remained skeptical about religion after his teenage years. As he said in an interview, he felt that all religions demonstrated their irrelevance during the Great Depression, and his work in various progressive social movements replaced the role of religious belief in his life.

In late 2004, battling an undisclosed form of cancer, pneumonia, and congestive heart failure, he was hospitalized, then released into hospice care at his sister's New York apartment in January of 2005. He insisted on returning to his home in Roxbury, Connecticut, where he died at the age of eighty-nine on the evening of February 10, surrounded by his children and his companion, Barley. Within hours of his death, reported the *New York Daily News*, Rebecca and Daniel Day-Lewis ordered Barley to vacate the premises.

Miller was buried at Roxbury Center Cemetery.

ROALD DAHL

Willy Wonka's creator lost his faith in religion after being counseled by a former Archbishop of Canterbury. When Roald Dahl and his wife, the actress Patricia Neal, lost their seven-year-old daughter to measles encephalitis, they sought comfort from an old friend recently retired from the highest ecclesiastical office in the Anglican community. As Dahl recalled the episode in a *Daily Telegraph* interview,

he asked the former Archbishop if his daughter's beloved dog would be with her in heaven. The churchman disapproved of the very question. "From that moment on," said Dahl, "I'm afraid I began to wonder whether there really was a God or not."

Baptized as a Lutheran in a family of Norwegian immigrants, Dahl was born September 13, 1916, in Cardiff, Wales. He was sent to boarding schools, where he was educated as an

Anglican. He shunned university and went to work for Shell Oil in Tanganyika, then joined the RAF when World War II broke out. After being badly injured when he crashed his plane, he was posted as an air attaché to Washington, D.C., where he engaged in a little espionage on the side as a British spy, had affairs with countless glamorous women (including playwright Clare Boothe Luce and cosmetics queen Elizabeth Arden), and met the British writer C. S. Forester. Forester wanted to write an article about Dahl's war exploits, but Dahl wrote his own account of his adventures, which Forester sold to the *Saturday Evening Post* for $900.

Dahl went to work for Disney in Hollywood, where he wrote an RAF story called *The Gremlins.* It attracted the attention of Eleanor Roosevelt, and Dahl became a frequent visitor at the White House. At a dinner party hosted by Lillian Hellman, Dahl met Neal, on the rebound from ending an affair with Gary Cooper, her co-star in *The Fountainhead.* Neal, who would go on to win an Oscar in *Hud,* accepted Dahl's proposal. The pair had five children before she suffered a series of debilitating strokes in 1965. Dahl spent months overseeing her recovery, but despite this tender devotion, the couple divorced bitterly in 1983. Dahl then married Felicity Crosland, a close friend of Neal's—at least until then.

Among Dahl's best known works, mostly darkly humorous stories ostensibly for children, are *James and the Giant Peach,* *Charlie and the Chocolate Factory* (also known as *Willy Wonka and the Chocolate Factory*), *The Fantastic Mr. Fox, Matilda, The Minpins,* and *The Vicar of Nibbleswicke.* He also wrote novels and short stories aimed at an adult audience.

Dahl's interests were wide-ranging and, according to his widow, included greyhound racing, breeding budgerigars, medical inventions, orchids, onions, gambling, golf, fine wine, music, art, and antiques. In 1986, he turned down the honor of an OBE, hoping (in vain, as it turned out) to achieve a knighthood instead.

In 1990, Dahl was diagnosed with a rare blood disorder called myelodysplastic syndrome, in which inadequate blood cells are produced, often resulting in severe anemia, internal bleeding, susceptibility to infection, and bone-marrow failure. Shortly before his death, Dahl wrote in a newsletter to his fans: "I've been a bit off colour these last few months, feeling sleepy when I shouldn't have been and without that lovely old bubbly energy that drives one to write books and drink gin and chase after girls." He died on November 23, 1990, in Oxford, at the age of seventy-four.

Dahl was given what his family called a "sort of Viking funeral," and was buried in the cemetery of St. Peter and St. Paul's Church in Great Missenden, Buckinghamshire, along with his snooker cues, a bottle of fine burgundy, chocolates, pencils, and a power saw.

HAROLD PINTER

Master of the pregnant pause, Harold Pinter was a Nobel Prize-winning playwright and also an actor, director, and screenwriter. Born October 10, 1930, to a Jewish tailor and his wife, and raised in Hackney in the East End of London, Pinter received a grammar-school education, then briefly attended drama schools before  embarking on a career as an actor. He was fined for refusing military service as a conscientious objector. Anti-war activism, much of it directed bitterly against the United States, played a prominent role throughout Pinter's life.

His career as a playwright began in 1957 with a one-act play called *The Room*. This was followed by a West End production

of *The Birthday Party*, which closed after only eight performances. In 1960, *The Caretaker* was an enormous hit, establishing his reputation as a major playwright. Pinter's thirty-odd
plays, noted for their economical use of language, naturalistic
dialogue with poetic qualities, abundant pauses, and a sense
of mystery with menace lurking beneath the surface, include
The Dumb Waiter, *A Slight Ache*, *The Homecoming*, *No Man's
Land*, *Betrayal*, *Old Times*, *Landscape*, and *Silence*. Among his
screenplay adaptations are *The Servant*, *The French Lieuten-
ant's Woman*, *The Trial*, *The Last Tycoon*, *The Pumpkin Eater*,
and *Sleuth*. He continued to work as an actor on stage, and in
film and television.

In 1956, Pinter married the actress Vivien Merchant, with
whom he had a son, Daniel. After affairs with journalist Joan
Bakewell and author Antonia Fraser, Pinter left Merchant in 1975
and married Fraser five years later. Merchant died of alcoholism
in 1982. Daniel, who had changed his name from Pinter to Brand,
was estranged from his father from 1993 until Pinter's death.

Pinter was awarded the Commander of the British Empire
(CBE) in 1966, but declined a knighthood offered in 1996 by
the government of Conservative Prime Minister John Major.
Although he regarded Labour Prime Minister Tony Blair as a
"war criminal," Pinter did accept the award of Companion of
Honour in 2002, saying "I do not regard it as having any political connotations at all."

During the last eight years of his life Pinter fought a range
of diseases, including esophageal cancer, leukemia, septicemia,
an auto-immune disease known as pemphigus, and liver cancer,
from which he died. A onetime heavy smoker, he was diagnosed
in 2001 with cancer of the throat and esophagus, for which
he received surgery and chemotherapy and recovered fully. In
2002, he learned of the leukemia and pemphigus, which caused
frequent coughing fits, loss of appetite, muscular weakness and
frequent falls.

In 2005, Pinter was awarded the Nobel Prize for Literature, but was too ill to attend the ceremony in Oslo, sending a recorded video message instead. While working on the speech, he received a call with blood test results and was told to go immediately to the hospital, where he was placed in intensive care. Doctors told him that his autoimmune disease was rapidly shutting down his breathing. "I then realised, for the only time in my life actually, that I was on the point of death," he later told an interviewer in *The Guardian*. "You don't think at all. You just experience it. What you do, in my case, is that you fight and fight to stay alive." Doctors managed to pull him through on this occasion, but Pinter remained frail.

In a memoir called *Must You Go?*, published two years after his death, Pinter's wife, Antonia, recounted his final weeks. In November of 2008, Pinter learned he had a cancerous tumor on his liver and was told he would have to give up alcohol. He did so, "heroically," until December 17, when his doctor told him the cancer was so far advanced that there was no point in avoiding drink. When they got home, Pinter asked Antonia to fetch a bottle of champagne, and as he sipped it, he said, "Oh, the enjoyment of this glass! I had forgotten how absolutely lovely champagne was."

On Sunday, December 21, the Pinters had lunch at Scott's Restaurant in Mayfair, and Harold was in good spirits, although suffering some mental confusion. That night he watched a television play by David Hare and commented on Kate Winslet's "vigorous, intelligent acting." The next day, he was admitted to Hammersmith Hospital, and he died there on Christmas Eve at the age of seventy-eight, as his wife held his hand.

The funeral, on an icy New Year's Eve, was a thirty-minute secular graveside ceremony at Kensal Green Cemetery with about fifty mourners, including Tom Stoppard, Edna O'Brien, and Ronald Harwood. Pinter's son did not attend. A devout atheist, Pinter had planned the event to include no religious aspects. Actor Michael Gambon read passages from Pinter's work, actress Penelope Wilton read from James Joyce's "The Dead" and T. S. Eliot's "Little Gidding," actor Matthew Burton read a poem about Pinter's beloved game of cricket, and Pinter's step-granddaughter, Stella Powell-Jones, read a poem by Pinter dedicated to his wife. At the end of the readings, a teary Antonia Fraser advanced to the grave and, looking down at the coffin, quoted Horatio's words over the body of Hamlet:

> Now cracks a noble heart. Good night, sweet Prince,
> And flights of angels sing thee to thy rest.

Owing to Pinter's anti-religious views, a senior church official objected to his being memorialized in Poets' Corner of Westminster Abbey, according to an account in the *Daily Telegraph*. In an effort to overcome such objections, a family member cited a mildly pro-religious feeling once expressed by Pinter: "I derive something I can only call an actual aesthetic pleasure from certain ceremonies and a great deal of religious music, and even the physical presence of being in churches." Pinter added that he sometimes accompanied his Roman Catholic wife to mass.

JOHN UPDIKE

Sex and religion were dual themes that pervaded the writing of John Updike. Sex scenes in his novel *Rabbit, Run* were so explicit that his publisher, Alfred A. Knopf, insisted that they be expurgated. (They were restored in later editions.) Updike's religious bent was evident in an early short story, *Pigeon Feathers*, about a boy who anguishes in fear over death.

His dread is resolved after he shoots some pigeons, and as he admires the divine craftsmanship in the beauty of their feathers, he has a sudden epiphany that God intends mankind to be immortal.

Updike was born on March 18, 1932, in Reading, Pennsylvania, was raised as a Lutheran in nearby Shillington, and at thirteen was moved with his family to an eighty-acre farm near Plowville. He wanted to be a Disney cartoonist when he grew up, and after high school, where he was valedictorian and class president, he attended Harvard University, where he drew cartoons for the *Lampoon.* He married a Radcliffe student named Mary Pennington, with whom he had four children between 1955 and 1960. He studied drawing on a fellowship at Oxford University and also began to write short stories, one of which was accepted in the *New Yorker.* After the birth of his first child he accepted a staff position on the *New Yorker* and shifted his interests from cartoons to writing.

During the 1950s, Updike published dozens of essays, poems, and short stories. His first novel, *The Poorhouse Fair*, was followed by a steady stream of works, including more than fifty books over the next half century. Among them are *The Centaur*; *On the Farm*; *Rabbit, Run*; *Couples*; three *Rabbit* sequels; *Bech: A Book* (and two sequels); and *The Witches of Eastwick.* He is one of only three authors—the others being William Faulkner and Booth Tarkington—to win the Pulitzer Prize for fiction twice (for *Rabbit Is Rich* in 1982 and *Rabbit at Rest* in 1991).

In 1974, Updike and Mary divorced, and in 1977, he married Martha Bernhard. They settled in Beverly Farms, Massachusetts, where they lived until his death.

Updike remained an active churchgoer all his life, first as a Lutheran, then a Congregationalist, and later as an Episcopalian. He joked about his lifelong "tour of Protestantism," but his stern search for religious truth is reflected in a passage from his 1989 memoir *Self-Consciousness*, in which he contemplates death and the impossibility of reaching any conclusions about the nature of an afterlife. "Every attempt to be specific about the afterlife," he writes, "to conceive of it in even the most general detail, appalls us."

A longtime cigarette smoker, Updike had health problems that included emphysema and bronchial asthma, as well as psoriasis, claustrophobia, and dental problems. In *Self-Consciousness*, he writes of what he calls "deference" to his various ailments, having given up smoking "in deference" to his emphysema, salt and coffee because of hypertension, and alcohol owing to adverse interaction with methotrexate, a medication for psoriasis. Alluding to the futility of trying to prolong life indefinitely, he quotes Frederick the Great's exhortation to his reluctant troops before battle: *"Hunde, wollt ihr ewig leben?"* ("Dogs, do you wish to live forever?")

Sadly, Updike was not destined to live forever, not on earth at any rate, but to succumb to lung cancer. In November of 2008, he was hospitalized at Massachusetts General Hospital in Boston, and in the new year, he moved to a hospice in Danvers, Massachusetts, where he died on January 27 at the age of seventy-six. In "Requiem," a poem he wrote about his impending death that was published posthumously, he referred to his "overdue demise," adding that "death is real, and dark, and huge."

Updike's funeral was at St. John's Episcopal Church in Beverly Farms, where three hundred mourners attended a simple service consisting of four hymns, some prayers, and several readings from Updike's works—all selected by Updike before his death. There was no eulogy. The *Reading* (Pennsylvania) *Eagle* reported that his wife, Martha, was in the first row of the church, and Mary, his ex, was a few rows back. Updike was cremated, and some of his ashes were buried in Manchester, Massachusetts, near his home, and some later interred at the Robeson Lutheran Church Cemetery near his boyhood home in Plowville, Pennsylvania, under a marker carved by his son Michael.

SYLVIA PLATH

Poet Sylvia Plath attempted suicide on three occasions; the third time was the charm. Born October 27, 1932, in Boston, Massachusetts, Plath had a history of mental illness and depression since childhood. She first attempted to end her life while she was a student at Smith College. On that occasion, she wrote a note saying she was going for a long walk, retrieved sleeping pills from the safe where her mother kept them, swallowed a good many of them, retreated to the cellar of her home, and fell into a coma. Family members heard a groan from the cellar and rushed Sylvia to a hospital, where she recovered. Two years later, she graduated *summa cum laude* from Smith.

Plath received a Fulbright Scholarship to study in England at Cambridge University, where she met fellow poet Ted Hughes. They were married in 1956. In 1960, Plath published *Colossus*, her only verse collection during her lifetime, and the same year gave birth to a daughter. A son followed in 1962, the same year that Hughes left Plath for aspiring poet Assia Gutmann Wevill, who was a tenant in the Hugheses' London flat. His desertion prompted Plath's apparent second suicide attempt, albeit a bit halfhearted, in which she ran her car off the road at a deserted airfield.

In January of the following year, using the pseudonym Victoria Lucas, Plath published her semi-autobiographical novel,

The Bell Jar. It received lackluster reviews, and thereupon she made her third suicide attempt, this one successful.

Plath and her two children, a two-year-old and an eight-month-old infant, had taken up residence at 23 Fitzroy Road in north London. In early February, she told her physician, Dr. John Horder, that she felt depressed, describing her feeling as "owls' talons clenching my heart." Dr. Horder prescribed anti-depressants and visited her daily, while trying without success to have her admitted to a hospital. It has been suggested by friends that the medication prescribed for her had been known to worsen her condition in the United States, but in England it had a different brand name, which Plath did not recognize.

On Thursday, February 7, having fired her au pair, Plath went with the children to stay with friends, Jillian and Gerry Becker. As Plath's biographer Carl Rollyson recounts in *American Isis*, Plath met Hughes on Friday evening at the Fitzroy Street flat after sending him what he called a "farewell love letter." She told him she was leaving the country and would never see him again. When they met, she took the letter from him and burned it, then told him to leave.

On Sunday, February 10, Gerry Becker drove her and the children back to Fitzroy Street, leaving them there about seven o'clock in the evening. Dr. Horder called to check on her and told her that he would send a nurse to come and assist her at nine o'clock on Monday morning. Around midnight, Plath borrowed some stamps from her downstairs neighbor, Trevor Thomas, and asked him what time he would be going to work in the morning.

Sometime between four-thirty and five-thirty in the morning, Plath left water and food in her children's room and opened their windows. She put a note with Dr. Horder's contact information on the baby carriage. She then sealed the kitchen from the rest of the house with tape and wet towels under the door, turned on the gas jets on the kitchen stove, and put her head into the oven.

When the nurse arrived the next morning, she was able to get into the flat with the help of a workman. They found Plath dead of carbon monoxide poisoning. She was thirty years old.

Describing herself as a "pagan Unitarian, at best," Plath attended both the Unitarian and Methodist churches in her youth, but strayed from religious belief after the death of her father when she was eight. In England, she occasionally attended the Anglican parish church, and she was buried in the churchyard of St. Thomas the Apostle in Heptonstall, West Yorkshire.

Hughes was devastated by her death and felt the sting of blame for the suicide from many of Plath's admirers. Six years later, Hughes's paramour, Assia Wevill, also committed suicide after killing the pair's four-year-old daughter.

Hughes oversaw the posthumous publication of much of Plath's work, including her highly regarded poem collection called *Ariel*. Hughes was married again in 1970, to a nurse named Carol Orchard. He was named Britain's Poet Laureate in 1984, and he died of cancer in 1998. Plath and Hughes's son, Nicholas, committed suicide in 2009. Their daughter, Frieda, a painter and poet, is also a trained bereavement counselor.

JOE ORTON

Joe Orton was the bad boy of British theatre. Not only were his plays irreverent, iconoclastic, and bawdy (some would say obscene), but his off-stage pranks were equally outrageous. He and his lover, Kenneth Halliwell, delighted in borrowing books from the public library and making outlandish alterations in the blurbs and illustrations before returning them. Among their capers were pasting a monkey's face in the middle of a rose on the cover of a horticultural book, substituting David's painting of Marat dead in his bath for a police photo of a contemporary murder site, and replacing a photograph of the distinguished Poet Laureate Sir John Betjeman with a picture of a heavily

tattooed, nearly naked man. Orton's death, however, was not an occasion for mirth; it was like a scene from a horror movie.

This *enfant terrible* first saw the light of day on New Year's Day in 1933 in Leicester, England. His family was of modest means, and Joe grew up in public housing on a council estate. He attended the local primary school, took a secretarial course when he was barely a teenager, and went to work as a clerk. He became interested in theatre, joined an amateur society, and then decided to study at the Royal Academy of Dramatic Art.

That's where Orton and Halliwell met and soon became lovers. After each of them had a stint in provincial repertory theatres, they moved into a flat in Islington, a London suburb, and began their respective writing careers, supporting themselves with odd jobs and Halliwell's inheritance. To Halliwell's annoyance, Orton led a promiscuous sex life, his romantic trysts taking place mostly in public toilets. When he was not thus occupied, Orton, abetted by Halliwell, amused himself with the library hoaxes, for which the pair were eventually charged with malicious damage, fined £262, and sentenced to six months in prison—an unusually severe penalty, Orton claimed, "because we were queers."

Orton proved to be an original voice in British theatre— harshly anti-establishment, irreligious, sexually graphic, and usually hilarious. His first success, among his several black comedies, the erotic *Entertaining Mr. Sloane*, won the backing of upper-crust playwright Sir Terence Rattigan and top London agent Margaret Ramsay, who shepherded Orton's career and often advised him in personal matters.

Orton's next play, *Loot*, satirizing the police, the justice system, religion, and attitudes toward sex and death, had a dismal tryout tour in the provinces, but after a thorough rewrite, it opened in the West End in 1966 to rave reviews and played 342 performances, winning several awards. During early 1967 Orton was putting the finishing touches on his final play, *What the Butler Saw*.

Meanwhile, Halliwell's writing career was going nowhere. His jealousy of Orton became obsessive, and he lapsed into severe depression. John Lahr's biography of Orton, *Prick Up Your Ears*, recounts the circumstances of his murder with gruesome detail.

On the morning of August 9, 1967, Orton was scheduled to meet with the film director Richard Lester to discuss a screenplay he was going to write for The Beatles. A car was sent to pick him up. At 11:40 a.m., the chauffeur knocked on the door of Orton and Halliwell's flat and received no answer. He phoned his supervisor and was told to try once more. He did so, then peeked through the letter slot in the door. What he saw chilled his blood.

Halliwell's body was lying nude on its back in the center of the room, spattered with blood. Orton's was on his bed, the skull crushed. The bad boy playwright was dead at the age of thirty-four.

Police later pieced together this account of what had happened: On August 5, Orton had met a friend at a pub and told him he wanted to end his relationship with Halliwell, but was fearful of raising the subject with him. Halliwell, heavily dependent on anti-depressant medication, was to see a psychiatrist on the morning of August 9; his regular doctor spoke with him at ten o'clock the night before to confirm the appointment. Halliwell told him, "I'm feeling better. I'll go see the doctor tomorrow morning." Sometime in the early morning hours of August 9, Halliwell bludgeoned Orton to death, delivering nine blows to his head with a hammer—an action that allegedly inspired The Beatles's song "Maxwell's Silver Hammer." Halliwell then took his own life by swallowing twenty-two Nembutal capsules, washed down with grapefruit juice to speed their action.

Orton was cremated on August 18 in a ceremony at Golders Green Crematorium, attended by about twenty-five people, including playwright Harold Pinter, who delivered a eulogy. Orton's ashes were blended with those of Halliwell, who had been cremated the previous day. According to a memoir by Dennis Dewsnap, Orton's sister was mixing the ashes and said, "A little bit of Joe, and a little bit of Kenneth." Then she added some more ashes from each container, saying, "Perhaps a little bit more of our Joe, and then some more of Kenneth." Orton's agent, Margaret Ramsay, impatient to get on with it, snapped, "Come on, dearie, it's only a gesture, not a recipe."

SUSAN SONTAG

"Everyone who is born," wrote Susan Sontag in *Illness as Metaphor*, "holds dual citizenship in the kingdom of the well and in the kingdom of the sick." Sontag became a citizen of the latter kingdom on three occasions, when cancer tried to kill her. The third time, the cancer succeeded.

Sontag was born Susan Rosenblatt in New York City on January 16, 1933. Her parents were fur exporters in China, and she spent her early years in New York with grandparents. She became Susan Sontag when her mother married U.S. Army Captain Nathan Sontag after her father's death when she was five. Hoping to relieve Susan's asthma, the family moved to Tucson, Arizona, where Susan grew up. She graduated from North Hollywood High School, attended the University of California at Berkeley, and then transferred to the University of Chicago, where director Mike Nichols became her best friend.

At seventeen she married Philip Rieff, a Chicago sociology instructor; the marriage lasted eight years and produced a son, who was later his mother's editor as well as a writer. Sontag did graduate work in literature, theology, and philosophy at Harvard, Oxford, and the University of Paris, studying with such academic powerhouses as Perry Miller, Paul Tillich, and Iris Murdoch. In Paris, Sontag met the playwright María Irene Fornés, with whom she moved back to New York and remained with for seven years. Sontag later had a relationship with photographer Annie Leibovitz.

Sontag's books include four novels—*The Benefactor*, *Death Kit*, *The Volcano Lover*, and *In America*—a short story collection, several plays, and nine works of nonfiction, among them *Against Interpretation*, *Illness as Metaphor*, *Where the Stress Falls*, *Regarding the Pain of Others*, and *At the Same Time*. She also directed films and plays and wrote numerous articles for journals including the *New Yorker*, the *New York Review of Books*, and the *Nation*. Her copious honors include a MacArthur Fellowship (also known as a "genius grant") and numerous literary awards in Germany, Israel, Italy, and France.

Although Sontag was born into a Jewish family, she said she never set foot in a synagogue until she was in her twenties. She feared death more than anything, according to her son, David Rieff, in his memoir about his mother's final illness, *Swimming in a Sea of Death*. He quotes Simone de Beauvoir: "Whether you think of it as heavenly or earthly, if you cling to living immortality is no consolation for death." Rieff adds, "My mother was equally unpersuaded and unconsoled."

Sontag's first brush with the Grim Reaper was in the 1970s, when she was diagnosed with breast cancer. She opted for radical surgery and aggressive therapy. "When it came to cancer treatment," Rieff said of her, "more was always better."

Uterine cancer struck in 1998, and once again Sontag conquered it and remained cancer-free for six more years.

In 2004, Sontag learned that she had myelodysplastic syndrome, a condition that involves inadequate production of certain blood cells and leads to anemia and bone marrow failure. Sontag's reaction on the way home from hearing the diagnosis was, "Wow." Later in the year, the disease evolved into acute myelogenous leukemia, a relatively rare form of blood cancer.

Again Sontag fought vigorously, enduring a painful bonemarrow transplant at the University of Washington Hospital in Seattle. The transplant was not successful, and Sontag returned to Memorial Sloan Kettering Hospital in New York. According to her son, she spent her last seven weeks there in agony, her body covered with sores. She wanted no one to say that she was dying, but she could not evade the awful truth, and on December 28, 2004, Susan Sontag died at the age of seventy-one.

She had a "horror of cremation," according to her son, and he decided to bury her in the Paris that she loved, in Montparnasse Cemetery, near Simone de Beauvoir, Jean-Paul Sartre, Samuel Beckett, and Charles Baudelaire.

NORA EPHRON

Even though it is rare, the same disease that caused Susan Sontag's death, acute myelogenous leukemia, carried off Nora Ephron eight years later. Ephron was diagnosed in 2006 and lived six years with the disease, but almost no one knew she was ill.

Born May 19, 1941, in New York, she was one of four daughters of Henry and Phoebe Ephron, writers of frothy Broadway comedies and slick Hollywood movies. Nora grew up in Beverly Hills and then went to Wellesley College. She married three times, first to writer Dan Greenburg, then to Watergate journalist

Carl Bernstein, and finally to yet another writer, Nicholas Pileggi, whose screenplays include the award-winning *Goodfellas.* "Writers are interesting people," she later said.

Nora followed the family trade ("Everything is copy," her mother told her), beginning as a newspaper reporter and magazine writer and then turning to books and screenplays. She earned three Oscar nominations for her work on the screenplays of *Silkwood,* *When Harry Met Sally . . . ,* and *Sleepless in Seattle.* Her last film was *Julie & Julia,* about TV chef Julia Child. Ephron's marriage to and acrid divorce from Carl Bernstein formed the basis of *Heartburn,* a novel and screenplay that starred Meryl Streep and Jack Nicholson. Her bestselling books include *I Feel Bad About My Neck* and *I Remember Nothing.* Theatre works were *Imaginary Friends*; the long-running *Love, Loss, And What I Wore* (with sister Delia); and the posthumously produced *Lucky Guy.*

Born into a Jewish family, Ephron nonetheless followed her mother's advice to avoid both sororities and organized religion. Speaking of *Julie & Julia,* she quipped, "You can never have too much butter—that is my belief. If I have a religion, that's it." In *I Remember Nothing,* written when Ephron knew she was suffering from a probably fatal disease, she mused on death's inevitability: "Everybody dies. There's nothing you can do about it. Whether or not you eat six almonds a day. Whether or not you believe in God." Ephron lamented her own lack of any religious faith, acknowledging that "a belief in God would come in handy."

While being treated for her leukemia at New York Presbyterian Hospital, Ephron developed pneumonia, from which she died on June 26, 2012, at the age of seventy-one. She had pre-planned a memorial service—including how long each speaker was allotted and what the topic of the speech was to be. The event was on a warm, sunny July 8 at Lincoln Center's Alice Tully Hall. The star-studded list of mourners included Barbara Walters, Diane Sawyer, Steve Martin, Martin Scorsese, Rob Reiner, Alan Alda, Jon Hamm, Meg Ryan, Charlie Rose, Martha Stewart, Mayor Michael Bloomberg, and Ephron's ex, Carl Bernstein. They sipped pink champagne and heard speakers Meryl Streep, Tom Hanks, Rosie O'Donnell, and several others pay tribute. Martin Short urged those present to be more like Ephron—"read everything, savor everything, talk to the person on your left, embrace laughter like it's a drug, drink more pink champagne, and yes, brush up your style."

Ephron was cremated and her ashes scattered.

ROGER EBERT

No one has ever written more extensively and eloquently about his own mortality and how to approach it than the movie critic Roger Ebert. He lived more than a decade with life-threatening diseases and devoted thoughtful commentary to their ramifications in a Facebook page, a widely read blog, a Twitter account with more than 800,000 followers, and a memoir, *Life Itself*, published the year before he died.

Born June 18, 1942, in Urbana, Illinois, Ebert was the son of an electrician and a bookkeeper. He attended St. Mary's

Catholic Elementary School, where he served as an altar boy; Urbana High School; and the University of Illinois at Urbana-Champaign. After a year's study on a Rotary Club fellowship at the University of Cape Town in South Africa, he began graduate studies at the University of Chicago, and at the same time went to work as a reporter for the *Chicago Sun-Times.*

In 1967, he was named the *Sun-Times* film critic. He became widely known, with fellow critic Gene Siskel of the *Chicago Tribune*, on a TV series known for its "thumbs up" (or "down") reviews. Ebert was known as the "fat one with horn-rimmed glasses," and Siskel was the "skinny bald one." Author of twenty books, Ebert won the first Pulitzer Prize ever given for film criticism and is the only movie reviewer with a star on the Hollywood Walk of Fame.

A member of Alcoholics Anonymous, Ebert gave up alcohol in 1979. He didn't marry until he was fifty, after his mother died, explaining he was afraid of displeasing her. His bride, attorney Chaz Hammelsmith, became coproducer of Ebert's various enterprises.

Illness struck Ebert in 2002, when he was diagnosed with papillary thyroid cancer, for which he had successful surgery, but in 2003, cancer returned in his salivary gland. More surgery was followed by radiation. Cancer struck yet again in 2006, this time in his right jaw, leaving him unable to eat, drink, or speak. He began to use a computerized device that sampled his own voice from previous recordings.

In 2008, Ebert underwent further surgery in an attempt to restore his voice, but it was not successful. Nonetheless, he resumed his career fulltime, and began to write about life and death in various online social media.

"I know it is coming," he wrote, "and I do not fear it, because I believe there is nothing on the other side of death to fear."

But Ebert clung to a vestige of his boyhood Catholic faith and refused to accept the label of atheist or agnostic. He said that he still considered himself to be a Catholic—"lock, stock, and barrel"—except for the proviso that "I cannot believe in God." He added that he still lay awake at nights pondering the ultimate questions, feeling more content with the question than he would be with an answer.

In December of 2012, Ebert was hospitalized with a fractured hip. Then he came down with pneumonia. He spent several months shuttling between hospital and the Rehabilitation Institute of Chicago. On April 2, 2013, he announced in his blog that he was taking what he called a "leave of presence" from his duties, because recurring cancer had been found and would require radiation. He insisted he would continue to review the movies that he wanted to review. But more reviews were not to come. Two days later, on April 4, as Ebert was preparing to leave the Rehabilitation Institute to return home, he suddenly died. "He looked happy," his wife recalled. "He looked peaceful, and he looked young." He was seventy.

A funeral mass was celebrated at Chicago's Holy Name Cathedral on the rainy morning of April 8. Illinois Governor Pat Quinn, Chicago Mayor Rahm Emanuel, Ebert's widow, Chaz, and his stepdaughter, Sonia Evans, were among the speakers. The homilist, the Reverend John F. Costello, said that Ebert wrestled with "the mystery of faith," not as someone rejecting God, but as one seeking further knowledge. The Reverend Michael Pfleger ended the service by declaring, "The balconies of heaven are filled with angels saying, 'Thumbs up.'"

Image Credits

AGATHA CHRISTIE from plaque at Torre Abbey, Torquay, licensed under GNU Free Documentation License Version 1.2, via Wikimedia Commons; HART CRANE photo courtesy of Hart Crane Papers, Rare Book & Manuscript Library, ©Columbia University in the City of New York, used by permission; ROGER EBERT photo ©Sound Opinions, Chicago Public Radio, 2007, licensed under Creative Commons Attribution-Share Alike 2.0 Generic, via Wikimedia Commons; NORA EPHRON photo ©David Shankbone, 2010, licensed under Creative Commons Attribution-Share Alike 3.0 Unported, via Wikimedia Commons; GRAHAM GREENE photo ©Baron Wolman/Iconic Images, used by permission; CHRISTOPHER MARLOWE drawing, courtesy of anonymous artist; THOMAS MERTON photo by John Howard Griffin, used with permission of the Merton Legacy Trust and the Thomas Merton Center at Bellarmine University; JOE ORTON photo ©Mirrorpix; HAROLD PINTER screenshot from Nobel Prize lecture, 2005, ©Illuminations Films, licensed under Creative Commons Attribution-Share Alike 3.0 Unported, via Wikimedia Commons; SYLVIA PLATH photo by Eric Stahlberg, courtesy of Mortimer Rare Book Room, ©Smith College, used by permission; DOROTHY L. SAYERS photo used by permission of The Marion E. Wade Center, Wheaton College, Wheaton, IL; SUSAN

S<small>ONTAG</small> photo ©MDC Archives, 1994, licensed under Creative Commons Attribution-Share Alike 3.0 Unported, via Wikimedia Commons; D<small>YLAN</small> T<small>HOMAS</small> photo courtesy of The Poetry Collection of the University Libraries, University at Buffalo, The State University of New York, used by permission.

Public Domain:

E<small>LIZABETH</small> B<small>ARRETT</small> B<small>ROWNING</small> printed in *Little Journeys to the Homes of Famous Women*, 1916; R<small>OBERT</small> B<small>ROWNING</small> printed in *Little Journeys to the Homes of English Authors*, 1916; M<small>ARGARET</small> F<small>ULLER</small> printed in *Eminent Women of the Age*, 1869; S<small>AMUEL</small> J<small>OHNSON</small> from a painting by Joshua Reynolds, printed in *A Dictionary of the English Language*, 1785; B<small>EN</small> J<small>ONSON</small> portrait by Robert Seymour/Thomas Mosses, c. 1830, Library of Congress Prints and Photographs Division, reproduction number LC-USZ62-138132; P<small>ERCY</small> B<small>YSSHE</small> S<small>HELLEY</small> printed in *Browning's England*, 1908.

Via Wikimedia Commons: L<small>OUISA</small> M<small>AY</small> A<small>LCOTT</small> photo, 1857; W. H. A<small>UDEN</small> photo: Library of Congress, Prints and Photographs Division, Carl Van Vechten Collection, 1939, reproduction number LC-USZ62-42537; A<small>UGUSTINE OF</small> H<small>IPPO</small>, from *The Hundred Greatest Men*, 1885; F<small>RANCIS</small> B<small>ACON</small> portrait by Jacobus Houbraken, 1738; S<small>AMUEL</small> B<small>ECKETT</small> photo by Roger Pic, 1977; R<small>OBERT</small> B<small>ENCHLEY</small> photo *Vanity Fair*, c. 1919; M<small>IGUEL DE</small> C<small>ERVANTES</small> portrait by Juan de Jauregui y Aguilar, 1600 (not authenticated); S<small>AMUEL</small> T<small>AYLOR</small> C<small>OLERIDGE</small> from *Letters of Samuel Taylor Coleridge*, 1895; N<small>OËL</small> C<small>OWARD</small> photo: Library of Congress, Prints and Photographs Division, Bain Collection, before 1940, reproduction number LC-DIG-ggbain-38534; R<small>OALD</small> D<small>AHL</small> photo: Library of Congress, Prints and Photographs Division, Carl Van Vechten Collection, 1954, reproduction number LOT 12735, no. 273; J<small>OHN</small> D<small>ONNE</small> after a miniature by Isaac Oliver, c. 1616; A<small>RTHUR</small> C<small>ONAN</small> D<small>OYLE</small> photo from *Current History of the War*, 1914; G<small>EORGE</small> E<small>LIOT</small> portrait by Frederick William

Burton, 1864, printed in *The Works of George Eliot*, 1910; WILLIAM FAULKNER photo: Library of Congress, Prints and Photographs Division, Carl Van Vechten Collection, 1954, reproduction number LC-DIG-ppmsca-10445; JOHANN WOLFGANG VON GOETHE portrait by Luise Seidler, 1811, from *Bibliothek des allgemeinen und praktischen Wissens*, 1905; OSCAR HAMMERSTEIN II photo by Al Aumuller, staff photographer, New York World-Telegram & Sun Collection, 1948, Library of Congress, Prints and Photographs Division, reproduction number LC-USZ62-126707; THOMAS HARDY photo: Library of Congress, Prints and Photographs Division, Bain Collection, ca. 1910-15, reproduction number LC-DIG-ggbain-13585; HORACE drawing from *Bibliothek des allgemeinen und praktischen Wissens*, (1905); BEN JONSON etching by George Vertue, after Gerard van Honthorst, 1730; JAMES JOYCE photo by C. Ruf, c. 1918, Cornell Joyce Collection; FEDERICO GARCÍA LORCA photo by unknown photographer, 1913; MOLIÈRE drawing from *Bibliothek des allgemeinen und praktischen Wissens*, 1905; JOHN HENRY NEWMAN drawing by Jane Fortescue Seymour, c. 1875, printed in *The Great Testimony Against Scientific Cruelty*, 1918; OVID drawing by Auréola; THOMAS PAINE drawing by George Romney, c. late 18th century, National Archives; DOROTHY PARKER photo by unknown photographer, c. 1918-22; EZRA POUND photo by Alvin Langdon Coburn, 1913, from *More Men of Mark*, 1922; CARL SANDBURG photo by Al Ravenna, staff photographer, New York World Telegram & Sun Collection, 1955, Library of Congress, Prints and Photographs Division, reproduction number LC-USZ62-115064; JAMES THURBER photo by Fred Palumbo, staff photographer, New York World-Telegram & Sun Collection, 1954, Library of Congress, Prints and Photographs Division, reproduction number LC-USZ62-112049; JOHN UPDIKE photo: George Bush Presidential Library, 1989; EVELYN WAUGH photo: Library of Congress, Prints and Photographs Division, Carl Van Vechten Collection, 1940, reproduction number